CW00544908

Mazda MX-5 Miata Performance Portfolio 1998-2005

Compiled by R M Clarke

ISBN 185520 7117

BROOKLANDS BOOKS LTD.
P.O. BOX 146, COBHAM,
SURREY, KT11 1LG. UK
sales@brooklands-books.com

A-MZ98PP

www.brooklands-books.com

Printed in China

ACKNOWLEDGEMENTS

Brooklands have been publishing automotive works of reference for over 40 years and this book brings our total of titles to over 700. Our earlier MX-5 Performance Portfolio, covering the years 1989 to 1997, proved to be very popular with enthusiasts and we are hoping that this new volume, covering the second generation cars, will prove to be equally successful.

Our thanks as always go to the world's leading publishers of motoring journals for allowing us to include their valuable and copyright road tests and other stories which make up our portfolios. We are indebted in this instance to the managements of *Autocar, Automobile Magazine, Car, Car and Driver, Car South Africa, Evo, Motor Australia, Motor Trend, NZ Classic Cars, Road & Track, Road & Track Specials, Top Gear, Wheels* and *What Car?* for their ongoing support.

R.M.Clarke

Mazda really created a storm in the international sports car market when it released the original MX-5, also known as the Miata. It really did re-awaken people's interest in sports car wind-in-the-hair motoring. There were fears expressed by the media that the replacement would not "keep the faith," so to speak. But we are glad to report that Mazda did not stray from the straight and narrow and with the second edition MX-5 presented a sports car that further enhanced the driving experience while at the same time keeping that particular "look" that denotes the model all over the world.

In true Japanese tradition, the MX-5 is an extremely user friendly sports car that caters for a wide range of driving temperaments from those who simply enjoy the car's great looks and don't care about performance to those who have to tinker and make it go faster and handle better. In its off the showroom floor form it is suitably rapid and handles with a great deal of surety. In outright performance terms it mirrors its great rival, the MG TF, insofar as it sprints from 0-60 mph in around 8 seconds with a top speed of 120 mph.

The aftermarket people quickly saw the potential for a higher performance variant of the MX-5 and were soon offering turbocharged editions that were lightning quick. Mazda took a while to come to the party and through Mazdaspeed offered a turbocharged edition that pumped out 178 bhp at 6000 rpm in the American market. Its 0-60 mph time was reduced to 6.8 seconds although top speed was still under 130 mph, it just got there much sooner!

Amazingly, and against all predictions, sales of the MX-5 increased internationally with the release of the second edition. America in particular, has been a fertile ground for Mazda as it continues to dominate its market segment. Nobody else gets close.

The Mazda MX-5 Miata is an icon sports car and one the company can be very proud of. And as Mazda enthusiasts you will enjoy reading the knowledgeable comment and views presented here.

Gavin Farmer

CONTENTS

1999 Mazda MX-5 Miata

ALL WE WANT FOR CHRISTMAS.

BY JEAN JENNINGS

Hiroshima, Japan—

A gorgeous British racing green Mazda MX-5 Miata wrapped in a big red velvet bow. A fire-engine red Miata with a festive evergreen wreath on the hood. Images of sugarplums dance through our heads this holiday season. There would be no sweeter treat than taking yuletide delivery of the masterfully reworked Mazda Miata.

Yes, masterfully reworked. That was the biggest concern, correct? That somehow, the new Miata (which had to happen sometime) would miss the incredible, indelible high-water mark of the original. A car we have enthusiastically lauded in print year after year as "one of the best cars a person could ever own," a car that "feeds our automotive soul like no other car does," a car that will "hold its own over the long run," and a car that "reaches out to the perpetual teenager in all of us." A magic car.

What was going to happen to our first *Automobile Magazine* Automobile of the Year (1990), the only car to have ever been named to the *Automobile Magazine* All-Stars list seven years in a row—every single year of its life? Only good things, it turns out.

One can imagine the almost paralyzing trepidation faced by the design and engineering teams given the task of reinventing Mazda's standard-bearer, the car that gives

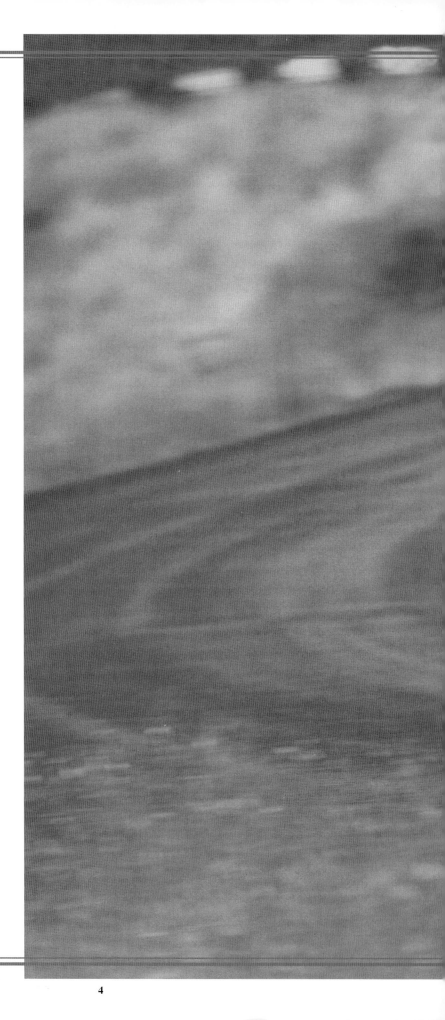

1999 MAZDA MX-5 MIATA

Front-engine, rear-wheel-drive roadster
2-passenger, 2-door steel body
Base price (estimated) $19,500

ENGINE:
16-valve DOHC 4-in-line, iron block,
   aluminum head
Bore x stroke 3.27 x 3.35 in (83.0 x 85.0 mm)
Displacement 112 cu in (1839 cc)
Compression ratio 9.5:1
Fuel system sequential multipoint electronic injection
Power SAE net 140 bhp @ 6500 rpm
Torque SAE net 119 lb-ft @ 5500 rpm
Redline 7000 rpm

DRIVETRAIN:
5-speed manual transmission
Gear ratios (I) 3.14 (II) 1.89 (III) 1.33 (IV) 1.00
   (V) 0.81
Final-drive ratio 4.10:1

MEASUREMENTS:
Wheelbase 89.2 in
Track front/rear 55.9/57.0 in
Length x width x height 155.3 x 66.1 x 47.3 in
Curb weight 2249 lb
Coefficient of drag 0.36
Fuel capacity 12.7 gal
Cargo capacity 4.8 cu ft

SUSPENSION:
Independent front, with double wishbones, dampers,
   coil springs, anti-roll bar
Independent rear, with double wishbones, dampers,
   coil springs, anti-roll bar

STEERING:
Rack-and-pinion
Turns lock to lock 3.3
Turning circle 30.0 ft

BRAKES:
Vented front discs, rear discs
Anti-lock system

WHEELS AND TIRES:
14 x 5.5-in steel wheels
185/60R-14 Toyo tires

PERFORMANCE (manufacturer's data):
0–60 mph in 8.0 sec
Top speed (estimated) 120 mph

COMPETITORS:
BMW Z3
Mercedes-Benz SLK230
Porsche Boxster

1999 MAZDA MX-5 MIATA

Mazda reason to still be alive. Or perhaps they reveled in the opportunity to be the heroes who would revitalize one of the truly iconic cars of the past two decades.

Heroes they are: The new Miata is lighter, faster, stronger, and quieter. Side by side, new car and old, the 1999 Miata muscles its way into your vision to the exclusion of the delicately drawn original. Almost nothing remains in terms of body parts but the A-pillars; the body is lower, with shorter overhangs, and the front air intake has been reshaped. Wind-buffeting pop-up headlamps have been replaced with shallow oval fixed headlights, and the taillights are shapelier as well. The sills bulge slightly, the midsection looks more substantial, and the wheels fill nicely bulging wheel wells (the old Miata's add-on wheel-well lips in the rear are gone). The entire look is organic, voluptuous.

To answer complaints about space efficiency and utility, there are bigger door pockets, a larger console bin, cup holders (!), and more trunk space now that the battery and spare are stacked under the floor.

It is a different car than it was, yet the Miata's original spirit of joy, simplicity, and "oneness between horse and rider" (as so eloquently stated by Toshihiko Hirai, the Miata's original product program manager) remains intact.

Having fought the good fight to maintain the simple sweetness of the original Miata concept, Mr. Hirai is long gone—he left in 1993 to teach engineering at rural Ōita University. In his wake, the Miata underwent a number of changes, some of them modest in scope, some more aggressive: different colors; special performance packages; optional ABS; upgraded stereo systems; power

Top left: The Miata's 1.8-liter engine gets an extensive redesign, yielding slightly higher horsepower and torque figures. Combined with an overall weight savings, it feels noticeably stronger than its predecessor.

steering, windows, antenna, and mirrors; retuned suspension; dual air bags; and side-door-beam protection.

The biggest upgrade was in the 1994 model year, when the Protegé's 1.8-liter engine was popped into the Miata's engine bay for an instant 12-bhp boost. Brakes, clutch plate, shocks, dampers, and anti-roll bars were beefed up to handle the additional power, and steel braces were added to the suspension front and rear and inside the cockpit behind the seats. A further power boost of five horsepower came in the 1996 model, bringing the total to 133 bhp.

Extensive redesign of that 1.8-liter engine (variable intake, larger-diameter intake and exhaust ports, higher-compression pistons, new cam profile, new cylinder head with knock control) raises the new Miata's horsepower figure to 140. Torque improves from 114 to 119 pound-feet, climbing longer after

3000 rpm to its 5500-rpm peak. The improved power, combined with weight savings of 44 pounds, enables the Miata to rip off an eight-second run from 0 to 60 mph, an improvement of 0.7 second. Weight distribution is still a sporting 50 percent front, 50 percent rear.

A five-speed manual transmission is still standard equipment, but reverse gear has been moved directly south of fifth gear and now has a lockout. Changes to the shift linkage reduce shift-handle vibration and make the little shift lever even smoother and quicker to operate. The knob has been reshaped to better fit the palm. You can still order a Miata with a four-speed automatic transmission (sacrilege), but only those clueless about operating a manual would want it.

There were some fifteen to twenty tweaks to various steering, suspension (the same sophisticated double wishbones at all four corners), and structural components, mostly to improve roll characteristics, straight-line stability, handling feel, and ride comfort. "Twisting and static rigidity is pretty much the same as in the old car," says Takao Kijima, product program manager. "But bending rigidity is up ten percent."

Among the most important changes:
• the front pillars, side sills, and transmission tunnel were bolstered, increasing bending rigidity;
• the front and rear cross bars were reshaped to improve rigidity;
• the tie-rod ends, upper and lower control-arm pivot points, and rear-hub supporting arms were all moved;
• the steering-gear mounting was changed;
• the dampers and springs were changed and the bump-stop material was switched from rubber to urethane;
• the old Mazda steering wheel was replaced by a smaller leather-wrapped steering wheel from Nardi that includes a center-mounted air bag.

We had a very brief and hush-hush opportunity to wheel a Miata prototype around Mazda's Miyoshi test track. Seeing the car for the first time was like watching a sequel to a great movie: It was wonderful, but missing the dramatic impact of meeting for the first time. Still, we had a great afternoon, buoyed by the success of the new Miata's more nimble and connected handling performance on a variety of road conditions, its stronger and more willing engine, its isolation from chattery road surfaces, and its much-improved body structure.

The Miata's top has also been reworked. Amazingly, it is two pounds lighter despite the addition of a glass window (a defroster is optional). But what happened to the little handle that allowed you to reach over your shoul-

The introduction of a smaller and very attractive three-spoke leather-wrapped steering wheel from Nardi improves the look of the interior. The shift lever (and linkage) has also been redesigned for better operation. Numerous other changes to the interior increase its space efficiency and utility.

1999 MAZDA MX-5 MIATA

der from the front seat and pull the top back up? Consider this an official plea for its return.

Back and forth we jumped, from old to new. Ride? Check. Performance? Check. Noise? Check. Bigger 195/50R-15 tires as an option? Better. The optional sport suspension's extra strut? Not for everyday. A high-performance R package coming? Check.

The beauty of the Miata remains: It is not a high-speed car but a lightweight, carefree cruiser with responsive steering and an exceptional gearbox. The makings of a huge success? Check.

How unusual it is to see this once iconoclastic, fun-loving band of rural Japanese carmakers now peppered from the top down with Ford executives representing the blue

The Miata Hall of Fame

WHERE ARE THEY NOW?

Toshihiko Hirai
Then: *Miata product manager and chief research engineer*
Now: *Professor of technology, Ōita University*
"Some people thought this simple idea was stupid. There might not be so many of these customers, but they have very strong feelings. It is like seeing your former lover thirty years later."

Bob Hall
Then: *Mazda's California product-planning office*
Now: *Automotive journalist at* Wheels Magazine *in Australia*
Concept requirements from a 1985 project report:
1. Responsive handling (car as an extension of the driver)
2. Snappy performance (feels aggressively fast)
3. Timeless design (looks as good in ten years as today)
4. Comfortable for two adults (with the utility a modern single wants)
5. Simple-to-use top (raise or lower in five seconds from driver's seat)
6. Affordable for all who love to drive

Mark Jordan
Then: *Designer, Mazda Research and Development (MRA) of Mazda North American Operations (MNAO)*
Now: *Assistant chief designer, MRA*
"The Miata was supposed to be an affordable, lightweight, fun-to-drive sports car that would appeal to American tastes. As long as every decision flowed from that idea, the car was going to maintain its identity. Sometimes a concept can stumble between the design and engineering teams. But not here. The engineers were as devoted to the concept as the designers."

Shigenori Fukuda
Then: *Vice-president of Mazda's West Coast product-planning office*
Now: *Managing director, Mazda Sangyo (in-house Mazda customizer)*
"For two years, our top managers hesitated to go ahead with the project. They had no idea whether it would be successful. Bob Hall's passion convinced us."

oval's 33.4 percent share of Mazda. One can only hope that Ford will bring to proud Mazda the stability, the business acumen, the money, and the light touch they brought to Jaguar, much to Jaguar's good fortune. Says Mazda's *gaijin* president, Henry Wallace: "My focus for the past three years has been on taking away concern of the unknown, on looking at policies and developing better efficiencies. Morale and expectations right now are pretty good."

So far, about 450,000 Miatas have made it into the hands of its adoring public, a phenomenal success in the very limited roadster category. The future looks bright to Mazda product planners, who expect demand to remain stable despite the BMW Z3, the Mercedes-Benz SLK, and the Porsche Boxster crowding the scene.

As for filling that Christmas wish list, Americans will have to wait for a spring delivery of the 1999 Miata. They will also have to wait for a firm price, though estimates are just above the current Miata's $19,125 base sticker. Worldwide production has already begun, though only Japan is scheduled for deliveries in this calendar year.

A nice set of fitted driving gloves may have to hold you 'til then.

DESIGN ANALYSIS

BY ROBERT CUMBERFORD,
AUTOMOTIVE DESIGN EDITOR

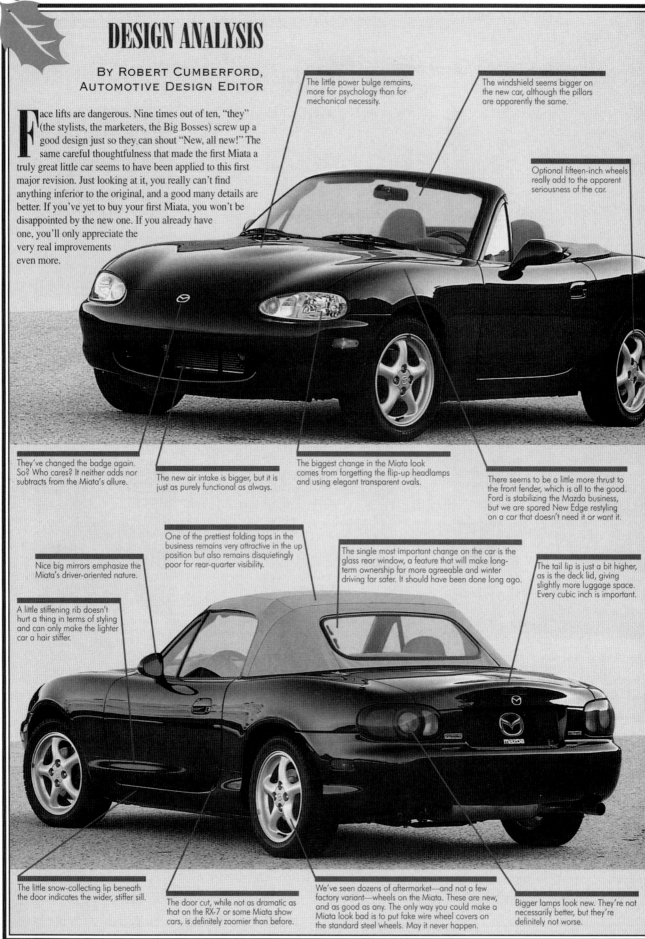

ace lifts are dangerous. Nine times out of ten, "they" (the stylists, the marketers, the Big Bosses) screw up a good design just so they can shout "New, all new!" The same careful thoughtfulness that made the first Miata a truly great little car seems to have been applied to this first major revision. Just looking at it, you really can't find anything inferior to the original, and a good many details are better. If you've yet to buy your first Miata, you won't be disappointed by the new one. If you already have one, you'll only appreciate the very real improvements even more.

The little power bulge remains, more for psychology than for mechanical necessity.

The windshield seems bigger on the new car, although the pillars are apparently the same.

Optional fifteen-inch wheels really add to the apparent seriousness of the car.

They've changed the badge again. So? Who cares? It neither adds nor subtracts from the Miata's allure.

The new air intake is bigger, but it is just as purely functional as always.

The biggest change in the Miata look comes from forgetting the flip-up headlamps and using elegant transparent ovals.

There seems to be a little more thrust to the front fender, which is all to the good. Ford is stabilizing the Mazda business, but we are spared New Edge restyling on a car that doesn't need it or want it.

One of the prettiest folding tops in the business remains very attractive in the up position but also remains disquietingly poor for rear-quarter visibility.

The single most important change on the car is the glass rear window, a feature that will make long-term ownership far more agreeable and winter driving far safer. It should have been done long ago.

The tail lip is just a bit higher, as is the deck lid, giving slightly more luggage space. Every cubic inch is important.

Nice big mirrors emphasize the Miata's driver-oriented nature.

A little stiffening rib doesn't hurt a thing in terms of styling and can only make the lighter car a hair stiffer.

The little snow-collecting lip beneath the door indicates the wider, stiffer sill.

The door cut, while not as dramatic as that on the RX-7 or some Miata show cars, is definitely zoomier than before.

We've seen dozens of aftermarket—and not a few factory variant—wheels on the Miata. These are new, and as good as any. The only way you could make a Miata look bad is to put fake wire wheel covers on the standard steel wheels. May it never happen.

Bigger lamps look new. They're not necessarily better, but they're definitely not worse.

PREVIEW TEST

Mazda MX-5 Miata

Where zing meets zest and makes whoopee.

BY PATRICK BEDARD

Once upon a time, sports cars roamed the earth, and they were hyperhip. This journal was there, evangelizing to the faithful under a different banner—we were *Sports Cars Illustrated* back then. And our spare pages were heavy with fevered imaginings of sports cars of the future, all of which were exactly like this updated-for-1998 Miata, only not as good. Not as cute, either.

They were not as good because, hey, we weren't stupid. Our credibility would have been shot into doilies had we raised the bar this high on basic goodness. No one back then would have believed a sports car could have the "start every day till six digits show on the odometer" reliability that we take for granted today, along with ache-free seats, toasty heaters,

and side glass that rises at the touch of a button.

Yet those imagined sports cars were to be exactly like this Miata—crazy fun to drive, frisky and zingy and quick to the touch. A sports car must have this essential zest, and the Miata captures it better than anything else on the road.

Whew. Take all this back-to-our-roots reminiscing as proof that this *new* Miata arouses all the right glands (if welcoming it onto our 10Best list this past January wasn't hint enough). For 1998, Mazda has gone back over the Miata it introduced for model year 1990, revising most details a little, but none of them very much, and— *hurrah!*—screwing up nothing.

Some changes are signs of the times. Hidden headlights were the fashion a

decade ago, and the Miata had 'em. Now, cars have sparkling lenswork in front, and none are more alluring than the Miata's almond eyes (getting rid of the retractor gizmos saved 12 pounds, too). Toward the rear, we see "shoulders" over the tires now and a saucy little flare at the top of the tail. We like the overall shape better, and so does the airstream; the drag coefficient drops to 0.36 from 0.39. In a deft bit of aero tailoring, lift has been reduced in front and slightly increased at the rear, so that both ends of the car now lighten their tire loads at nearly the same rate as speed climbs; handling changes less with speed now.

Speed is another quality of sports cars that's changed beyond imagining over the years. In our *SCI* days, the affordable

PHOTOGRAPHY BY JEFFREY G. RUSSELL

marques—the MGs, the Triumphs, the Fiats—topped out well under 100 mph. Now, the Miata is the only drop-top two-seater we'd put into the affordable class—about $24,000 here, with a heavy load of options. And it chases right up to a 123-mph top speed, 4 mph above our best first-generation Miata.

Displacement remains unchanged at 1840cc, but a new cylinder head lifts output by seven horsepower to 140; torque is up just over four percent. Both outputs peak at the same revs as before, and the 7000-rpm redline continues. This is very much a sports-car engine, with a torque curve that keeps rising till 5500 rpm. That late peak gives you a payoff for working the lever and keeping the revs raging.

Zero to 60 has dropped under 8.0 seconds now, to 7.9, compared with the 8.2-second clocking of our best previous Miata.

"So what?" some of us ask. Impressive acceleration numbers have never been the fun part of little top-down two-seaters.

High fashion, then and now: Hidden headlights were must-haves in 1990; today, it's designer spectacles.

And top speed is purely academic. Call this the *sensualist's* view of sports cars. We love the tingle of revs and the snick of the shifter and the feel of a machine as it nears its limits, the slip-slide of the tires on the blacktop. These are joys *SCI* savored, and they're the forbidden fruit of today's powerful cars with their grippy tires. You can't treat yourself to much redline time when five or six seconds of flat-pedaling will punch through every speed limit in your state.

The "g" guys think differently. They measure their car fun according to the g meter, and more is better. The Miata, to most g guys, is a peashooter car without much appeal.

Except that this one has the optional Sport suspension with bright yellow Bilsteins and the 195/50VR-15 Pilot SX Michelins (Mazda says tire and suspension tuning of production cars may be slightly different

THE VERDICT

Highs: Light, snick-quick controls; born to heel-and-toe; knows all the sports-car moves.

Lows: Optional Sport suspension is stiff-legged and grippy all out of proportion to the engine's thrust.

The Verdict: An almond-eyed cutie that will show you a very good time.

from this preproduction test car). It clings to the skidpad up to 0.89 g and brakes down from 70 mph in only 174 feet. Those are pretty impressive numbers, enough to lift a peashooter into respected territory.

The sensualists, though, hold to their vision of driving fun. We want a supple suspension that doesn't hammer the body into quivering responses to the bumps. We want to feel the tires slip, and to feel them fade toward steering unresponsiveness as the limits approach. *We want drift angles.* And we want them at speeds that don't raise too many eyebrows on those twisty roads.

The Sport package fights that goal. The 50-series Michelins are so grippy that drifts last for just microseconds, and they finish violently as the tires regain traction and snap the Miata back into line. More compliant shocks and the higher-profile

185/60R-14s of the standard suspension will greatly enhance these pleasures.

Still, *SCI* would have celebrated the Sport option as a perfect solution for weekend autocrosses (called gymkhanas in the old days). The "competition" sports car had a special swagger then. Imagine the Miata with a roll bar and black tape over its almond eyes.

Sports-car fun is more than drift angles, of course. The shifter has to be just right. "Toggle-switch action." That was the favored description. Mazda has reduced friction in the shifter and narrowed the free play. The stubby lever moves in short arcs, with definite stops at the ends of its travel. Gears are changed with a *snick*. The quick, light clutch travel plays right along. The brake pedal is firm to the touch. And have pedals ever been better placed for heel-and-toe operation? Not in our memory.

Even the turn signals join in the sporty mood. The lever is rigid, and it stops crisply at its travel limits.

The cockpit seems slightly more hospitable to tall drivers now, although Mazda doesn't claim any improvements. The left-foot rest is in the correct place and rock-solid, exactly right for a sports car. This preproduction Miata had leather-covered seats, which probably will not be available in combination with the Sport package. The buckets provide lateral restraint appropriate to this car's mission. Drivers up through six feet will find this a good place to work.

Gone are the bright trim bezels that circled the Miata's round instruments just as

A Nardi wheel! Old-timers will frown because the classic Nardi had metal spokes, but hey, Mazda, thanks for remembering.

COUNTERPOINTS

In eight years, the Miata has lost its similarly priced competition and gained a bunch of rivals at twice its price. Even so, this new Miata fares well against them. Its performance now surpasses that of a four-cylinder Z3, its steering is less twitchy than before, and its chassis is as nimble as ever. An average driver can attack a twisty road in a $20,000 Miata and slide the car around like a Mille Miglia vet. The same driver in a $40,000 Boxster may go faster, but the wheels will probably never slip and it will feel like normal driving in fast forward. If you're a mere mortal who wants to feel like a driving pro, the Miata's tough to beat.
— *Frank Markus*

When people ask me, "What's your favorite car?" I never hesitate. "Miata," I reply. I like it simply because it's fun to drive—nothing made me giggle like a Miata. This updated Miata is faster and corners harder, but does that make it more fun? I say no. With the Sport package, there's way too much grip for even the more powerful motor to overcome, making any sort of power slide a genuine feat to pull off. If you do slide, it catches too abruptly—no fun. The body rolls less, but I loved the way the old car pitched around corners. Don't get me wrong, I'm all for more performance, but if it doesn't make driving more fun, which is this car's mission, what's the point?
— *Larry Webster*

When details of the new Miata first began to leak to the world, I was convinced Mazda had made some bad decisions. Grainy pictures arriving over the Internet were worrisome. Now, I can't remember what all the worry was about. Not only is this newest Miata easier on the eyes, but it's more fun to drive, too. Gone is the darty steering, the too-small trunk, and the plastic rear window. Those things that we loved the Miata for in the first place—precise shifter, rev-happy motor, nimble handling—have all been improved. It's so good I'm considering trading in my '90 model, but only if I can have one retrofitted with pop-up headlamps.
— *Jeffrey Dworin*

they circled the dials of MGs and Triumphs in the traditional-roadster days. Mazda has yielded to today's expectation of blackness, arriving at a cockpit that's matte-finished and completely unglittery and probably better for it. Still, a bit of character departed with the chrome rings.

The center console now offers holders for two cups, although having to keep the console lid open during use limits their convenience.

The old Miata held the record for ease of downing and upping the roof, until now. The new one is better. The weight to be lifted is reduced by about two pounds. And the new glass rear window eliminates all concerns about what folding it up—and

dust—would do to the previously used plastic window when it was back there rustling around in the stowed position.

A neat little windblocker is always in place behind the seats, ready for deployment, ready to block the swirling currents that blow forward over the rear deck. Just hinge it up when dropping the top. It's unexpectedly effective, given its small height. As traditional sports cars go, this is a relatively undrafty cockpit, better than

the BMW Z3's, we think.

With the top down, the exhaust takes on a surprisingly hard bark at full power, and the scenery doesn't rush past so quickly that you're afraid to grab another gear, and, oh, what the hell, maybe another. The shifter is really perfect, and you can do all that heel-and-toe throttle blipping as you brake hard for your driveway. *SCI* would have written up this Miata to the rapture redline. ●

C/D TEST RESULTS

ACCELERATION
	Seconds
Zero to 30 mph	.2.4
40 mph	.3.8
50 mph	.5.6
60 mph	.7.9
70 mph	.10.5
80 mph	.14.1
90 mph	.18.7
100 mph	.24.8
110 mph	.37.3
Street start, 5–60 mph	.9.2
Top-gear acceleration, 30–50 mph	.10.7
50–70 mph	.11.1
Standing ¼-mile	.16.1 sec @ 84 mph
Top speed (drag limited)	.123 mph

BRAKING
70–0 mph @ impending lockup ....174 ft
Fade ....**none** light moderate heavy

HANDLING
Roadholding, 300-ft-dia skidpad ....0.89 g
Understeer .... minimal **moderate** excessive

FUEL ECONOMY
EPA city driving ....**23 mpg**
EPA highway driving ....**29 mpg**
C/D observed fuel economy ....**21 mpg**

INTERIOR SOUND LEVEL
Idle	.53 dBA
Full-throttle acceleration	.80 dBA
70-mph cruising	.75 dBA
70-mph coasting	.75 dBA

MAZDA MX-5 MIATA
Vehicle type: front-engine, rear-wheel-drive, 2-passenger, 2-door roadster

Estimated price as tested: $24,000 (estimated base price: $20,150)

Options on test car: leather seats, anti-lock brakes, power steering, windows, and locks, A/C, cruise control, Bose sound system with CD player, Sport handling package (includes 15-inch wheels and tires and Bilstein shocks)

Major standard accessories: rear defroster

Sound system: Mazda/Bose AM/FM-stereo radio/cassette/CD player, 4 speakers

ENGINE
Type ....4-in-line, iron block and aluminum head
Bore x stroke ....3.27 x 3.35 in, 83.0 x 85.0mm
Displacement ....112 cu in, 1840cc
Compression ratio 9.5:1
Engine-control system ....Mazda with port fuel injection
Emissions controls ....3-way catalytic converter, feedback air-fuel-ratio control, EGR
Valve gear ......belt-driven double overhead cams, 4 valves per cylinder, hydraulic lifters
Power (SAE net) ....140 bhp @ 6500 rpm
Torque (SAE net) ....119 lb-ft @ 5500 rpm
Redline ....7000 rpm

DRIVETRAIN
Transmission ....5-speed manual
Final-drive ratio ....4.10:1, limited slip

Gear	Ratio	Mph/1000 rpm	Max. test speed
I	3.14	5.1	36 mph (7000 rpm)
II	1.89	8.5	59 mph (7000 rpm)
III	1.33	12.0	84 mph (7000 rpm)
IV	1.00	16.0	112 mph (7000 rpm)
V	0.81	19.7	123 mph (6250 rpm)

DIMENSIONS AND CAPACITIES
Wheelbase ....89.2 in
Track, F/R ....55.9/57.0 in
Length ....155.3 in

Width	.66.1 in
Height	.47.3 in
Ground clearance	.4.5 in
Curb weight	.2380 lb
Weight distribution, F/R	.53.8/46.2%
Fuel capacity	.12.7 gal
Oil capacity	.4.0 qt
Water capacity	.6.3 qt

CHASSIS/BODY
Type ....unit construction
Body material ....welded steel stampings

INTERIOR
SAE volume, front seat ....46 cu ft
luggage space ....4 cu ft
Front seats ....bucket
Seat adjustments ....fore and aft, seatback angle
Restraint systems, front ....manual 3-point belts, driver and passenger airbags
General comfort ....poor fair **good** excellent
Fore-and-aft support ....poor fair **good** excellent
Lateral support ....poor fair **good** excellent

SUSPENSION
F: ....ind, unequal-length control arms, coil springs, anti-roll bar
R: ....ind, unequal-length control arms, coil springs, anti-roll bar

STEERING
Type ....rack-and-pinion, power-assisted
Turns lock to lock 2.7
Turning circle curb to curb ....30.0 ft

BRAKES
F: ....10.0 x 1.3-in vented disc
R: ....9.9 x 0.3-in disc
Power assist ....vacuum with anti-lock control

WHEELS AND TIRES
Wheel size ....6.0 x 15 in
Wheel type ....cast aluminum
Tires ....Michelin Pilot SX, 195/50VR-15
Test inflation pressures, F/R ....26/26 psi

MX-5 keeps what's best, changes the rest

Host of detail changes skilfully update Mazda's roadster but preserve original's spirit

MAZDA MX-5
On sale April
Price £17,000–£19,500 (est)
Category Roadster

The legions of loyal Mazda MX-5 fans can rest easy.

The new two-seat roadster, revealed last month at the Tokyo motor show, and on sale in the UK from April, has been successfully updated without sacrificing its classic appeal.

After eight successful years, the MX-5 deserved nothing less. It has helped keep Mazda's head above water during the vicious mid-'90s recession, and has introduced countless thousands to the pleasures of open-top sports car motoring.

Reluctant to tinker too much with a successful formula, Mazda has improved what it needed to and left well alone where it could.

Visually, the biggest change is the new face. Gone are the supercar-style pop-up headlamps (too expensive to make and occasionally unreliable) in favour of conventional lenses. But the rest of the skin is new, too – just two minor panels being carried over. Overall, 60 per cent of the car has been changed.

Despite this, Mazda has kept length, width and wheelbase almost identical to those of today's car. The basic platform is carried over, too, and so is the layout of the suspension.

It still uses double wishbones

Headlamps are change you'll notice first, but 60 per cent of car is new. Cockpit is no roomier

front and rear, although Mazda's engineers have tweaked them for better handling and ride, sharper steering and improved straight-line stability. We won't be able to assess the impact of the changes until our First Drive next spring.

But it is a safe bet that the already agile MX-5 will be better. Performance, though, is unlikely

Boot a touch bigger, space better used

to be much improved. Mazda has not revealed official performance figures yet, but with similar-output engines to today's and a similar weight, the MX-5 isn't going to turn into a rocketship.

Again, two engines are on offer – both all-aluminium, 16v four-cylinder units. The 1.8 will produce about 135bhp and the 1.6 about 110bhp. The 1.8, though, will be torquier than at present, thanks to a variable intake manifold that promotes low-speed pulling power.

Owners of the new cars should notice big improvements in refinement. Although the body is no stiffer than today's, the tweaked suspension apparently soaks up road bumps much better and Mazda claims 35 per cent less vibration. A redesigned manual fabric hood with a new

windscreen sealing strip is also claimed to reduce wind noise.

Owners bugged by poor rearward visibility through the plastic rear screen will be pleased to hear that a glass window with a defroster has been added.

They will also be glad that Mazda has improved crash worthiness. Front- and side-impact resistance are both helped by a tougher understructure and strengthened bodyshell.

These changes may have added 40kg of steel, but Mazda's engineers have shaved off a similar amount elsewhere. First to go was the rear strut brace (saving 5kg) and then seats lost 5kg, too. Less sound deadening, aluminium used for some parts such as bumper reinforcements and other detail changes saved the rest.

Twin airbags with belt pre-tensioners and anti-lock brakes complete the safety package. Side airbags won't be offered – they're unsuitable for a confined cockpit.

Not forgotten in the improvements is boot capacity, which grows from 4.38cu ft to 4.77. Available space is better used, too. There isn't any more room in the redesigned cabin, although the driving position has been lowered a fraction.

So, steady as she goes is the message from this new MX-5. Thankfully, the essentials that always made this two-seat sportster so much fun to drive don't appear to have been compromised. We look forward to its launch next spring.

Julian Rendell

MAZDA MX-5	
Engines	1.6 110bhp, 1.8 135bhp
Trim levels	tba

FIRST GLANCE

Thorough improvements have not been at the expense of character. A modern classic reworked

'99 MAZDA MIATA

RESTYLED, REVISED, REJUVENATED—BUT IS IT BETTER?/by Brad Long and Chris Walton

PHOTOGRAPHY BY BRAD LONG

FIRST DRIVE Ten years ago, Mazda jump-started the American love affair with the convertible sports car. Remember when people followed Miata transporters to dealerships and paid unbelievable markups for those first '89 Miatas?

The name "Miata" is German for high reward, but don't think that means Mazda is trying to compete in the same market with upscale, higher-priced two-seaters. It doesn't have to; the Miata is already the world's best-selling roadster and has nothing to prove—but it will, anyway. Although there have been numerous improvements to the car, what the new Miata "means," how it drives, and how it's priced all remain in line with the model's overall philosophy. Remarkably, the ragtop Miata has come a long way without forgoing its heritage as a fun-to-drive, back-to-basics two-seater. Yet, this destined-to-be-classic car is better than ever and shows no sign of being overlooked by the media, enthusiasts, or the fun-loving public in general.

Four design teams, the foremost two in Hiroshima, Japan, and Irvine, California, had the seriously tough task of spicing up the recipe without putting a bad taste in mouths of the over 450,000 satisfied worldwide customers—including the 30,000-member Miata Club of America. The more masculine-looking '99 model (there will be no '98) will be offered about the time you read this with five somewhat overlapping option packages encompassing a $6000 range in price: base plus Power Steering, Touring, Popular Equipment, Leather, and Sports packages. All Miatas will be powered by the same 1.8-liter inline-four, DOHC 16-valve engine, but equipped with varying degrees of posh and performance. Depending on the package, you may outfit your pint-size fun-mobile with everything from a four-speed automatic transmission, Bose audio system, leather, and ABS, to a Nardi steering wheel, fender flares, Bilstein shock absorbers, strut tower connector brace, and 195/50VR15 Michelin Pilot SX tires. Make no mistake: This is not your sister's Miata. Imagine the old one with

TECH DATA
'99 MAZDA MIATA

GENERAL
Location of final assembly	Hiroshima, Japan
Body style	2-door, 2-passenger
EPA size class	Two-seater
Drivetrain layout	Front engine, rear drive
Airbag	Dual

POWERTRAIN
Engine type	I-4, cast-iron block/aluminum heads
Bore x stroke, in./mm	3.3x3.4/83.0x85.0
Displacement, ci/cc	112/1839
Compression ratio	9.5:1
Valve gear	DOHC, 4 valves/cylinder
Fuel/induction system	Electronic multipoint fuel injection
Horsepower, hp @ rpm, SAE net	140 @ 6500
Torque, lb-ft @ rpm, SAE net	119 @ 5500
Horsepower/liter	76.1
Redline, rpm	7000
Transmission type	5-speed manual
Recommended fuel	Regular unleaded

DIMENSIONS
Wheelbase, in./mm	89.2/2265
Track, f/r, in./mm	55.7/56.7 / 1414/1440
Length, in./mm	155.3/3945
Width, in./mm	66.1/1679
Height, in./mm	48.4/1229
Base curb weight, lb	2299
Weight distribution, f/r, %	50/50
Cargo capacity, cu ft	5.1
Fuel capacity, gal.	12.7
Weight/power ratio, lb/hp	16.4

CHASSIS
Suspension, f/r	Upper & lower control arms, coil springs, anti-roll bar/upper & lower control arms, coil springs, anti-roll bar
Steering type	Rack and pinion, power assist
Ratio	18:1
Turns, lock to lock	3.2
Turning circle, ft	30.2
Brakes, f/r	Vented disc/disc, ABS optional
Wheels, in.	15 x 6.0, aluminum alloy
Tires	195/50VR15, Michelin Pilot SX

PERFORMANCE
Acceleration, sec	
0-30 mph	2.3
0-40 mph	3.8
0-50 mph	5.5
0-60 mph	7.9
0-70 mph	10.4
0-80 mph	13.7
Standing quarter mile, sec/mph	15.9/86.1
Braking, 60-0 mph, ft	122
Lateral acceleration, g	0.92
Speed through 600-ft slalom, mph	70.5
EPA fuel economy, mpg, city/hwy	25/29

PRICE
Base price	$19,770
Price as tested	$23,800
www.mazdausa.com	

a jolt of caffeine, a lower voice, and dancing lessons, and you'd come close—it's that much better.

We sampled both the Popular Equipment (pictured) and Sports versions with similar but different impressions of the two. While the Popular-equipped car was evidently more capable, more comfortable, and easier to drive than the vehicle it replaces, the Sport version provided some world-class performance figures.

The Miata's often-criticized (for its lackluster performance) powertrain receives a gentle massage (larger, straighter, variable intake ports, higher compression, and new-profile cam lobes) upping the output from 133 to 140 horsepower (138 in the Golden State). That's good enough to run 0-60 mph in 7.9 seconds (same as the BMW Z3 1.9), and tour the quarter mile a tenth quicker than BMW's lowest-priced droptop, at 15.9 seconds. If that doesn't convince you that Mazda has gotten serious about the Miata's performance, how about a wickedly fast cone-dodging display through the 600-foot slalom at 70.5 mph. Believe it or not, that's in the realm of the F355, NSX, 911, and even the record-holding Viper!

The little sportster's 0.92g lateral acceleration figure is enough to make your head spin, but when it stops, it'll do so from 60 mph in only 122 feet.

If you want to drive the Miata fast, you'd best like oversteer. (If not, perhaps we could show you something in a front-driver.) Autocrossers will rejoice because its at-the-limit handling retains the same spirited, wheels crossed-up, four-wheel-drift-master characteristics of the previous car, but the new, grippier tires push that time- and tire-wasting limit a bit farther away. Nevertheless, we found it every bit as catchable and well balanced as before.

Here's a list of major changes that make the second-generation Miata, or M2 to aficionados, even better:
• Total body makeover (retaining the essence of the previous car's character);
• Modest engine upgrade (boosting power to a more than adequate level);
• Repositioned steering mounts for more responsive control;
• Increased front and rear track widths (enhancing already impressive cornering stability);
• Mazda's so-called Innovative Power Plant Frame unites the engine, trans-

mission, and differential unit, virtually eliminating driveline lash and substantially quelling vibration;
• Easy-to-operate manual softtop with a new, glass window.

Saying we like the new Miata would be like saying that *wasabe* is a mild horseradish condiment from Japan. More succinctly, the new Miata is not a poseur; it's a genuine sports car and it's still at a bargain price. **MT**

1999 Mazda Miata

Substantial improvements to the world's favorite sports car

BY THOS L. BRYANT

THE TAIL END of the Mazda Miata prototype wiggled just a little as I went through a series of esses at the Miyoshi proving ground test track in Japan. The signal from the car was polite but firm: "You're going too fast for these conditions." As I eased off and the all-new Miata settled itself, a grin spread across my face. I've always loved the Miata, ever since it was introduced in 1989, but this new one is markedly improved.

The 1999 Miata is just being unveiled to the public at the Tokyo International Auto Show as you read this, and it will be coming to Mazda dealers in the U.S. this spring. Mazda, which has been the dominant seller of inexpensive sports cars in the U.S. since the Miata was introduced, certainly wants to retain that position. But it's equally clear that the Miata needed some serious revamping.

At Mazda's headquarters in Hiroshima, Takao Kijima, product program manager of the new model, outlined the goals and objectives: Retain the loyalty of the current buyers (mostly middle-aged men), entice new enthusiasts (women and younger men) and improve the car while retaining its virtues. Simple, no? Well, perhaps not, but Mr. Kijima's team seems to have pulled it off, based on my exposure to the prototype several months ago. The styling has been altered to give the Miata a somewhat more aggressive appearance, with some sharper edges and muscular bulges. The subtle styling changes also produced a slight improvement in the coefficient of drag (0.36 versus 0.39). Design chief Norihiko Kawaoka and chief stylist Koichi Hayashi took great pleasure in showing off the new styling treatments while we stood on the roof of one of the Mazda buildings—the same place, I think, where I first got a peek at the RX-7 in the Seventies.

Improvements were made in everyday utility of the Miata by increasing trunk volume by nearly 10 percent (via moving the battery and the spare tire beneath the trunk floor), adding storage space to the interior for odds and ends, and yet keeping the virtues of light weight and tidy dimensions. The new Miata weighs just a bit less than the previous one, and the only dimensions that have changed noticeably are front and rear track, both of which are wider.

The drivetrain was also the focus of attention as Mazda's engineering staff worked on improving the engine response, the sound of the exhaust and the crispness of gear changes. Although the engine now has higher compression (up from 9.0:1 to 9.5), a variable intake control system, a revised camshaft profile and a new cylinder head with a knock-control system and improved intake and exhaust ports, the result is a seemingly negligible gain of seven horsepower. But the difference in feel is significant, especially when combined with the refinements to the gearbox and shift lever as well as the suspension alterations.

■ Engine refinements produce 9.5:1 compression ratio and additional 7 bhp.

At Miyoshi, I first drove the current or "old" Miata, then the new one. The old version, always a delight to my driving senses, felt just fine, thank you. But when I moved to the new car, I was pleasantly surprised with its noticeably more taut feel in handling, steering and ride. The new Miata tackled the test track with a sharpness the previous car could not muster, leaving me with the sense that sports-car enthusiasts are going to love this. And those less inclined to push their Miata close to its limits will find the improvements in precision and firmness neither jarring nor upsetting.

The changes to the Miata's suspension geometry focused on lowering the front roll center, increasing front caster trail for improved stability, making the rear shock absorber stroke 10 mm longer and the afore-mentioned widening of front and rear tracks (10 mm front, 20 mm rear). The base wheel is still the same 14-in. disc with 185/60R-14 tires, but there are newly styled 14- and 15-in. alloy wheels as options. The previous 4-spoke steering wheel is no more, replaced by a 3-spoke leather-wrap steering wheel with airbag, and there is a wind deflector behind the seats to make top-down motoring even more pleasurable.

All these alterations to one of our favorite cars are improvements. The new Miata is a better car to drive, thanks to a little more power, a little more tautness, a little more sporting touch and a little more this and that inside and out. It's risky business to make changes to an icon such as the Miata, but Mazda has done it with intelligence and style. 🏎

■ The Miata's driving dynamics are roundly improved, with a touch more spirit and improved handling. The interior dimensions are unchanged but there is a new steering wheel design and more storage spots. Exterior styling is more muscular from stem to stern. Trunk space is also enhanced.

SPECIFICATIONS

Curb weight	2245 lb
Wheelbase	89.2 in.
Track, f/r	55.9 in./57.0 in.
Length	155.3 in.
Width	66.1 in.
Height	48.2 in.
Fuel capacity	12.7 gal.

ENGINE & DRIVETRAIN

Engine	dohc 4-valve inline-4
Bore x stroke	83.0 x 85.0 mm
Displacement	1839 cc
Compression ratio	9.5:1
Horsepower (SAE)	140 bhp @ 6500 rpm
Torque	119 lb-ft @ 5500 rpm
Fuel delivery	elect. port
Transmission	5-speed manual, 4-speed automatic

CHASSIS & BODY

Layout	front engine/rear drive
Brake system, f/r	10.0-in. vented discs/ 9.9-in. discs
Wheels	14 x 5½J
Tires	P185/60R-14
Steering type	rack & pinion, pwr assist
Suspension, f/r	upper & lower A-arms, coil springs, tube shocks, anti-roll bar/ upper & lower A-arms, coil springs, tube shocks, anti-roll bar

MAZDA MX-5 MIATA

The same basic formula taken to new heights

BY SAM MITANI
PHOTOS BY JOHN LAMM

P HENOMENON. BOOM. SENSATION. Call it what you will, but when Mazda unveiled its retro 2-seat roadster back in 1989, it triggered a shock wave in the automotive world. Not only was this Japanese car company reviving an automotive concept long considered forgotten, it was about to change the way people felt about driving—especially those not old enough to remember cars such as the Triumph TR4, Lotus Elan or even the MG. (And imagine, an affordable roadster that didn't require weekly visits to the mechanic!)

Everywhere the MX-5 Miata roadster appeared, people flocked. In Japan, eager buyers were forced to endure waiting periods of up to half a year. Here in the States, desperate buyers ponied up as much as $30,000 for a car that carried a sticker price of about $14,000.

And the Miata's popularity has hardly faltered over the years—competitors have come and gone, yet not one has seriously challenged its reign in the compact roadster segment. Needless to say, with the car experiencing so much success, Mazda took its time introducing a successor and managed to periodically feed our hungry curiosities with teasers like the M Roadster and the M Coupe (not to be confused with the BMW offerings). However, a change was inevitable.

Mazda finally faced the music last year when it announced a heavily revised Miata for model year 1999. One naturally assumed that the company would keep the car relatively unchanged; after all, why would anyone want to seriously mess with such a successful formula? But, according to those responsible for styling the new car, the case was not that simple.

"We needed to consider the different markets of the world when we approached the new Miata design," said Tom Matano, executive vice president of design and special products. "For instance, in Japan people are accustomed to seeing a completely fresh style after a model change, while in the States, it's common to see three generations of a certain model

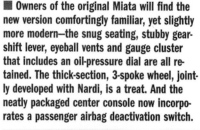

look remarkably similar. Therefore, we had to make the car look different yet still be recognizable as a Miata."

Back when this discussion took place, his words seemed a bit ambiguous. "So are you going to change it much or not?" I remember asking, a little impatiently.

"You'll see," he answered.

And indeed I did, at the new Miata's unveiling at the 1997 Tokyo Motor Show. At once, I recognized the original model's pill-bug shape, although the front end wore a dramatically different mask, one with exposed oblong headlights in place of the large square "pop-ups." Mazda designers exercised more caution with the car's profile; with the exception of a new swooshing doorline, there's not much here to distinguish it from the previous model. The new Miata's rear sports a similar overall design, but the taillight treatment has been freshened and a Millenia-esque trunklid gives it a sporty, upscale demeanor.

The new Miata has grown slightly, though its wheelbase remains at 89.2 in. Curb weight is up 140 lb. to 2,470,

while its overall length, width and height are 155.3, 66.0 and 48.3 in., respectively, giving the roadster a bit more space for occupants. Trunk space has been slightly increased, thanks mainly to a floorplan stamping that incorporates a

recessed well for the spare tire.

A slick three-spoke Nardi steering wheel complete with airbag highlights the changes inside. Also, the dashboard has been completely restyled, with more curves and a new center-

THE COMPETITION

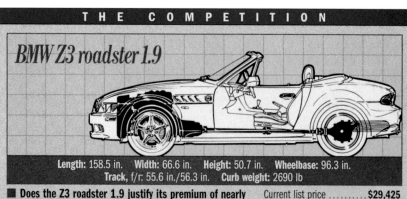

BMW Z3 roadster 1.9

Length: 158.5 in.   Width: 66.6 in.   Height: 50.7 in.   Wheelbase: 96.3 in.
Track, f/r: 55.6 in./56.3 in.   Curb weight: 2690 lb

■ Does the Z3 roadster 1.9 justify its premium of nearly $10,000 over the Miata? The two are virtually neck-and-neck in acceleration, but the definitive nod goes to the BMW in cornering and braking performance. And love or hate the Z3's flared hood, beady headlights and somewhat reptilian side vents, it packs a much stronger visual punch than the Mazda. Factor in status and that certain Teutonic precision of the Z3's chassis, and the decision suddenly becomes much more difficult. *(Tested: 1/96)*

Current list price	$29,425
Engine	dohc 1.9-liter inline-4
Horsepower	138 bhp @ 6000 rpm
Torque	133 lb-ft @ 4300 rpm
Transmission	5-speed manual
0–60 mph	8.1 sec
Braking, 60–0 mph	118 ft
Lateral accel (200-ft skidpad):	0.91g
EPA city/highway	23/32 mpg

1999 Mazda MX-5 MIATA

IMPORTER

Mazda Motors of America, Inc
P.O. Box 19734
Irvine, California 92713

PRICE

List price	$19,770
Price as tested	22,670

Price as tested includes std equip. (dual airbags, AM/FM stereo/cassette); Touring package (pwr steering, pwr windows & mirrors, 14-in. alloy wheels) $1550, air cond ($900), dest charge ($450).

0–60 mph	8.0 sec
0–¼ mi	16.1 sec
Top speed	123 mph*
Skidpad	0.83g
Slalom	61.2 mph
Brake rating	good

TEST CONDITIONS

Temperature	75° F
Wind	calm
Humidity	35%
Elevation	1100 ft

SCALE: 10 IN.(254mm) DIVISIONS
DRAWING BY TIM BARKER

ENGINE

Type	cast-iron block, alloy head, **inline-4**
Valvetrain	dohc 4 valve/cyl
Displacement	112 cu in./1840 cc
Bore x stroke	3.27 x 3.35 in./ 83.0 x 85.0 mm
Compression ratio	9.5:1
Horsepower (SAE)	**140 bhp @ 6500 rpm**
Bhp/liter	76.1
Torque	**119 lb-ft @ 5500 rpm**
Maximum engine speed	7000 rpm
Fuel injection	elect. sequential port
Fuel	unleaded, 87 pump oct

CHASSIS & BODY

Layout	**front engine/rear drive**
Body/frame	unit steel
Brakes	
Front	**10.0-in. vented discs**
Rear	**9.9-in. discs**
Assist type	vacuum
Total swept area	330 sq in.
Swept area/ton	252 sq in.
Wheels	cast alloy, **14 x 6JJ**
Tires	Yokohama ADRAN A-460, **185/60R-14 32H**
Steering	**rack & pinion**, pwr assist
Overall ratio	15.0:1
Turns, lock to lock	3.2
Turning circle	30.2 ft
Suspension	
Front	**upper & lower A-arms,** coil springs, tube shocks, anti-roll bar
Rear	**upper & lower A-arms,** coil springs, tube shocks, anti-roll bar

DRIVETRAIN

Transmission			**5-speed manual**
Gear	Ratio	Overall ratio	(Rpm) Mph
1st	3.14:1	13.50:1	(7000) 34
2nd	1.89:1	8.13:1	(7000) 56
3rd	1.33:1	5.72:1	(7000) 80
4th	1.00:1	4.30:1	(7000) 106
5th	0.81:1	3.48:1	est (6535) 123*
Final drive ratio			4.30:1

Engine rpm @ 60 mph in 5th 3200
*Electronically limited.

GENERAL DATA

Curb weight	**2470 lb**
Test weight	2620 lb
Weight dist (with driver), f/r, %	52/48
Wheelbase	89.2 in.
Track, f/r	55.7 in./56.7 in.
Length	**155.3 in.**
Width	**66.0 in.**
Height	**48.3 in.**
Ground clearance	4.3 in.
Trunk space	6.1 cu ft

MAINTENANCE

Oil/filter change	7500 mi/7500 mi
Tuneup	30,000 mi
Basic warranty	36 mo/50,000 mi

ACCOMMODATIONS

Seating capacity	**2**
Head room	36.5 in.
Seat width	2 x 19.0 in.
Leg room	42.0 in.
Seatback adjustment	45 deg
Seat travel	8.0 in.

INTERIOR NOISE

Idle in neutral	50 dBA
Maximum in 1st gear	78 dBA
Constant 50 mph	72 dBA
70 mph	77 dBA

INSTRUMENTATION

150-mph speedometer, 8000-rpm tach, coolant temp, oil temp, fuel level,

ACCELERATION

Time to speed	Seconds
0–30 mph	2.6
0–40 mph	4.0
0–50 mph	5.7
0–60 mph	8.0
0–70 mph	10.6
0–80 mph	13.7
0–90 mph	17.7
0–100 mph	23.2
Time to distance	
0–100 ft	3.2
0–500 ft	8.7
0–1320 ft (¼ mi):	16.1 @ 86.5 mph

FUEL ECONOMY

Normal driving	est 26.0 mpg
EPA city/highway	25/29 mpg
Cruise range	est 305 miles
Fuel capacity	12.7 gal.

BRAKING

Minimum stopping distance	
From 60 mph	146 ft
From 80 mph	270 ft
Control	very good
Pedal effort for 0.5g stop	na
Fade, effort after six 0.5g stops from 60 mph	na
Brake feel	excellent
Overall brake rating	good

HANDLING

Lateral accel (200-ft skidpad)	0.83g
Balance	mild understeer
Speed thru 700-ft slalom	61.2 mph
Balance	mild understeer
Lateral seat support	excellent

Test Notes...

■ Around the skidpad, the new Miata is exquisitely balanced, responsive to the least steering nudge and throttle squeeze. Lifting the throttle induces quick, but catchable, oversteer.

■ Through the slalom, the Miata's front and rear ends don't function in concert as much as we'd like, though the steering's quick responsiveness makes corrections easy.

■ Under heavy braking, this non-ABS-equipped Miata tended to easily lock its rear wheels from 80 mph. Interior noise (top-up) is still plentiful, but the Miata's ride quality seems improved.

Subjective ratings consist of excellent, very good, good, average, poor; na means information is not available.

■ There are traces of the sorely missed RX-7 in the Miata's flanks and tail, and perhaps a bit of the MX-6 in the Miata's exposed, almond-shape headlamps. The sturdy 1.8-liter twincam inline-4 continues, massaged to produce 140 bhp.

dash cluster that neatly houses the ventilation system, stereo and a small key-operated switch that deactivates the passenger airbag. And, best of all, say goodbye to zipping and unzipping the rear window every time you lower or raise the top; Mazda has incorporated a new glass window into the car's manually operated soft top.

So far, so good. But the most important question remained: Did Mazda retain the fun-to-drive character of the original?

My chance to put the new car—in this case, equipped with the Touring package—through its paces came on the secluded roads of the island of Hawaii—a fully appropriate setting for the debut of this new roadster.

Upon twisting the car's ignition key, you're greeted by a delightful *blluurp* of the exhaust. The sound is reminiscent of the original Miata's, yet something about it is different.

"The new Miata has a completely new exhaust system. We did like the sound of the old one, but we found that there were still 'bad' or 'unpleasant' sounds mixed in. Therefore, we refined the exhaust note until all the bad noises were eliminated. If you listen to the exhausts of the old and new car one after the other, you'll find that the new one sounds much more pleasant," said Takao Kijima, program manager of the new Miata.

Punch the throttle and the car snaps off the line with verve, chirping its Yokohama A-460 185/60R-14 rear tires (the Leather and Sport versions come with 195/50R-15s, wrapped around 15-in. alloy wheels). As you reach freeway speeds, it feels like the new Miata is decidedly quicker than the previous model. And it is. Thanks to seven more bhp (now 140) and five more lb.-ft. of torque (now 119) from the car's 1.8-liter twincam inline-4, the new Miata smokes the previous version by nearly a second to 60 mph and runs the quarter-mile in 16.1 sec. And changing gears, always a pleasing experience, is even better in the new Miata because of the shifter's improved linkage and shorter throws.

Around the hills near Waimea, the new Miata displayed its penchant for winding roads. The chassis has been stiffened slightly—torsion and bending rigidity have been upped 7 and 1 percent, respectively—helping the new car feel more stable through corners and exhibit better turn-in feel. Mazda engineers increased the camber for less understeer, and tuned the upper and lower A-arm suspension for less body roll. Thus, the new car feels tighter and more agile than the previous version. At the test track, the Miata registered 0.83g around the skidpad and ran the slalom at 61.2 mph.

The 1999 Miata comes in four basic versions: base; Touring; Leather, which includes leather trim and 15-in. alloy wheels; and Sport, a lightweight version for those keen on competition (stiffer springs, less weight, fewer amenities). The base car will carry a price tag of $19,770, making it still one of the most affordable sports cars on the market. And although the nimble-roadster concept is no longer ground-breaking news, Mazda has definitely raised the bar in the affordable roadster segment—making it all the more difficult for the batch of new competitors (see "Rising Sun," January 1998, and the Kia Elan First Drive elsewhere in this issue) to knock the Miata off its throne. I'd say the odds are against them. ◉

Base MX-5 is anything but

Mazda MX-5 1.6
PRICE £15,520
ON SALE End of April

The new Mazda MX-5 1.8 was everything we had hoped it would be, convincingly topping last week's group test against the MGF, Fiat Barchetta and BMW Z3. But of the 430,000 cars sold since the MX-5's launch eight years ago, it is the 1.6 that has accounted for most sales.

And for the launch of the new model, it's the 1.6 that has had the more thorough going over. The outgoing 1.6, with a mere 88bhp on tap to power the 1010kg roadster, turned in peppy but unremarkable performance (60mph in 10.6sec and 109mph flat out). That's reasonable, but not enough to scare any self-respecting hot hatch.

More muscular performance is the order of the day for the new model. Power has climbed by a healthy 22 per cent to 108bhp at 6500rpm, with the torque peak of 99lb ft arriving at a high 5000rpm. The engine block is little changed, retaining the 78.0/83.6mm bore and stroke, but improvements to the mechanical friction and breathing resistance, as well as a compression ratio of 9.4:1 (up from 9.0:1) account for the power increases. With kerb weight up by a mere 5kg, to 1015kg, the performance now has a much harder edge.

The dash to 62mph is down by 0.9sec to 9.7sec and top speed rises 9mph to 118mph. It feels even quicker, not least because of the eager engine, which sounds both richer and creamier than its big brother. Our only criticism is the gearing – higher than that of the 1.8iS, with third running to over

Lights front and rear have changed

85mph. The 1.6 could do with a more sporty set of ratios – especially as the beautifully crisp gearbox makes cog-swapping a joy.

The Mazda's ride and handling are impeccable; in fact, the MX-5 is so much fun to drive that it's hard to resist the

Low-slung cabin is dark and simple

temptation of a long blast. Heel and toeing is a delight thanks to the well-placed pedals.

The only criticism the enthusiast could have is a surfeit of grip. The test car rode on optional 195/50 R15 rubber, highlighting the car's natural balance but giving too much adhesion for the tail-out brigade. The standard 185/60 R14 Yokohamas may be a better bet.

The downside of that is the wheels. The standard items are cheap and ugly steel rims, but the optional five-spoke alloys look the business – £440 well spent. Another option worth considering is the wind blocker that fits behind the seats. It looks small and ineffective but

MX-5 1.8's Nardi wheel not for 1.6

cuts cabin bluster almost completely.

With an on-the-road price of £15,520, group 11 insurance and combined economy of 34.9mpg, the MX-5 1.6 is as sensible as it is attractive. It could yet prove to be the pick of the range.
Oliver Marriage

Power in 1.6 has climbed to 108bhp

FACTFILE

0-62mph	9.7sec
Top speed	118mph
Combined mpg	34.9

HOW BIG?

Length 3975mm	**Width** 1680mm		
Height 1225mm	**Wheelbase** 2265mm		

ENGINE

Type 4 cyls in line, 1597cc
Installation Front, longitudinal, rear-wheel drive
Max power 108bhp at 6500rpm
Max torque 99lb ft at 5000rpm
Gearbox 5-speed manual

CHASSIS

Suspension Double wishbones, coil springs, anti-roll bar (front); Double wishbones, coil springs, anti-roll bar (rear)
Steering Rack and pinion, power assisted 2.6 turns lock to lock
All manufacturer's figures

VERDICT

Improvements to lusty 1.6-litre engine make it sound good and go well. Gearing could be a little bit more sporty, but, at £15,520, this could just be the pick of the range.

MX-5 is a driver's delight – very grippy and neutral on 15in rubber

MAZ 1074

Story: **Angus Frazer** Photography: Paul Debois

The old **MX-5** was a real **gas**. It was **the** car to give you a **tankful** of pure roadster **fun**. Then **everyone** else got **in** on the act. **Two-seater** soft tops like the Fiat **Barchetta** and Rover **MGF** sprung up but they **didn't** quite make the **grade**. So the question is, is the **newly**-revamped **Mazda** really

AS GOOD AS IT GETS?

Cool '60s-style lights and silver paint, ooh I feel dizzy with desire

British racing green, low-slung lines, new lights, hmm, not too bad

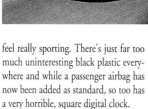

Purple paint, red interior, cream dials, oh dear I feel a bit blurrrgh

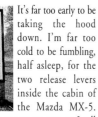

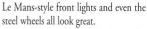

It's far too early to be taking the hood down. I'm far too cold to be fumbling, half asleep, for the two release levers inside the cabin of the Mazda MX-5. But this is a sports car test, so I tell myself I must. At least the hood folds away with little resistance and we're off, escaping the suburbs before dawn.

There are no cheery pop-up headlamps to light the way, for this is the new MX-5, the £18,775 1.8iS version to be exact. It's got a new, slightly wider body, a new interior and more equipment. But the familiar pop-up lamps have popped their clogs. They've gone, along, it would seem at first glance, with all the interesting bits from the interior. OK, so there's a Nardi steering wheel but it's too big to

feel really sporting. There's just far too much uninteresting black plastic everywhere and while a passenger airbag has now been added as standard, so too has a very horrible, square digital clock.

A traffic-free run out to the M4 improves my mood and gives me the chance to work that tiny, stubby little gear lever. It feels good; I can snick up and down through the ratios just by moving a hand, not a whole arm. The heater, cranked up to full power, is toe-burningly effective. The new wind deflector behind the back seats does its job, too, and the journey from London to Membury services – the rendezvous point with the Mazda's rivals, a £17,995 MGF and a £15,824 (but left-hand-drive) Fiat Barchetta – passes with reasonable civility for a small open-top sports car on a cold morning.

The others (cheats) have arrived with their hoods up. I feel I can eat my fry-

up with a clearer conscience. After breakfast, it's time to get sorted. A quick perusal of the MX-5's boot – bigger now, thanks to a space-saver under the floor – reveals a tonneau cover and with a little bit of tugging and plenty of button-popping, it's soon in place. Folding the hood down on the MGF is easy, but getting the tonneau cover on is not. No matter how it's tugged and stretched, it never quite covers all the bits it should.

Dispensing with the Fiat Barchetta's hood is infinitely more satisfying. Unlike the others, it folds completely out of sight into its own little compartment behind the seats, creating one very pretty sports car. The Barchetta looks like you could just get in it and drive straight back to the '60s. It's not just the retro bodyshape, the detailing is also superb – the slender, pop-out door handles, the twin rear lights, the

Le Mans-style front lights and even the steel wheels all look great.

There are some smart details on the MGF too, like the fuel filler cap, the rear side air intakes, the front grille, the twin exhaust pipes and the five-spoke alloy wheels. But its looks are just too frumpy and too high-sided to be considered a true classic. It's almost more of a cabriolet than a sports car.

While the MX-5 could never be mistaken for anything other than a sports car, it has lost a lot of its character. That nose could now belong to any number of cars – Mazda MX-3 and Hyundai Coupe included. A power bulge on the bonnet of a car with only 138bhp is plain silly, and the new curved-up boot-lid lip, which admittedly accommodates a third-level brake light, looks out of place too.

Transferring to the Fiat, I spend a minute or so familiarising myself with

the Barchetta's interior before my departure. It's simply fabulous. Whereas the Mazda's cabin looks like it popped out of a plastic moulder, each item in the beautiful little Fiat seems carefully, even lovingly crafted. The three sunken instrument dials – with the rev counter fittingly positioned in the middle – scream 'sports car' at you. The air-vents and the heater controls also look excellent. Even the stereo looks right, although like the Mazda's, it's a little bit fiddly to use with gloves on. And the Barchetta's silver body colour contrasts cleverly yet simply with the black interior.

Smart as it is, once on the go I'm yearning for the Mazda's heater – the Barchetta's doesn't do as good a job at keeping the tops of my legs warm. The Fiat does have the better driving position, though, thanks to an adjustable steering wheel – something none of the

others offer. The seats are good, too, so once settled in, it's not a cabin that you find yourself in a great hurry to vacate. Leave it I must, though, for our little convoy has wound its way into Sedge Moor services and it's time to put the MGF through its paces.

I know I'm sitting in the F, because there are five interior badges to remind me of the fact. One on the plastic steering wheel, one on the dashboard (for the passenger), one on the speedo, one on the rev-counter and one, of course, on the back of the tax disc holder. This is overkill, but so is the whole of the interior design.

The purple colour of the exterior looks fine, but to then blend in cream and purple dials with red seat and door trim is just awful. It looks like something an imprisoned pimp who attended a few – but not enough – design classes might have come up with.

Before I can start to feel forgiving, I discover the driving position is bad too. The lower half of my left leg is jammed against the transmission tunnel while both my thighs rub the steering wheel. The seat needs more side support as well, and the MGF doesn't keep out quite as much wind as the Mazda. It does at least feel solid and stable on the motorway and its Hydragas suspension gives a smoother ride than either the Fiat or the even firmer Mazda.

There's only so much that can be learnt from driving a car along a motorway, though, so we pull off, swap machines and continue on smaller roads towards Exmoor. The first lesson learnt is that the Fiat has no brakes. As a result the MGF almost ends up losing its rear tail lights.

Of course the Barchetta does have brakes: vented discs at the front, solid discs at the rear and standard ABS; it's

just that, compared with the MGF and the MX-5, they don't feel very good. They took the longest distance to stop at the test track and the pedal has to be pushed hard and far before anything seems to happen. The feel from the MGF's pedal is much more convincing, although the pedal itself feels awkwardly high and anti-lock comes as a £685 option. The Mazda's brakes were the best when tested and the pedal has a superb feel to it – just brush it and the brakes bite immediately. It also comes with ABS as standard.

The country lanes show up some shortcomings in gearboxes as well as brakes. The Barchetta's 'box, for instance, is OK when it's not rushed, but try changing down fast from third to second to first and it can baulk and refuse to engage. Changing gear in the MGF is a more reliable experience, although its saloon-car-like long throw

doesn't come close to rivalling that short, snappy, direct shift of the MX-5.

Scudding along the quiet back roads, far away from the madding rumble of the motorway crowds, we could have easily slipped back in time. Wonderfully, the illusion isn't ruined at all when we pull into Frederick Charles Awcock's *Black Cat Garages and Tea Gardens* near Bampton. Built in 1926, it's not the sort of petrol station that feels the need to sell Pot Noodles and pregnancy-testing kits.

Fred tells us how, in the height of the tourist season, he needs to get up at five o'clock on a Sunday morning to get a decent run over the local roads on his Hesketh motorbike. We're luckier. The first of the *caravanus horriblis* species has yet to come crawling out of hibernation. Best, then, not to waste such good roads. Time to pull on hats and coats and gloves again, for even

though the sun is shining, it's going to be pretty cold up there on the moors.

Cold maybe, but still empty and twisty enough for a hot-blooded drive, and what a merry dance the nimble MX-5 leads the Barchetta and MGF. When it comes to precision and response, the Mazda is still king, although there are noticeable changes over the old – not all of them good.

Power steering is now standard across the range, which is good as the old, non-assisted system did tend to get heavy in slow corners. The new system allows just the merest hint of delay before the car responds and maybe it could do with a bit more feel, but there's no questioning the MX-5's sharpness into corners. The Japanese car retains its excellent all-round independent double-wishbone suspension, although the geometry has been modified and the track widened. The

1.8iS also comes with very grippy 195/50 R15 Michelin Pilot rubber.

For outright cornering ability and grip, the new MX-5 is an improvement over the old, but – and it's a sizeable but – some of the fun has gone. To put it simply, it's no longer as easy to get the tail out. We're not talking fantasy 80mph opposite-lock slides here, just the sort of quick, tail-out tweak on the exit of a bend that made the old car such fun. You just can't do it any more on a dry road without some serious provocation, which is a shame. All the same, the MX-5 is still more fun to drive than its rivals here.

The Barchetta, like some pasty-faced delinquent dragged from the shopping mall and forced on a twenty-mile hike over the moors, does not respond well to hard work in an unforgiving rural environment. It's front-wheel-drive chassis – the only one here – has the

least sophisticated suspension of the three, with MacPherson struts at the front and trailing arms at the rear. It puts up a valiant effort, but the type of bumpy, twisty roads which leave the Mazda unscathed, vanquish it in the end. It grips quite well but its steering is too imprecise and it suffers from too much body roll to shine on such roads.

With its mid-engined layout and double wishbone Hydragas suspension, one might expect the MGF to be the brightest star here, but that's not how it feels. It rides better than the others, and when worked hard its handling is competent, safe and effective. But it never truly comes alive in your hands the way the Mazda does. The variable power-assisted steering is light at low speeds and gets heavier when you corner harder, but you want feel as well as weight from steering, and the MGF provides only the former. Although

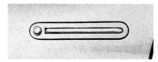

Fiat has steel wheels but they look great, as do the door handles

Mazda has most powerful engine, but it doesn't sound that great

Handle, boot and mirror are the only bits without an MG badge

rear-wheel drive, it's much more prone to understeer than oversteer, in the dry at least. It's safe and efficient, but not particularly exciting, involving or fun.

Like little children all too happy and unaware in their evening play, dusk has crept upon us. As the suns sets, the air grows cold around us and the darkness spreads out from the thorny moorland hedges. Quickly the moor seems a sinister place and it's time, I reckon, to motorvate with all haste to a strong-walled, strong-aled local hostelry.

For sheer 'lets get out of here quick' ability, there's not much to separate the three cars. All have four-cylinder, 16-valve engines and all posted very similar 0-60mph times at the track.

The MX-5 should have fared better; it's 1.8-litre engine has had a power hike from 128 to 138bhp and Mazda claims 0-62mph in 8.0 seconds. Ours took 8.9 to 60mph, though when we

figured it the car still had very low mileage and we had to treat it with consideration for its youth. On the road, though, with a few more miles racked up, it feels quickest of the three and would be my choice for escaping foes – real or imagined. It's a shame it has such a harsh, uninspiring cry to it.

Both the 130bhp Barchetta and the 118bhp MG sound better, with the Rover proving the smoother of the two as well. The Fiat's engine needs plenty of revs but it is, as they say, 'up for it'. The MGF is not only hampered by a lack of power but also quite tall gearing. It's fine on long straight roads, exercising its long legs up to the 7,000rpm red-line, but the gearing doesn't make for snappy overtaking or sharp acceleration away from any of those moorland beasties.

But we all make it safely to the pub and sit there, contentedly sipping our

Exmoor Ale by a big fire while supper is being cooked, watched over by stuffed examples of those who didn't escape the moor so lightly.

The next morning is a fine one to be alive on. It really does feel like Spring. The sort of day when you feel just a little bit smug, hood-down in a sports car, feeling the wind on your face. It doesn't last, though, and all too soon the weather has changed to dark and cold. It's time to pull the hoods up and head for home and warmth.

The Mazda is best for high-speed, hood-up motoring. It's the only one with a proper glass rear window and is easily the quietest of the trio. The Barchetta makes too much noise and it's all too easy to clonk your head on the hood hinges in the narrow cabin.

The MGF's levels of wind noise are tolerable, but if they annoy you too much in the winter months, you can

always purchase the £1,125 hard top, which is an advantage the MGF offers over the other two. Sadly it's about the only major one, for considering it costs almost £18,000, the MGF is not a terribly well equipped car. True, it's the only car here to have an alarm as well as an immobiliser, but you can't have electric mirrors – standard in the other two – and anti-lock brakes are optional, while again, they're standard on both the Barchetta and MX-5.

But what the MGF really lacks is any special magic. Its exterior and interior styling are nowhere near as appealing as the Fiat's and as a driving package it can't really compete with the Mazda. Despite its clever engineering, it wins no special place in our hearts.

Then what about the Fiat? It's a car you could be tempted to buy straight out of the showroom without ever taking it for a drive, so sexy does it

Sadly, living with a sports car isn't all sun-kissed driving days, there are more practical issues to consider, too. All these cars have standard immobilisers, but only the MGF provides an alarm too. Thieves won't be interested in the Barchetta's unique-size stereo but you need to remember to remove the panel from the Rover and the front from the Mazda's stereo. Stowage space in the Barchetta is measly, average in the MGF and better in the MX-5. All have enough bootspace to carry a week's shopping or enough luggage space for two for a week's hols

TOPS AND TAILS	Fiat Barchetta	Mazda MX-5	Rover MGF
Performance			
0-30mph (secs)	2.9	2.9	2.8
0-40mph (secs)	4.5	4.7	4.4
0-50mph (secs)	6.4	6.5	6.5
0-60mph (secs)	8.7	8.9	8.8
0-70mph (secs)	11.6	11.8	12
0-80mph (secs)	14.9	14.9	15.9
0-90mph (secs)	19.9	19.7	21.2
0-100mph (secs)	26.3	25.5	29.2
Max speed, mph	118.1	119.2	117.7
Standing 1/4 mile (secs)	16.7	16.7	16.7
30-50mph in 3rd/4th	5.3/7.8	5.2/7.4	5.5/7.5
50-70mph in 5th	10.5	11.6	12.1
30-70mph thru' gears	8.7	8.9	9.2
Braking 70-0mph (ft)	175.5	164.9	167.9
Costs			
On the road price/Insurance group	£15,824/16	£18,775/13	£17,995/12
Replacement hood	£580	£429	£448
Test mpg/combined mpg	29.0/33.2	28.9/33.2	32.7/38.3
Service interval/Warranty	9,000/1yr unltd	9,000/3yr/60k	12,000/1yr unltd
Equipment			
Airbag driver/passenger	yes/no	yes/yes	yes/option
Alarm/immobiliser	option/yes	no/yes	yes/yes
Alloy wheels/ABS	no/yes	yes/yes	yes/option
Power steering/Radio cassette	yes/yes	yes/yes	yes/yes
Central locking/remote	yes/option	yes/yes	yes/yes
Electric windows/mirrors	yes/yes	ye/yes	yes/no
Glass rear window/hard top	no/no	yes/no	no/option
Technical			
Engine/capacity (cc)	4-cyl dohc 16v/1,747	4-cyl dohc 16v/1,839	4-cyl dohc 16v/1,796
Max power (bhp @ rpm)	130 @ 6,300	138 @ 6,500	118 @ 5,500
Max torque (lb/ft @ rpm)	121 @ 4,300	119 @ 4,500	122 @ 3,000
Transmission	5-speed man, fwd	5-speed man, rwd	5spd man, rwd
Front brakes/Rear brakes	vent disc/solid disc	vent disc/solid disc	vent disc/solid disc
Front suspension	MacP strut	dble wshbone	dble wsh + hydragas
Rear suspension	trailing arms	dble wshbone	dble wsh + hydragas
Wheels	15x6.5 J steel	15x6 J alloy	15x6 J alloy
Tyres	195/55 R15	195/50 R15	205/50 R15
Dimensions L/W (mm)	3,911, 1,640	3,975, 1,680	3,911, 1,626

look both inside and out. Yes it comes with left-hand drive only and yes, it has a hefty group 16 insurance rating, but it only costs £15,824. Surely that's enough to make it win here?

Almost, but not quite, for when you do take the Barchetta out of the showroom expecting a tight, invigorating sports car drive, it just can't deliver. It doesn't drive badly, far from it, but its vague handling and sloppy gearbox are too far removed from what a proper sports car should feel like. No matter how much it tears at the heart strings, we can't give victory to something that looks every inch a sports car, but doesn't quite go like one.

So that leaves the Mazda in first place. At £18,775 it's the most expensive here but also the best equipped and the most powerful. However, the winning margin is not as large as it ought to be. You can argue that it hasn't lost its looks, only changed them, but what can't be denied is that it has lost a lot of its identity and character. It's lost some of its driving fun too, by being no longer so easy to provoke sideways in classic sports car style.

Fortunately, the old Mazda had such reserves of driving fun in the first place that it can afford to lose a little and still be the best, and by a long way at that. It still sticks true to the simple formula of a just-powerful-enough, front-mounted engine and brilliant, sharp rear-wheel-drive handling. And that's probably where Rover and Fiat and anyone else needs to start, if they are ever going to build a sports car than can beat it □

Mazda MX-5 1.6i

Get your laughing gear warmed up for the 1.6-litre MX-5. And if you feel like making any jokes about this convertible being a hairdresser's car, the last laugh could be on you, because hairdressers obviously have excellent taste – and more fun behind the wheel than you'd ever imagine. With a pert, cheeky, roadster body, coupled with rear-wheel drive and a lusty 110bhp engine, the 1.6i makes for huge dollops of entertainment – especially when it's drizzling.

On the tight and twisty stuff the MX-5 does take a little getting used to. It's a much more challenging drive than the average hatch, and woeful tales about rear-wheel drive and wet weather ensure you keep your wits about you. But if you want to learn about life after front-wheel drive – and find out what all those magazine road-testers have been raving about for years – the baby Mazda's a great place to start. Add the incredibly flexible and free-revving engine to the mix and the MX-5 is a delightful drive – both on country lanes and faster-moving motorways (although the wind noise might irritate after a while).

The top-of-the-range 1.8iS version costs an extra £3255 and will give you 138bhp underfoot. You'll also get: a set of 15in alloys (which are an option on the 1.6) rather than the 14in steel wheels, along with electric mirrors and windows. central locking, a limited slip diff and anti-lock braking. Not forgetting a stereo, leather steering wheel and front and rear mudflaps! Add the wheels and the mudflaps, though, and you'll be hard-pushed to tell them apart.

The top end speed of both cars isn't vastly different with only 5mph between them but if it's a quick acceleration buzz you're after, the 1.6 is a little way behind in the traffic light grand prix (though the stylish looks of the reshaped MX-5 should keep people staring at the bodywork long enough to give you a head start).

The most memorable feature of the MX-5 is the glorious gearbox – and the 1.6 gets that too. The short shift is switch-like but smooth and you'll be changing up and down through the gears at every available opportunity. And even unavailable ones.

Maybe you'll bemoan the lack of creature comforts, but what we're looking at here is a serious driver's tool. Drive it hard and fast or drop the top and take it easy; the MX–5 is equally able to oblige. As for spending the extra £3255 on the 1.8 version, why bother?

MX-5 1.6i provides nearly all the magic of the more expensive models, and that means a corking rear-drive chassis, a keen, 16v twin-cam engine, and a gearshift that's as sweet as any you'll find. Cockpit is back-to-basics, but that suits the character of the car right down to the ground

MX-5	1.6i	1.8iS
Price	£15,520	£18,775
Insurance group	11	13
Max power	109bhp	138bhp
	@ 6500rpm	@ 6500rpm
Max torque	99lb ft	120lb ft
	@ 5000rpm	@ 4500rpm
Power to weight	108bhp/ton	134bhp/ton
0–60mph	9.7secs	7.4secs
Max speed	118mph	123mph
Cosmetic costs?	Alloy wheels £440. Mudflaps £106	

Mazda MX-5

MODEL TESTED 1.6i **ON-ROAD PRICE** £15,520
TOP SPEED 122mph **0-60MPH** 8.9sec
30-70MPH 9.0sec **60-0MPH** 3.2sec **MPG** 29.2
FOR Terrific handling, great steering, crisp gearchange, neat hood
AGAINST No anti-lock brakes, seats short on support

The average lifespan for a Japanese sports car is somewhere between four and five years, after which a newer, faster, better version is introduced which often renders the outgoing model obsolete. And then there's the Mazda MX-5.

It is safe to say that without the unprecedented sales success of Mazda's seminal roadster, cars like the BMW Z3, MGF and Fiat Barchetta might never have been given the go-ahead. When the MX-5 unexpectedly carved its way into the hearts of hundreds of thousands of people worldwide, BMW, Fiat and Rover needed no further encouragement to begin crafting their own interpretations on Mazda's elegantly simple theme.

The fact that it has taken Mazda nine years to replace the MX-5 – it was unveiled in February 1989 – is testament to the genius of the original design. But spare a thought for the designers and engineers

at Mazda's Hiroshima headquarters: replacing this car will have been one of their toughest assignments ever.

The result of all their deliberations is a car that's a little heavier and a little fatter in most directions than its predecessor. But that's not any cause for concern, as we shall see. Beneath its curvy

Alloys of test car cost £440 extra

Styling perhaps not as cute as old car's, but body far stiffer and stronger

new skin – to some eyes less attractive than before – the new MX-5 is a much-improved car. That's some achievement when you consider how good the old car was, even on the day Mazda announced its departure from the price lists.

The main engineering changes are to the bodyshell and chassis, which have been stiffened considerably. In truth, however, there isn't a single aspect of the new car that hasn't been either modified or replaced, even though the basic front engine/rear drive formula with double wishbone suspension all round has been left well alone.

While the range-topping 1.8-litre MX-5's engine has

been extensively tweaked to uncork a more useful 138bhp, our test car's old 1597cc 16-valve twin-cam engine has simply been refined to produce 108bhp at 6500rpm and 99lb ft of torque at 5000rpm, fractionally up from before. The result is that performance has improved in both cases – slightly in the case of the 1.6, significantly in the 1.8.

For example, the new 1.6 MX-5 takes 8.9sec to reach 60mph from rest and 9.0sec to get from 30-70mph, whereas the old one needed 9.1sec and 9.5sec respectively. And the new car has a top speed of 122mph, compared with its predecessor's 114mph, indicating that the new shape is much more

aerodynamic than before (although no Cd figure was available to us).

The new MX-5 is also considerably more flexible in the higher gears, an area in which the old 1.6 was not strong. The 50-70mph lug in top gear has been cut by more than a second to 12.8sec, while the 30-50mph amble in fourth is now 8.2sec, which sounds poor beside the old car's time of 7.5sec, until you take into account the latest car's longer overall gearing – 19.7mph per 1000rpm in top versus 18.8.

Unsurprisingly, this has also had the benefit of reducing overall mechanical noise levels quite dramatically on the motorway, especially with

Small lip distinguishes new boot

the hood up. The engine has always been free-revving and smooth in operation, but the combination of longer gearing and internal engineering improvements has made it even better subjectively, the end result being one of the slickest small sports car drivetrains there is. This feeling is heightened when the quality of the gearchange is taken into

account, which, if you can believe it, is even crisper than before.

What initially separated the MX-5 from its army of impersonators was its simple but beautifully effective blend of well-balanced front-engined, rear-drive handling, refreshingly uncorrupted steering and good, sharp brakes. Although it wasn't especially rapid across

country, it was one of the most fun cars you could possibly wish to drive hard over a good road. And in the wet it was plain fantastic. The good news is that fundamentally it's very much business as usual for the new car; Mazda has simply polished away one of two of the old car's less smooth edges.

There is, if anything, even more fluidity to the way the ◗

Retro-style eyeball vents are still there; gearchange is better than ever

ENGINE

Layout 4 cyls in line, 1597cc
Max power 108bhp at 6500rpm
Max torque 99lb ft at 5000rpm
Specific output 68bhp per litre
Power to weight 108bhp per tonne
Torque to weight 99lb ft per tonne
Installation Front, longitudinal, rear-wheel drive
Construction Aluminium head, iron block
Bore/stroke 78.0/83.6mm
Valve gear 4 valves per cyl, dohc
Compression ratio 9.4:1
Ignition and fuel Electronic ignition by Mazda, sequential multi-point fuel injection

GEARBOX

Type 5-speed manual by Mazda
Ratios/mph per 1000rpm
1st 3.14/5.2 **2nd** 1.89/8.7 **3rd** 1.33/12.0
4th 1.00/16.0 **5th** 0.81/19.7
Final drive ratio 4.10:1

MAXIMUM SPEEDS

5th 122mph/6000rpm **4th** 112/7000
3rd 84/7000 **2nd** 61/7000 **1st** 36/7000

ACCELERATION FROM REST

True mph	sec	speedo mph
30	3.0	31
40	4.5	42
50	6.4	52
60	8.9	62
70	12.0	73
80	15.7	83
90	21.0	94
100	28.2	105

Standing qtr mile 16.9sec/82mph
Standing km 30.6sec/102mph
30-70mph through gears 9.0sec

ACCELERATION IN GEAR

mph	5th	4th	3rd	2nd
10-30	–	–	6.7	4.2
20-40	12.3	8.6	6.1	4.0
30-50	11.6	8.2	6.0	4.0
40-60	11.6	8.5	6.0	4.6
50-70	12.8	9.0	6.3	–
60-80	14.5	9.4	7.2	–
70-90	17.0	10.5	–	–
80-100	20.8	13.2	–	–

STEERING

Type Rack and pinion, power assisted
Turns lock to lock 2.7

CONTROLS IN DETAIL

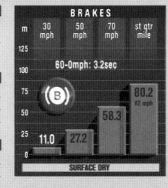

1 Good to see that retro eyeball vents are still there **2** Air conditioning can be specified for an extra £1395 **3** Rifle-bolt gearchange is even sharper than before **4** Dials no longer chrome rimmed. sadly **5** Leather-rimmed wheel adjusts for height: it's slightly larger than before **6** Seats more comfortable than those of old car but could do with more support

SUSPENSION

Front Double wishbones, coil springs over dampers, anti-roll bar
Rear Double wishbones, coil springs over dampers, twin anti-roll bars

WHEELS & TYRES

Wheel size 5.5Jx14in
Made of Cast alloy
Tyres 185/60 HR14 Yokohama A-460
Spare Space saver

BRAKES

Front 255mm ventilated discs
Rear 251mm discs
Anti-lock Not available

BRAKES

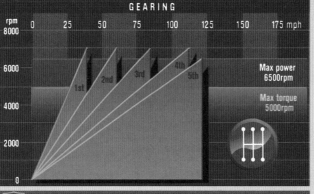

60-0mph: 3.2sec

m	30 mph	50 mph	70 mph	st qtr mile
	11.0	27.2	58.3	80.2 (82 mph)

SURFACE DRY

GEARING

Max power 6500rpm
Max torque 5000rpm

FUEL CONSUMPTION

TEST RESULTS

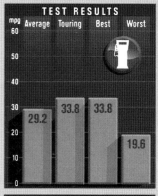

	Average	Touring	Best	Worst
mpg	29.2	33.8	33.8	19.6

GOVERNMENT CLAIMS

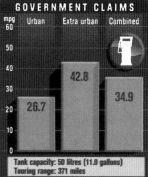

	Urban	Extra urban	Combined
mpg	26.7	42.8	34.9

Tank capacity: 50 litres (11.0 gallons)
Touring range: 371 miles

NOISE

SPL dB (A)	idle	30 mph	50 mph	70 mph	Full accl n
	n/a	n/a	n/a	n/a	n/a

SURFACE N/A

LAYOUT

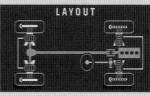

AUTOCAR road tests are conducted using BP Unleaded or BP Diesel Plus with additives to help keep engines cleaner

Body 2dr roadster **Cd** n/a **Front/rear tracks** 1405/1430mm **Turning circle** 9.7m **Min/max front leg room** 990/1090mm **Min/max front head room** 990mm **Interior width** 1360mm **Min/max boot width** 1060/1260mm **Boot length** 560mm **VDA boot volume** 144 litres/dm³ **Kerb weight** 1004kg **Weight distribution f/r** 49/51 per cent **Max payload** 240kg

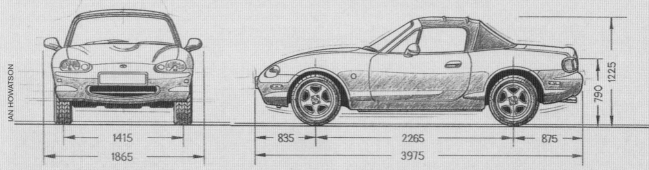

IAN HOWATSON

1415
1865
835
2265
875
3975
122.5
790

Revised 1.6-litre engine produces 108bhp, 99lb ft; performance improved

◀ latest car can string together a series of fast, sweeping corners that aren't especially well surfaced, the one handling area in which the old car was a little suspect. Partly due to the greater chassis stiffness but mainly, we suspect, due to the superior damping qualities of the latest suspension, the new car is markedly better at absorbing shocks when it's loaded up in a corner. Consequently, it's even less likely to be upset on or near the limit of its pleasingly skinny 185/60 HR14 Yokohama tyres.

And even when it does let go it is extremely benign, leaning gradually into a friendly understeering attitude that can only be transformed into catchable oversteer by closing the throttle sharply mid-corner. Power oversteer isn't on the menu in the dry in the less powerful 1.6 version (it's just about achievable in second gear corners in the 1.8), although in

the wet the inherent balance of the chassis immediately comes to the fore, allowing neat oversteer slides to be provoked without raising the pulse by more than a beat or two. Incidentally, no form of traction control is fitted, a move by Mazda which we applaud, if only because it displays a refreshing degree of confidence in the car's natural basic handling balance.

The brakes are also shorn of electronic trickery unless you specify the most expensive 1.8iS model – in other words, there's no anti-lock system. And that's not such good news when it's wet. But at least the basic pedal feel and weighting are well judged, making it difficult to lock the wheels in the dry unless you're clumsy with the pedal.

In order to keep the price down, Mazda chose not to fit an electric hood, going instead with a similar set-up to the

Pop-up lights have been ditched

excellent manual system of the old car. Flick open a couple of catches and away it goes, the main difference now being that the rear window is made of glass rather than plastic and contains a heating element. A neat, easy-to-fit tonneau cover goes over the hood when it's down, and for an extra £149 there's a wind blocker that sits behind the front seats to minimise buffeting in the cabin.

Inside, the new car retains most of, though quite not all, its predecessor's simple charm. The adjustable leather steering wheel is a little bigger in diameter and the seats are

slightly more biased towards comfort than support, but the biggest difference is the disappearance of the chrome rings around the edge of the dials. The knowledge that the new dials are bigger and easier to read and that the eyeball vents are just as retro in design as before does much to offset the chrome's absence, though.

Which leaves just the price and specification to potentially spoil things. Wisely, Mazda has made no such error here. Although the alloy wheels of the test car cost £440 extra, everything else is standard, including twin airbags and an alarm/immobiliser, a vital piece of kit on a soft top that lives in a town centre. At £15,520 on the road, it's fine value indeed and makes the £21k BMW Z3 1.9 look plain expensive.

Mazda has done it: replaced the irreplaceable. And with a car that is even better to drive than its forebear. That's some achievement.

Well-made hood fits very snugly; refinement levels are much improved

WHAT IT COSTS

On-road price	£14,865
Total as tested	£15,520
Cost per mile	41.0p

EQUIPMENT
(**bold** = options fitted to test car)

Automatic transmission	–
Metallic paint	£250
Anti-lock brakes	–
Airbag driver/passenger/side	●/●/–
Remote central locking	●
RDS radio/CD player	●/–
Electric hood	–
Air conditioning	£1395
Detachable hard top	£1475
Heated rear window	●
Wind blocker	£149

● standard – not available

INSURANCE

Group	11
Typical quote	£280

WARRANTY
3 years/36,000 miles, 6yrs anti-corrosion

SERVICING

Interim 9000 miles/12 months, £7 parts	
Major 54,000 miles/2 years, £86 parts	

Handling, ride and fun factor are all improved – no mean achievement for Mazda

Britain's best budget roadster ★★★★

Today, we have the capability to produce a sports car that can travel in excess of 300km/h. Its braking, acceleration, steering and navigation can be monitored for maximum safety by an onboard computer; advanced structural materials, seatbelt pre-tensioners and whole clusters of cockpit airbags would endow it with greater passive safety than any light aircraft.

We can build such a sports car. It's just that, in today's environment, we couldn't really drive it anywhere. The notion of driving as a skill and a pastime has been trampled by over-zealous policing, nice round numbers, non-existent driver training and road networks that have failed to evolve with the cars they're supposed to serve.

However here are two small, relatively affordable sports cars that owe much to the tradition of Lotus founder Colin Chapman. One is the Mazda MX-5, a spiritual successor to the Lotus Elan but with standards of quality, rigidity, reliability and sophistication that Chapman could not have imagined in 1962 when he produced his Elan. The other is a new Lotus, as the young Colin Chapman would have a new Lotus be.

SET TO SSSPRINT

These two sports cars are quite different in personality. Yet, as **MICHAEL STAHL** discovers, in their own ways they both deliver the true thrill of sports driving

WARWICK KENT

The interior of the MX-5 is considerably better soundproofed than the Elise but slightly noisier than its more expensive predecessor.

Both these cars, it could be argued, are the *real* sports cars of the cop-conscious '90s. Both have been acclaimed for their mix of agility and stability, their compromise between cornering and comfort, their foolproof responses. They may not be the fastest of cars, but their blacktop-to-backside communication ensures they're the most fun.

These two quite different roadsters – the practical, mass-produced, front-engined Mazda MX-5 and the pricey, purposeful, mid-engined Elise – have both been hailed as handling benchmarks. So who's zooming who?

The $74,996 Elise has all the hallmarks of a Chapman classic,

screw-you sports car design. The two-seater uses an innovative spaceframe of extruded aluminium sections, bonded together with epoxy glue. The bare chassis weighs just 70kg. The whole, completed car only weighs 736kg.

It's been acclaimed as the new benchmark in handling and responsiveness; major car manufacturers buy Elises to show their suspension teams how good it gets. Double wishbones at each corner with coil-over-dampers are nothing unusual on race cars (nor is it unprecedented on road cars), but the Elise has certainly tidied up the textbook.

Brakes, likewise, are conventional discs – but decidedly unconventional in being the first production fitment of aluminium metal matrix composite discs. Like the rack and pinion steering, the Elise's brakes get by without any power assistance. Its tyres are Pirelli P-Zero Asimmetricos, the fronts 15-inch, the rears 16s.

In Lotus tradition, power comes from a relatively unsexy, mass-produced engine, in this case the Rover K-series 1.8 litre, twin cam 16-valve unit shared with the base-model MG-F sporty and, indeed, the Land Rover Freelander. Bog-stock as you'll find it in the Elise, it produces a modest 88kW at 5500rpm and 165Nm at 3000rpm. Hardly anything for Enzo to envy.

With sod-all to weigh it down, though, the Rover motor's output becomes one half of a pretty spectacular weight-to-power ratio. Each kilowatt has just 8.1kg to carry; while still more than the (roughly) 5 or 6kg burden of each Ferrari F355 or Porsche 911 kilowatt, it puts the Elise in front of the Porsche Boxster (8.3 kg/kW), the BMW Z3 2.8 (9.2), Mercedes-Benz SLK 230 Kompressor (9.3), MG-F VVC (9.9) and, for that matter, the recently revamped Mazda MX-5 (9.7 kg/kW).

Ah, the MX-5. A darling of ours since the launch of the original in 1989, the little Mazda has since been uprated to 1.8 litres (in late-'93) and, in March this year, was superseded by a new model still owing much to the old. The new car has put on just 45kg in weight, an apparently small price for a stiffer chassis,

increased power and torque (now 106kW and 165Nm), slightly broader track widths (10mm front, 20mm rear), Michelin Pilot SX 195/50R x 15 rubber, improved roof with a glass rear window and a 40 percent larger boot.

Actually, it's a small price to pay in financial terms, too, for the new MX-5 which lobs in at only $39,800 – more than $3000 cheaper than the outgoing model. Mind you, one can feel and hear where the money's come out, with sadly harsh and unsupportive seating and evidently more engine, tyre and rear suspension noise getting into the cabin.

There again, compared with the Elise, the MX-5 almost lets you hear the ticking of the digital dashboard clock. Unequipped with any soundproofing, the Elise provides an overwhelming aural experience. Bare aluminium surrounds the driver, save for small rubber foot-mats, plastic door trim inserts and some ($1700 optional) leather trim on the seats, sills and dash.

The Elise's cabin does a fair job with what it's got. Once you've manoeuvred your left leg between the steering wheel and the sill, fallen arse-first into the seat and dragged your right leg after you, the virtually fixed driving position is quite reasonable.

The Elise's one-piece moulded racing buckets have you fairly

A TRAILBLAZING TRADITION

Lotus has not only tried, but has produced all the logical basic vehicle layouts on the small, light weight sports cars developed by the company bar the rear-engine, rear drive setup favoured by Porsche. The original Elan used a traditional front-engine, rear drive design. The Elan of the 1980s became the first Lotus to use front-wheel drive and the latest small Lotus road car Stahly is writing about here relies on the mid-engined layout which first appeared on a road-going Lotus in the Europa of the mid 1960s.

The original Elan is one of the best remembered Lotus road cars, and not only because Emma Peel from *The Avengers* drove one. When the small, backbone-chassised roadster appeared at Earls Court in 1962, it indeed created quite a fuss. Though technically less adventuresome than the original Elite (with its unique fibreglass monocoque construction), the Elan was considerably more affordable than the Elite had been, due in no small part to the fact that Lotus was using its own, albeit Ford-based, engine in the new car (see Retro, page 122). The car offered magnificent balance, though by modern standards the grip was just so-so. But the thing was such a delight to drive on the tyres of the day, you wouldn't care even in one today.

The 'new' Elan had rather protracted development. The car was originally rumoured to be designed around a Toyota engine and gearbox. However, Toyota's interest was displaced by General Motors which eventually bought the Hethel-based car-maker. Corporate myth has it that this required a redesign of the 'new' Elite around an Isuzu 1.6 litre engine and transaxle, with a delay from the original target launch a side-effect. The front-drive Elan was dynamically a damn good front-driver (as you'd expect something from Lotus to be), but despite the off the shelf powertrain it was expensive to build and the timing was unfortunate, as the car appeared around the same time as the MX-5's debut, causing some traditionalists to say the MX was the car Lotus 'should' have built.

Now, with the Elise, Lotus has once again stepped into trail-blazing mode with a car that's not so much a replacement for the previous Elans as it is a Lotus Seven for the 21st century. Perhaps more toy-like than a mainstream car, there's some impressive technology in the Elise, such as the aluminium chassis which relies upon TIG welding and structural adhesives to stay in one piece. *BH*

The interior of the Elise takes minimalism to the extreme – don't expect soft seat cushion or noise insulation. A crane helps in getting in or out.

LIVING WITH THE ELISE

Odd thing about the Elise – eulogised by British mags for its superb balance, adroit handling and brilliant performance, it was the car everyone wanted to drive at first. But after a couple of days in the *Wheels* garage, there were no more fights for the keys. "I'm over it," was the common response.

Maybe we're soft, but we found the Elise was – quite literally – a pain in the arse to live with. You need to be contortionist to get into the bloody thing – especially with the roof on – and the race-style bucket seats have negligible padding. The reality is the Elise is harsh, cramped and uncomfortable.

There's nothing wrong with building a minimalist sports car. What annoys is the obvious lack of attention to detail in other areas that stamps Lotus, for all its engineering flair, as little more than a jumped up kit-car maker.

Surely it's possible to build a minimalist sports car with a hood that's light, simple and easy to use. Or a HVAC system that doesn't sound like a threshing machine chewing gravel. Especially for 75 grand – and that doesn't include the optional radio, leather trim, driving lights and metallic paint on our test car...

All of which throws the new MX-5 into sharp relief. On anything other than a race track, it's damn near as much fun to drive as an Elise, a helluva lot easier to live with and costs half as much. The MX-5 proves building a great sports car isn't as hard as Lotus would have us believe. And that building an MX-5 is a lot more than Lotus could manage. *A MacK*

well reclined but, despite their body-hugging form, there's perhaps only 5mm of padding beneath the upholstery. The driver's seat alone gets a rubber-bulb inflater with which to vary lumbar support, but it doesn't stop tailbone ache.

Everything you touch in the Elise makes a noise. You move the seat – it's adjustable for fore-aft slide only – and the locking pins clunk through the bare floor. Turn on the ventilation fan (loud whirr), slide the control onto heat (a frizzing sound), depress the clutch pedal (metallic clunk against the floor), press the brakes (squeal).

Of course, out on the road most of this will be drowned out in the aural assault from the mid-mounted engine and from the thrashing and clunking transmitted directly between the suspension and the floor.

One major letdown in the tactility department is the long, rubbery gearshift action, which feels little different from a stock, front-drive hatchback's. Everything else is lively when the Elise hits the road. The unassisted but comfortably firm steering has virtually no freeplay at the straight-ahead – it shuffles and jiggles in your hands like an early-model 911's and is super-quick, if still linear, just off-centre.

The overriding feeling from the Elise on the road is of its light weight. Hard to explain, but one can sense that the thing accelerates so fast, darts like a rat into corners and stops like a stomped cockroach - not because it's big and powerful and super-grippy, but because it's not slowed in any direction by much inertial mass.

With very little dive, squat or roll in the suspension, it's like hitting a golf ball: One second it's stationary, the next, it's simply on the move.

For all its feeling of lightness and agility, however, the Elise isn't one to hit a bump and bounce off the road; it holds its line impressively even on choppy surfaces, although the crashing and banging tends to temper your speed.

The new MX-5 feels a lot like the old one – only better. Straight-line performance is little changed, the slight increase in power output more than offsetting the slight increase in weight.

The steering is actually as heavily weighted but initially much slower than the Elise's, exacerbated by the Mazda's large, airbagged wheel. However it is no less linear in its turn-in, and not lacking in its feedback, either. Funnily enough, the Mazda has fewer turns lock-to-lock (2.5 versus the Elise's 2.7) and a smaller turning circle. But, either way you slice it, the MX-5's 330kg weight deficit is bound to show in the immediacy of its responses.

It's more conventional, dare we say car-like, in the manner of its shifting loads during direction changes – you don't turn it into corners, you set it up into corners. Which is not to say that the MX-5 wants for much once it's there.

But what of the pure, hard-arsed technicalities of handling? The things that can be measured by impressively expensive and needlessly complex test equipment? Jolly glad you asked, because I wanted a fang around Eastern Creek.

The Elise was faster. By around eight seconds per lap, circulating in the 1:59s against the Mazda's 2:06 – this latter number, a second faster than the previous model MX-5 in *Wheels'* handling fest. A 1:59 lap was also one second quicker than the Porsche Boxster, half a second faster than the Subaru Impreza WRX and eight seconds faster than the MG-F, powered by the up-spec, 108 kW, VVC variable-valve version of the Elise's engine.

But interestingly, although it always felt like it, the Lotus wasn't faster than the Mazda everywhere. Its mid-corner speeds and lateral G limits weren't so vastly superior to the MX-5's.

On studying our *Wheels* numbers, the Lotus was reliably pulling lateral Gs about 10 percent higher than those of the heavier, skinnier-tyred Mazda. But where the Lotus makes up a lot of its time is through its ability to brake far later and harder – like, 0.9G where the Mazda will squirm at 0.7 – and accelerate sooner and faster. Both, of course, are functions of its having less inertia.

In fact, the Lotus got so quickly out of Eastern Creek's Turn 2 left-hairpin that its nose would push wide through Turn 3, the open right-hander that immediately follows. A classic, mid-engined feel to the front end.

The odd, small bite out of the Elise's G-analyst cornering diagrams illustrates the rear end's sensitivity to road camber. Also quite typical of a mid-engined machine, the Lotus can get twitchy on a trailing throttle or on a falling road camber.

At two particular corners on the Eastern Creek circuit – the flip-flop left Turn 5 and the left-crest Turn 8 over Corporate Hill – the Lotus would lead nicely into the corner and progressively take up the load on the outside before its rear end stepped out quite assertively. Again, it felt like the world's lightest Porsche 911 and, like the Porsche, requires some degree of throttle input pretty much all of the time to keep its tail-end stable. It's go-karty, but you've got to stay on top of it.

The Mazda, by comparison, feels even slower than seven seconds per lap around here. Which is intended as a compliment, because this car is just so easy, so stable and foolproof in its handling. Despite its much greater body roll, suspension movement and generally slower responses, it's got to be the safer bet for over-enthusiastic drivers on unpredictable road surfaces.

Push the Mazda too fast into a corner and it'll simply wash off the speed in understeer; get totally out of the gas in mid-corner and it'll lazily slew it off in oversteer. You just wheel the Mazda into a corner, hook it straight onto the limit of its lateral adhesion and let it hang there for a fraction, before feeding in the gas and looking for the concrete on your exit.

Its power output is quite sufficient to propel it efficiently and

EASTERN CREEK

	Mazda MX-5	Lotus Elise
Turn 1	143.2km/h; 0.90G	137.5km/h; 0.79G
Turn 2	63.4km/h; 0.96G	68.4km/h; 0.98G
Turn 3	104.0km/h; 0.86G	111.9km/h; 1.00G
Turn 4	101.1km/h; 0.99G	102.1km/h; 1.00G
Turn 5	96.0km/h; 1.01G	93.6km/h; 1.04G
Turn 6	112.9km/h; 0.45G	114.2km/h; 0.45G
Turn 7	74.9km/h; 0.97G	75.2km/h; 1.02G
Turn 8	112.4km/h; 0.98G	114.0km/h; 1.03G
Turn 9	62.5km/h; 1.08G	61.4km/h; 1.02G
Turn 10	132.6km/h; 0.76G	137.9km/h; 0.68G
Turn 11	82.3km/h; 0.90G	86.0km/h; 0.90G
Turn 12	87.3km/h; 1.04G	91.0km/h; 1.04G
Lap	2:06.4sec	1:59.9sec
Price	$41,670 (as tested)	$80,150 (as tested)
Engine	1.8 litre longitudinal four	1.8 litre transverse four
Max power	106kW at 6500rpm	89kW at 5500rpm
Max torque	165Nm at 4500rpm	166Nm at 3000rpm
Power to weight	9.68kg/kW	8.12kg/kW
Length	3975mm	3726mm
Wheelbase	2265mm	2300mm
Weight	1026kg	723kg
0-100km/h	8.76sec	7.12sec
SS 400m	16.39sec at 135.6km/h	15.17sec at 141.9km/h

unspectacularly out of corners with little worry of wheelspin.

I lost a couple of kilograms driving the Lotus – not because it's hard work to drive, because it isn't. Rather, the pure annoyance of having to get in and out of this car kept me from stopping at the shops on my way home. On the pure aggravation of entry and egress alone, the Lotus dumps a bucketful of charm points.

As a Sunday morning or club sport car, however , the new Lotus clearly steps up the game that its predecessor of 40 years ago invented.

And the MX-5? What you're buying in the little Mazda sure doesn't feel like $35,000 less. Its blend of fun and forgiveness brings true sports car fun within reach of more people, yet the hard, scientific evidence shows that it's hardly shamed in the handling stakes. Four decades ago, the Lotus 7 tried to teach us that sports cars aren't necessarily about horsepower, but handling. Today, we have a new pair of prodigies proving the point. **⚙**

MAZDA'S perfect 10

The refinements and new features built into the 10th Anniversary MX-5 underscore the excellence of this beloved roadster

Birthday presents don't come any sweeter than this. Forget the cake and candles, and the daft paper hats. Ten years after releasing the original MX-5 to a startled but appreciative market, Mazda has come up with a new version of the world's best value sports car which has subtly improved the whole package.

Yep, the MX-5 has been on the road 10 years since the first volume production cars rolled off Mazda's Hiroshima line in April 1989. There's been a model change since then, of course, after exactly 431,543 examples of the original MX-5 were sold up until November 1997.

To mark the small sports car's 10th anniversary, Mazda has released a special edition called, not surprisingly, the 10th Anniversary. Unlike plenty of other one-off production runs, this MX-5 adds far more than just a new pinstripe and free air-conditioning. This one has got real mechanical improvements and,

STORY | **Jonathan Hawley**
PHOTOS | **Stuart Grant**

after a good drive of the 10th Anniversary, it's fair to say they go some way towards making a great car even better.

Chief among these improvements is the adoption of a six-speed manual gearbox in place of the usual five-speeder. The transmission changes entail more than just the addition of an extra tall overdrive gear; all six have been bunched closer together to give crisper acceleration and fill any holes in the power delivery of the 1.8-litre, 16-valve engine.

The engine itself has had most of its moving internals balanced and blueprinted to promote smoothness, although Mazda still quotes the same 106 kW power output of mainstream MX-5s. Nevertheless, on the road it is immediately obvious there's more verve, thanks largely to the shorter and closer spaced lower gears.

Extra acceleration is evident on the road (if not in the figures) and

shuffling back two or three cogs through the six-speed heading into a corner is even more inspiring because of the holes which have been filled in the torque delivery. On the drag strip the Correvit shows little improvement over the five-speed, a result of extra time-sapping gear changes which negate the leverage of lower ratios in the lower gears.

The anniversary model also has Bilstein gas shock absorbers and a brace linking the front suspension struts. It sounds like a recipe for race-car like handling and a rocky ride, but that is not the case. If anything, the ride quality is more compliant and there's less of the scuttle shake and body shimmy which affects every

it remains true to the original concept – to bring a cheesy grin to the driver's face

convertible car, including the MX-5.

As well as new hardware, there's plenty of fruit. Blue is the colour theme, from the mica paintwork, the seats, gearknob and steering wheel, and even the fabric of the roof. Buyers even get a letter from Mazda president James Miller, a key ring and a scale model of their car for the mantlepiece.

Probably the best thing about the 10th Anniversary, however, is that it remains true to the original concept of the MX-5, which is to bring a big cheesy grin to the driver's face. Blipping the throttle and climbing up and down the gearbox was never as much fun, and the handling has a razor sharp, seat-of-the-pants feel, all accompanied by a rasping exhaust note and new 100 km/h hairdo.

It all seems in line with the original MX-5 idea of low weight, tight dimensions and ample feedback from all parts of the car equalling brilliant sports performance. It isn't until you look at the specification of that first car in 1989 – self-winding windows, 1.6-litre engine and plastic rear window included – that you realise the car has grown bigger and more plush. But only a little.

Perhaps the most interesting indicator of the MX-5's success is the announcement that BMW has dropped four-cylinder versions of the Z3 from its Australian line-up. It isn't often BMW is forced to play catch-up, and rarer still that it misses the mark, but if the Z3 was meant to better the MX-5 then it has failed in its mission. An extra $25,000 might have brought BMW owners the luxury and prestige they crave, but on a given stretch of road an MX-5 will eat them any place, any time.

The good news is that at $46,920 the 10th Anniversary MX-5 is still a bargain compared with the $39,800 Mazda asks for the standard car.

The bad news? All 150 which were allocated to Australia out of the 7500-strong production run have been snapped up and sold, so there ain't no more. Keep an eye on the classifieds if you want one, or ask your friendly Mazda dealer if his snouts can snuffle one out. Being hooked on an MX-5 isn't hard, and the little things which make up the anniversary version have sharpened its blade to the finest of cutting edges. **᭢**

acceleration

0-10	0.60
0-20	1.19
0-30	1.73
0-40	2.24
0-50	2.97
0-60	4.03
0-70	4.95
0-80	6.10
0-90	7.21
0-100	8.71
0-110	10.24
0-120	11.80
0-130	14.21
0-400m	16.35 @ 137.6 km/h

body
two-door roadster

drive
rear

engine
1.8-litre 16-valve DOHC in-line four

power
106 kW at 6500 rpm

torque
165 Nm at 4500 rpm

bore x stroke
83 mm x 85 mm

compression ratio
9.5:1

weight
1040 kg

weight/power
9.8 kg/kW

specific power
57.6 kW/litre

transmission
six-speed manual

final drive
3.636:1

suspension
independent by double wishbones, coil springs and anti-roll bar (f&r)

length / width / height
3975/1680/1225 mm

wheelbase
2265 mm

track
1415 mm (f); 1440 mm (r)

brakes
255 mm ventilated discs (f); 251 mm solid discs (r)

wheels
15 x 6-inch alloy

tyres
Michelin Pilot SX, 195/50 R15

fuel capacity
48 litres

price
$46,920

FIRST TEST

MAZDA MIATA 10TH ANNIVERSARY EDITION

EVEN BETTER WITH A SIX-SPEED/by Matt Stone

Has it really been 10 years since Mazda reinvented the classic British sports car? Ten years since igniting a roadster revival that's still spawning new models? Yes, it has. And the fact that more than half a million Miatas have since hit the world's highways proves the concept was indeed a good one. So Mazda is celebrating these milestones with a commemorative model dubbed—appropriately enough—the Miata 10th Anniversary Edition.

But while most such "special editions" amount to little more than not-so-special paint, floor mats, and maybe a decal or two, Mazda has gone the extra mile by making substantive hardware upgrades. The most significant is a new six-speed close-ratio transmission that really sweetens up the Miata's already lively, communicative driving experience.

First gear is a bit shorter than that of the standard five-speed, and the rear-axle ratio is taller (3.91:1 ver-

sus 4.30:1). Fifth gear now becomes 1:1, with sixth being the overdrive. This allows closer ratio spacing between first and fourth, meaning less rpm drop-off as you're going through the gears. Another benefit is slightly more relaxed cruising—rpm at 60 drops from about 3200 revs to an even 3000.

While the power output of the 1.8-liter DOHC four is certainly appropriate for a sporting roadster, you won't confuse its torque curve with a Viper's either. So the new tranny really helps make the most of what the engine has to offer. You'll be shifting more, but that's okay: The Miata's stubby gear change is quicker and slicker than ever, so rowing the box is part of the fun. Performance from 0 to 60 mph improves 0.4 seconds over the five-speed version.

Mazda raided its own parts bin and poured the best of it into its Miata birthday cake. The suspension tuning, adjustable strut tower brace, Torsen limited-slip differ-

The Miata's cabin continues to be businesslike, yet sporty. We found the new suede-ish seat inserts to breathe better than typical vinyl or leather.

MAZDA MIATA SIX-SPEED

GENERAL

Location of final assembly	Hiroshima, Japan
Body style	2-door, 2-passenger
EPA size class	Two-seater
Drivetrain layout	Front engine, rear drive
Airbag	Dual

POWERTRAIN

Engine type	I-4, cast-iron block/aluminum head
Bore x stroke, in./mm	3.27x3.35/83.0x85.0
Displacement, ci/cc	112/1839
Compression ratio	9.5:1
Valve gear	DOHC, 4 valves/cylinder
Fuel/induction system	EFI
Horsepower, hp @ rpm, SAE net	140 @ 6500
Torque, lb-ft @ rpm, SAE net	119 @ 5500
Horsepower/liter	76.1
Redline, rpm	7000
Transmission type	6-speed manual
Axle ratio	3.91:1
Final-drive ratio	3.30:1
Recommended fuel	Regular unleaded

DIMENSIONS

Wheelbase, in./mm	89.2/2266
Track, f/r, in./mm	55.7/56.7 / 1414/1440
Length, in./mm	155.3/3945
Width, in./mm	66.1/1679
Height, in./mm	48.4/1229
Base curb weight, lb	2299
Weight distribution, f/r, %	50/50
Cargo capacity, cu ft	5.1
Fuel capacity, gal.	12.7
Weight/power ratio, lb/hp	16.4

CHASSIS

Suspension, f/r	Upper & lower control arms, coil springs, anti-roll bar/upper & lower control arms, coil springs, anti-roll bar
Steering type	Rack and pinion, power assist
Ratio	18:1
Turns, lock to lock	3.2
Turning circle, ft	30.2
Brakes, f/r	Vented disc/disc, ABS optional
Wheels, in.	15 x 6.0, aluminum alloy
Tires	195/50VR15, Michelin Pilot SX

PERFORMANCE

Acceleration, sec	
0-30 mph	2.4
0-40 mph	3.7
0-50 mph	5.4
0-60 mph	7.5
0-70 mph	10.2
0-80 mph	13.3
Standing quarter mile, sec/mph	15.8/86.8
Braking, 60-0 mph, ft	131
Lateral acceleration, g	0.91
Speed through 600-ft slalom, mph	67.0
EPA fuel economy, mpg, city/hwy	24/29

PRICE

Base price	$26,900 (est.)
Price as tested	$26,900 (est.)
www.mazdausa.com	

ential, and high-pressure gas-charged Bilstein shocks come from the Sport suspension option; Michelin Pilots over polished 15-inch alloys complete the handling hardware. The Appearance Package's front air dam, side sills, and rear mud guards also are standard.

The entire ensemble is done up in an eye—and light—catching Sapphire blue-and-black color combination. Seating comfort is enhanced via grippy-and-breathable faux suede inserts, and the leather-wrapped steering wheel and shift knob are Nardi designer pieces. Chrome bezels highlight the speedo and tach, and all the gauges sport red needles. Blue is also the color of choice for the top and tonneau cover. Don't forget the obligatory special floor mats and a build-sequence number badge on the left front fender.

No British roadster of the '50s or '60s ever packed as much into a proper sports car interior as does the Miata. Particularly impressive is how Mazda manages to squeeze a powerful, crisp-sounding Bose audio system (with both CD and cassette players) and logically laid out, easy-to-use heating and air conditioning controls—into an area on the console that's only about two-thirds the size of this page.

No other major enhancements were required, as the Miata was redesigned—and substantially improved in just about every way—last year, as a '99 model. Final pricing has also yet to be announced, though expect it to be about double that of the original '90 Miata's $13,000 range. For now, you can only get the six-speed on the Anniversary model; Mazda is being coy about when it will be made standard or optional on other Miatas. So if you want one, don't dawdle: There'll only be 7500 10th Anniversary Edition Miatas built, just 3000 of which are earmarked for the U.S. market. **MT**

MAZDA
MIATA

Could this be *your* Miata?

BY JOHN MATRAS
PHOTOS BY BRIAN BLADES

What have they done to my Miata? Well, not my Miata, actually. The Miata. Although I do feel some ownership of the model by having driven one of the first in the country and having written about it lo these many years. And now they've changed it. They had changed it before, but those were upgrades, refreshes and embellishments. The 1999 Miata is new. The body panels are new, the chassis is stiffer and the engine more powerful. It's a different car.

But is it a better car? Carmakers have been known to refine the emotional purity out of a classic. And the Miata was one of those rare cars that hit the sweet spot in the emotional psyche of car lovers around the world. Well, rest easy. If you loved the original Miata—and you know you did—you'll be entranced by the new one.

Although the '99 Miata looks very similar to its predecessor, the details are different. Most noticeable are the exposed oval headlamps that replace the previous pop-up lamps. They make the front end a little more ordinary, perhaps, but at least the illuminated airbrakes—the pop-up lamps when raised—are gone. Other subtle refinements include more curves in the hood and fenders, a curved door cut line a la Miata show cars, and a raised lip on the decklid. A larger grille opening allows for more cooling air. Overall, the new Miata has a more aggressive look. If the old Miata smiled, the new one grins.

It has something to grin about. Under that new hood are 140 horses (less two in California, thanks to a "direct fit" catalyst in addition to the usual undercar cat). The compression ratio has been bumped to 9.5:1 and camshaft profiles are new. The iron-block/aluminum-head dohc 1.8-liter engine has a new cylinder head with larger, straighter intake and exhaust

ports with a new Variable Intake Control System that improves breathing and part-throttle operation. That may be, but what drivers will notice is the extra punch. It comes at some expense in harshness, but it's a reasonable trade-off. And the new engine still runs on regular 87-octane unleaded.

Mazda claims it has improved the 5-speed manual transmission by reducing the vibration of the shift knob and "making the gearchanges smoother and easier." Hmmm, has anyone ever complained about the Miata's shifting ... that is, other than competitors who have used the Miata's manual transmission as a benchmark? Mazda also changed the shift knob "to better conform to the driver's hand." How many times have carmakers made this claim?

Of course, the Miata has always been known for its balance of performance and handling, so the chassis was upgraded to match the added power. Mazda's innovative Power Plant Frame, basically a truss between the engine and differential, has been retained. Credit this appliance for the immediate response the

Miata has to the throttle, eliminating the usual need to wind up all the bushings from one end of the car to the other. But the new body, subjected to more extensive computer modeling than the original, has greater bending and torsional rigidity. Mazda added more gusseting to both ends of the center tunnel, to the side sills and at the base of the A-pillar. These aren't really felt, but a crisper-handling Miata results. The old Miata tripped lightly around corners; the '99 digs in and holds on like an Olympic square dancer in a power do-se-do.

Befitting a modern sports car, the brakes are ventilated discs front and rear, 10.0 and 9.9 in. diameter, respectively, perhaps the most fade-proof binders on any production automobile I've driven. You can jump on the middle pedal all day long and expect the same, strong effect every time. They're so good you don't have to think about them. You'll have brakes. Period.

The basic suspension remains double A-arm front and rear with anti-roll bars at each end, just like you'd do if you were designing a race car. A Sports Package is a must for the serious enthusiast, and it comes with bigger 15-in. wheels, a nifty 3-spoke NARDI leather-wrapped steering wheel, Torsen limited-slip differential, sport suspension with Bilstein shocks and a strut bar between the front suspension towers. Visual cues to a Sport Package- equipped Miata are the front air dam and rear decklid spoiler.

Mazda likes to throw the options at you in clumps. There's also the Power Steering Package that includes engine-speed-sensitive power steering and wheel trim rings for the base styled-steel 14-in. wheels. Add the Touring Package for power steering, 14-in. alloy wheels, the NARDI wheel and power windows and mirrors. The Popular Equipment Package includes the Touring equipment plus the Torsen limited-slip rear end (5-speed only), cruise control, power antenna, special wide-range speakers, power locks and the draft-stopping Windblocker. Up one more level is the Leather Package which includes 15-in. alloy wheels, tan leather seats and interior trim, a tan vinyl top and trick Bose audio system. The Bose system uses special compact

MAZDA

MIATA

PRICE

List price, all POE	$19,770
Price as tested	$22,450

Price as tested includes std equip. (dual airbags, lockable center console, rear defroster, remote fuel/trunk release, molded door trim with armrests, dual cupholder), air conditioning ($900), carpeted floormats ($80), HLEV emissions equipment ($150), Touring Package (pwr steering, pwr mirrors, pwr windows, alloy wheels w/locks, leather-wrapped steering wheel) ($1100), dest charge ($450).

ENGINE

Type	dohc 16-valve inline-4
Displacement	1839 cc
Bore x stroke	83.0 x 85.0 mm
Compression ratio	9.5:1
Horsepower, SAE net	140 bhp @ 6500 rpm[1]
Torque	119 lb-ft @ 5500 rpm[2]
Maximum engine speed	7000 rpm
Fuel injection	elect. sequential port
Fuel requirement	regular unleaded

GENERAL DATA

Curb weight	2299 lb
Weight distribution, f/r, %	50/50
Wheelbase	89.2 in.
Track, f/r	55.7/56.7 in.[3]
Length	155.3 in.
Width	66.0 in.
Height	48.4 in.
Trunk space	5.1 cu ft

CHASSIS & BODY

Layout	front engine/rear drive
Body/frame	unit steel
Brakes, f/r	10.0-in. vented discs/9.9-in. vented discs, vacuum assist
Wheels	cast alloy, 14x6
Tires	Yokohama ADRAN, P185/60R-14
Steering	rack & pinion, variable power assist
Turns, lock to lock	2.7
Suspension, f/r	upper and lower A-arms, coil springs, tube shocks, anti-roll bar/upper and lower A-arms, coil springs, tube shocks, anti-roll bar

DRIVETRAIN

Transmission	5-speed manual

Gear	Ratio	Overall Ratio	Rpm	Mph
1st	3.14:1	13.49:1	7000	34
2nd	1.89:1	8.12:1	7000	56
3rd	1.33:1	5.73:1	7000	80
4th	1.00:1	4.30:1	7000	106
5th	0.81:1	3.50:1	est 6535	123*

Final drive ratio	4.30:1
Engine rpm @ 60 mph, top gear	3200

*Electronically limited

ACCELERATION

Time to speed	Seconds
0–30 mph	2.6
0–40 mph	4.0
0–50 mph	5.7
0–60 mph	8.0
0–70 mph	10.6
0–80 mph	13.7
0–90 mph	17.7
0–100 mph	23.2

Time to distance	
0–100 ft	3.2
0–500 ft	8.7
0–1320 ft (1/4 mile)	16.1 @ 86.5 mph

BRAKING

Minimum stopping distance	
From 60 mph	146 ft
From 80 mph	270 ft
Control	very good
Overall brake rating	good

HANDLING

Lateral accel (200-ft skidpad)	0.83g
Speed thru 700-ft slalom	61.2 mph

FUEL ECONOMY

Normal driving	est 25.0 mpg
EPA city/highway	25/29 mpg
Fuel capacity	12.7 gal.

[1]CA 138 bhp @ 6500 rpm
[2]CA 117 lb-ft @ 5000 rpm
[3]w/alloy wheels

The 1999 Miata digs in and holds on like an Olympic square dancer in a power do-se-do.

components to minimize impact on luggage space.

Bose or no, the new Miata has loads more cargo room than its predecessor, now up to a whole 5.1 cu ft. That's exactly 42 percent more. If you need even more than that, you're packing too much to be driving a car like this. Another welcome improvement is the glass rear window with standard defogger. This may disappoint those who sell the lotions and potions that allegedly keep the old plastic rear windows transparent, but ordinary folks will be relieved of all the obsessive rituals required. The glass window doesn't even need to be unzipped. Just unlatch the header and push it back. Another triumph for modern man. Neatniks can install a soft boot, but for casual running around, the top lays mostly below the body contours, and with its easier operation, the top will get lowered more often.

After all, that's what driving an open car is all about.

Other interior changes include a larger console storage compartment with two built-in cupholders. The compartment still locks and houses the hood and fuel-door release, maintaining some security even with the top lowered. Mazda also changed the switches for the power windows, located on the console, so they are less likely to be pushed accidentally—not that this has ever been a problem for us. Most appreciated is the relocation of the interior lighting to the rearview mirror, rather than under the dash, where the weak lamps on the original Miata mostly illuminated one's shins. Incidentally, it's a sign of the times that the base audio equipment on the '99 Miata is an AM/FM stereo with a standard CD player. A cassette player for those oldies from the '80s is optional.

Yet, for all the changes, the '99 Miata is still a Miata. Certainly better, for one would expect Mazda to learn something from almost a decade of building the car (the Miata made its debut in the summer of '89). It's more powerful, but not so much as to overwhelm an improved chassis, and the exhaust still barks when one shifts gears. The price has gone up, but it's still affordable and, anyway, you're making more now than you did 10 years ago. All in all, the Miata still yields that essence of sports car, that one-on-one relationship with an automobile, the sky above and the road below, bottled in amber from a time of stringback gloves and snap-brimmed caps. The sartorial accouterments may have changed, but the thrill still remains in the driver's seat of a Miata. If you haven't had your Miata yet, maybe there's still time.

MAZDA MX-5

Perfect ten

It's the most popular roadster of all time, and 10 years down the track Mazda has released a birthday version of the car that saved its life

Drive it hard, hang it out, the MX-5 loves it

Nothing earth-shattering, but power's fine

A BIT OF A SUCCESS STORY, THE MX-5. And a bacon-saver. For if it wasn't for the smash-hit sales of the little sportster, the corporate world of Mazda, even given all Ford's protective mothering, would be a rather bleak and austere place.

Half a million MX-5s have now rolled off the production line in 10 years, making it the most successful roadster of all time: a fact Mazda, not surprisingly, is keen to celebrate. Hence the rather garish-looking car you see here, as Mazda commemorates its 10th anniversary with, yes, you guessed it, a limited-edition model based on the top-of-the-range 1.8S. Yet, for once, this is a limited edition that 'serious' owners – of whom the MX-5 has attracted many over the years – might actually want to consider. Because, once you've navigated your way past the laughable polished wheels and boy-racerish, Nardi leather-covered steering wheel and gear lever, the car has a close-ratio, six-speed gearbox (available for the first time outside the Japanese market) which makes the roadster even more fun to drive.

Great handling and massive, grin-factor motoring have always been part of the MX-5 magic, and the new gearbox, along with detailed suspension changes and new Bilstein shockers, have made the car even more pointable and exploitable. Probably because it has been around for so long

with only mild body-sculpting changes, the MX-5 rarely seems to attract the headlines it deserves for its handling prowess... suffice to say that it remains one of *the* best and most controllable sports-cars ever to have stepped sideways in the line of duty (see GBU entry page 186). This 10th Anniversary model has only strengthened that claim, the ratios making it even more responsive to hard driving on twisty roads, while the change is one of the best you'll find in a car with sporting pretensions – quick, efficient and completely fuss-free.

Indeed, those last words sum up the

Okay, it's a little blue-suede OTT, but there's a CD player...

MX-5 nicely, and go a long way to explain why it has become such a phenomenal success. Everything that the MX-5 needs to do well as a small roadster, it excels at – but not through complicated technology or design. Its engine – the latest 1.8-litre 16V unit – is not particularly advanced or powerful at 140bhp, yet it delivers easily and readily. The interior is functional and well-designed, even if the Anniversary model does have blue, suede-look seats, chromed surrounds on the speedo and rev-counter, carbonfibre-look trim on the centre console and – crikey, this is a bit modern – a

CD player. The hood-opening mechanism, which operates in seconds and is still one of the most practical of any roadster, is fiddle-free, despite the fact it's manually operated. Think of a nimble, reliable MGB for the '90s and you're not far off.

According to Mazda folklore, the building of the MX-5 was a close-run thing, and it was nearly pipped to production by an MPV project. If it had been, of course, the chance to buy this – the latest and probably the best MX-5 ever assembled – would have been denied you... although that might still be the case. Just 600 Anniversary models will be sold in the UK (of which half have already been reserved), from a total production run of 7500. Each buyer receives a special 'Owner's Certificate' signed by, wait for it, one James E Miller, president of Mazda Motor Corporation, no less. Maybe that's why there's such a limited number of the limited edition. Any more, and poor old Mr Miller would be too busy inscribing his moniker to run the company.
ROB MUNRO-HALL

MAZDA MX-5 10TH ANNIVERSARY ★★★	
Price:	£21,100
Engine:	1839cc dohc 16V four, 140bhp, 162lb ft
Performance:	123mph, 8.4sec 0-60mph, 32.0mpg
On sale in UK:	Now

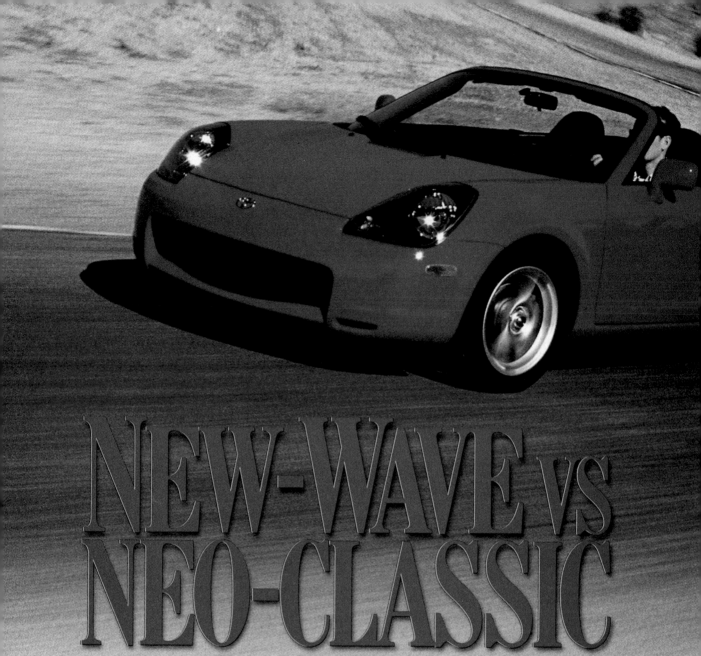

NEW-WAVE VS NEO-CLASSIC

How does the Toyota MR2 Spyder compare with the Mazda MX-5 Miata?

BY DENNIS SIMANAITIS
PHOTOS BY JEFF ALLEN

COMPARISON ROAD TEST

IN KEEPING WITH VARIous Federal Disclosure Acts bandied about these days (this is, after all, an election year), I begin this Comparison Test with the following statement: I have been and am now an owner of a Mazda MX-5 Miata. In fact, this spans almost a decade, as ours was R&T's original Long Termer. Not that such ownership, a priori, puts the Toyota MR2 Spyder at a disadvantage. In fact, familiarity with

a car can sometimes breed if not contempt, at least indifference.

So it was with an open mind—"sieve-like," some say—that I teamed up with Executive Editor Douglas Kott for a day of open-car fun at the Streets of Willow at Willow Springs International Raceway followed by some entertaining driving through Los Padres National Forest west of there.

The cars

THE ORIGINAL MAZDA MX-5 MIATA (see R&T, March 1989) was patterned

after the classic sports car. Today, more than 500,000 Miatas around the world have made it something of a classic on its own right. Changes over the past 10 years have included increases in displacement, in power and, alas, in weight (but then who am I to talk). Two years ago, the car received restyling that eliminated pop-up headlights, opened its grille, widened its rear flanks and added rocker panel contouring. A relocated spare tire gave rather more useful trunk space; a glass rear window offered long-term integrity and

clarity. As we found in our April 1998 Road Test, the new Miata was still the definitive lightweight affordable open sports car. And, amazingly, for a long time it had this niche all to itself.

But no longer. Directly targeted against the now-classic Miata is a new-wave counterpart, the Toyota MR2 Spyder. Derived from the MR-S show car first seen at Tokyo 1997, the MR2 is a Porsche Boxster for the masses. It also pays homage to the first-generation MR2—and avoids some of the sins of success besetting its bigger, heavier and more expensive immediate predecessor.

We were impressed with this new MR2 in our December 1999 cover story. "Toyota is definitely back on the sports-car scene," said Sam Mitani "The MR2 Spyder is sure to make foreheads sweat in Mazda's corporate boardrooms." So why not increase the pressure by putting these two lightweight affordable open sports cars precisely head-to-head?

Different tacks, same course

THESE TWO CARS PROVED TO BE DIFferent in personality, though they are akin in spirit. First and foremost, each is an absolute ball to drive. There's an immediacy of controls and environment that says, "This is fun, not just transportation!"

Second, each by today's standards is quite affordable. Our MR2 carries a base price of $23,098 plus its $455 destination charge. Its impressive list of standard features includes ABS, air conditioning, electrically actuated windows and locks, electric steering assist, a tilt steering wheel, a cockpit-rear-mounted wind deflector and a good quality AM/FM/cassette/CD sound system. Alas, for those with bothersome commutes, there's no automatic transmission offered.

A Miata is also quite affordable, and it comes in considerably more possible variations. At one extreme is the $21,245 Miata (with cloth seats, 14-in.

alloys and appropriate power assist for steering, windows, mirrors and antenna). At the other is a newly arriving Miata Special Edition, limited to a series of only 3000, with 6-speed gearbox, Torsen limited slip, lots of wood and leather and a 200-watt Bose AM/FM/cassette/CD; price unannounced as I write this. Or, if one prefers, it would not be absurd to start with a Miata LS ($23,995), get its leather-trimmed seats, Bose audio and cruise control, and check off appropriate options to drive away with automatic transmission ($900), air conditioning ($900), ABS ($550), front air dam, side sills and rear mud guards of the Appearance Package ($595), rear spoiler ($295), foglamps ($250), carpeted floormats ($80) and, if you live in a less than temperate clime, the hardtop ($1500). Together with its $450 destination charge, this absolutely loaded luxo Miata skims close to $30,000. Our $26,420 Miata LS was rather more to R&T liking, though I personally would have swapped the $595 styling add-ons for $550 ABS, which our test car didn't have.

On road

OF COURSE, WITH NICE SUNNY DAYS beckoning, the first order of business is putting down the top. Each is utterly manual with a pair of over-center latches. The Miata's top is perhaps a little easier to manage from the driver's seat, the MR2's requiring a final push to lock it in place. On the other hand, in scissoring down, the MR2's top stows with its forward portion outer-side-up and looks rather more finished, even without a tonneau cover.

Cruising along at freeway speeds, there's a marked contrast in optimal wind control within these two open cockpits. At 70 mph, for instance, the MR2 is more pleasant with its side windows up; the Miata, with them down. The Miata's windshield has side wings that do an excellent job of keeping the wind from spilling in, and, in fact, putting up its side windows seems to increase the backdraft. Both cars have fold-up deflectors behind the seats. The efficacy of each could be felt, but if either were a stand-alone option, I'd save the money, buy a Tilley Endurable broad-brim hat and remember to use its chin strap at really elevated speeds.

Neither car is particularly long-legged. Again, using 70 mph as an example, the MR2 is turning 3500 rpm in 5th and the Miata's tach reads a tick over 3600 in this same gear. It's not that either 1.8-liter engine is straining, mind. Indeed, each approaches its red-line (MR2: 6750 rpm; Miata: 7000) with commendable smoothness. It's just that you recognize you're piloting small-displacement sports cars.

This term "small-displacement" also applies to the interiors, as neither car

■ Miata's interior and power-plant are old friends; its trunk is usefully proportioned.

offers an abundance of room for "stuff." With two people aboard, even something like an attaché case or knapsack becomes something of a logistical challenge.

The MR2 is particularly lacking in this regard. Behind its seats are two drop-down panels revealing a 2.8-cu.-ft. volume that's triangular in cross section and a little less than the width of the interior. A medium duffel bag will fit, provided it's not overly full; an airline carry-on of typical proportions won't. Up front in the spare-tire well is another tiny volume; maybe a smallish knapsack would fit; maybe not. And that's it—there's no storage aft whatsoever.

I know from firsthand experience that a Miata trunk will tote a week's groceries. However, the only way to get them home in an MR2 is to shop solo. With its spare tire now lurking below, the Miata's 6.1-cu.-ft. trunk presents a more regular volume than in *my* Miata (the 1990 one). However,

this same spare tire location decreases the depth of the trunk as well. Trade-offs, tradeoffs.

And track(s)

REAL ENTERTAINMENT WITH THESE two cars came at the Streets of Willow and, for Road Test Editor Patrick Hong, at our Pomona testing location. His cold hard numbers showed that the MR2 reached 60 mph in 7.3 seconds and passed the quarter-mile marker in 15.6 sec. and 88.4 mph. Corresponding data for the Miata are 8.0, 16.1 and 86.1, respectively. These latter are rather a surprise because, in truth, the

---

In My Opinion...

DENNIS SIMANAITIS, Engineering Editor

What a quandary! Both of these cars are so much fun. However, I'm opting for the MR2 keys and here's why: The car's handling dynamics are outstanding, yet, like the Miata's, they're utterly approachable in ordinary driving. Its list of standard equipment, of things that I'd want, give it an inherent 10-percent advantage in price. True, its styling is a bit derivative, but I actually prefer the purity of line of the *original* Miata anyway. The MR2 interior offers a bit more room for two people—and I've got just the duffel bag for our occasional travel.

R2 SPYDER

Miata doesn't feel *that much* slower, but there you are.

Running through the gears is great fun in each of these cars. The engines are responsive and the exhaust notes are sonorous, the Miata's offering a bit more character, we thought. What's more, its shifter continues to be the absolute best in the world (note how it earned rare 10s from both Douglas and me in the ratings). The Miata's short throws are well-defined and it's a joy to stir the gears around. Toyota engineers haven't been napping, though. The MR2's shifter is almost as good—and for a mid-engine car, it's superlative.

For once, those of us with wider feet are rewarded: I found each car's pedals amenable to heel-and-toe (actually outside-of-shoe and sole) downshifts; Doug was less pleased with the Miata's.

While fooling with these artful activities around the Streets of Willow, we were held adequately in place by the driver's seat in either car. The Toyota's cockpit is a bit more spacious, especially for elbow-thrashing. Its seats are larger, yet better shaped to hold you in place.

Both cars are nimble in cornering, their steering communicating well the grip—or lack of same—of the front tires. In quantitative terms, the skidpad contest went to the Miata by a bare tick (0.92g versus the MR2's 0.91g). Weaving amidst slalom cones, the Miata again pipped the MR2, 62.7 mph to 62.6. Patrick reported that the Miata felt tossable and safe; the MR2 profited from smoothness (or otherwise it could spin).

Qualitatively, we sensed differences as well. The MR2 went exactly where we pointed it, its attitude capable of being predictably modulated by throttle. By contrast, we sensed that the Miata liked to play an entertaining game of toss-and-catch. Also, entering long sweepers with track-induced elan, it exhibited a jaunty two-step of its rear suspension, sort of a hop/set. We conjecture that this is traceable to lateral compliance in the Miata's array of

double A-arms, coils and anti-roll bar back there. The Toyota felt more linear in its acceptance of load, though more softly sprung as well.

This latter translated into a ride that was somewhat less firm under most conditions. Yet, almost paradoxically, the MR2 proved a bit more unsettled on ripples, and its straight-line stability wasn't as plumb-perfect as the Miata's.

Doug made a most cogent comment contrasting front-engine versus mid-engine handling: "The Miata," he said, "feels like it rotates around a point directly under its rearview mirror. The

MR2's yaw center is in the middle of its stowed roof panel."

Chasing each other around the Streets, we experienced nary a trace of brake fade in either car. The Miata's discs had an utterly linear feel; the MR2's felt a tad soft in initial application. However, the quantitative contest proved no contest at all—because of how our cars were outfitted. The MR2 was equipped with standard ABS, the Miata without its ($550) optional ABS. Skilled though Patrick is, his average distances for the Miata from 60 and 80 mph were a lengthy 150 and 282 ft.;

■ Quicker performance and more elbow room are countered by really limited stowage—unless you have precisely the right bag.

In My Opinion...

DOUGLAS KOTT, Executive Editor

Having long championed odd-looking cars with mid-engine configurations (my garage is home to a Porsche 914), naturally I've taken a liking to the MR2 Spyder. Offsetting its "Friendly Piglet" looks and fussy access to limited cargo space are its roomy cockpit, happy-to-rev inline-4 and sublime handling that's as forgiving as it is finely balanced. Yet my heart, as if to spite my brain, goes to the Miata. The classically redefined 1960s' roadster has weathered the decade (yes, decade!) well, a testament to the rightness of its design..

2000 Mazda MX-5 Miata LS

SCALE: 10 IN. (254mm) DIVISIONS
DRAWING BY TIM BARKER

List price/Price as tested: **$23,995/$26,420**
Price as tested includes std equip. (dual airbags, leather-trimmed seats and steering wheel, Bose AM/FM/CD w/in-door tweeters, cruise control; power windows, mirrors & door locks; glass rear window w/defog, air conditioning ($900), Appearance Package: front air dam, side sills, rear mud guards ($595), foglamps ($250), LEV emissions ($150), carpeted floormats ($80), dest charge ($450).

2000 Toyota MR2 Spyder

SCALE: 10 IN. (254mm) DIVISIONS
DRAWING BY TIM BARKER

List price/Price as tested: **$23,098/$23,553**
Price as tested includes std equip. (dual airbags, ABS, air conditioning, AM/FM/cassette/CD, pwr windows and locks), dest charge ($455).

General Data

	Mazda Miata	Toyota MR2 Spyder
Curb weight	**2385 lb**	**2250 lb**
Test weight	2520 lb	2415 lb
Weight dist (with driver), f/r, %	52/48	43/57
Wheelbase	89.2 in.	96.5 in.
Track, f/r	55.7 in./56.7 in.	58.1 in./57.5 in.
Length	155.3 in.	153.0 in.
Width	66.0 in.	66.7 in.
Height	48.4 in.	48.8 in.

Engine

Type	dohc 4-valve/cyl **inline-4**	dohc 4-valve/cyl **inline-4**
Displacement	1839 cc	1794 cc
Bore x stroke	83.0 x 85.0 mm	79.0 x 91.4 mm
Compression ratio	9.5:1	10.0:1
Horsepower (SAE)	**138 bhp @ 6500 rpm**	**138 bhp @ 6400 rpm**
Torque	**117 lb-ft @ 5000 rpm**	**125 lb-ft @ 4400 rpm**
Maximum engine speed	7000 rpm	6750 rpm
Fuel injection	elect. sequential port	elect. sequential port
Rec. fuel	unleaded, 87 pump octane	unleaded, 87 pump octane

Chassis & Body

Layout	**front engine/rear drive**	**mid engine/rear drive**
Body/frame	unit steel	unit steel
Brakes, f/r	**10.0-in. vented discs/ 9.9-in. vented discs;** vacuum assist	**10.0-in.. vented discs/ 10.4-in. vented discs;** vacuum assist, ABS
Wheels	alloy, **15 x 6JJ**	alloy; **15 x 6JJ f, 15 x 6½JJ r**
Tires	Michelin Pilot SX-GT, **195/50R-15 82V**	Bridgestone Potenza RE040; **185/55R-15 81V f, 205/50R-15 85V r**
Steering	**rack & pinion,** pwr asst	**rack & pinion,** pwr assist
Overall ratio	15.0:1	13.6:1
Turns lock to lock	2.7	2.7
Suspension, f/r	**upper & lower A-arms,** coil springs, tube shocks, anti-roll bar/**upper & lower A-arms,** coil springs, tube shocks, anti-roll bar	**MacPherson struts,** coil springs, tube shocks, anti-roll bar/**struts,** coil springs, tube shocks, anti-roll bar

Accommodations

Seating capacity	**2**	2
Head room	36.5 in.	37.0 in.
Leg room	42.0 in.	45.0 in.
Trunk space	6.1 cu ft	2.8 cu ft

Drivetrain

	Mazda Miata	Toyota MR2 Spyder
Transmission	**5-speed manual**	5-speed manual
Gear/Ratio/Overall/(Rpm) Mph		
1st, :1	3.14/13.50/(7000) 34	3.17/13.66/(6750) 35
2nd, :1	1.89/8.13/(7000) 56	1.90/8.19/(6750) 56
3rd, :1	1.33/5.72/(7000) 82	1.39/5.99/(6750) 80
4th, :1	1.00/4.30/(7000) 109	1.03/4.44/(6750) 108
5th, :1	0.81/3.48/est (6380) 123*	0.82/3.53/est (6450) 129
Final drive ratio	4.30:1	4.31:1
Engine rpm @ 60 mph in top gear	3100 rpm	3000 rpm

*Electronically limited.

Acceleration

Time to speed, sec		
0–40 mph	4.1	3.8
0–60 mph	8.0	7.3
0–80 mph	13.7	12.5
0–100 mph	23.0	20.6
Time to distance		
0–1320 ft (¼ mile)	16.1 sec @ 86.1 mph	15.6 sec @ 88.4 mph

Braking

Minimum stopping distance		
From 60 mph	150 ft	115 ft
From 80 mph	282 ft	204 ft
Control	good	excellent
Brake feel	average	excellent
Overall brake rating	average	excellent

Handling

Lateral accel (200-ft skidpad)	0.92g	0.91g
Balance	mild understeer	moderate understeer
Speed thru 700-ft slalom	62.7 mph	62.6 mph
Balance	mild understeer	mild understeer

Interior Noise

Idle in neutral	50 dBA	45 dBA
Maximum, 1st gear	82 dBA	81 dBA
70 mph	77 dBA	76 dBA

Fuel Economy

Normal driving	25.8 mpg	26.7 mpg
EPA city/highway	25/29 mpg	25/30 mpg
Fuel capacity	12.7 gal.	12.7 gal.

*Subjective ratings consist of excellent, very good, good, average, poor;
na means information is not available.*

The Results...

Performance		Mazda Miata	Toyota MR2 Spyder
Lap Times	50 pts.	49.3	50.0
0–60 mph	25 pts.	22.8	25.0
Braking, 60–0 mph	25 pts.	13.3	25.0
Slalom	20 pts.	20.0	20.0
Skidpad	20 pts.	20.0	19.8
Fuel economy	10 pts.	9.7	10.0
TOTAL	150 pts.	135.1	149.8

Performance points based on proportional scale.

Subjective Ratings		Mazda Miata	Toyota MR2 Spyder
Engine	10 pts.	8.0	8.5
Gearbox	10 pts.	10.0	8.5
Steering	10 pts.	8.5	8.5
Brakes	10 pts.	9.0	8.0
Ride	10 pts.	7.5	8.0
Handling	10 pts.	8.0	9.0
Controls	10 pts.	8.0	8.5
Build quality	10 pts.	8.5	9.0
Exterior styling	10 pts.	8.0	6.0
Interior styling	10 pts.	8.5	6.5
Seat	10 pts.	7.0	8.5
Trunk space	10 pts.	7.0	3.5
Noise	10 pts.	8.5	7.0
Driving excitement	10 pts.	8.5	9.0
TOTAL	140 pts.	115.0	108.5

Subjective ratings based on points awarded in each of 14 categories, by two editors.

Price		Mazda Miata	Toyota MR2 Spyder
List price	100 pts.	89.4	100.0

Points-range for price equals average points-range of other categories, with 100 being maximum.

Results		Mazda Miata	Toyota MR2 Spyder
Total points	390 pts.	339.5	358.3
(Total points ÷ 3.9)		87.1	91.9
STANDINGS		2 Mazda Miata	1 Toyota MR2 Spyder

corresponding distances for the MR2 were an amazingly short 115 and 204 ft.

Technology triumphs (and I told you earlier I'd prefer ABS to those silly side sills).

Capping our Streets of Willow fun were Doug's timed hot laps. The MR2 posted an average of 1 minute 8.08 seconds; the Miata, just a bit behind at 1 minute 8.95. (And before you Miata owners write Doug letters questioning his driving ability, fool with a decent stopwatch and check out just how small 0.87 sec. is.)

About the MR2, he said, "Is this the Toyota Elise? It corners and makes transitions with near-magical agility and fluidity. Its steering telegraphs the road surface with delicacy and detail."

After his Miata laps: "Compared with the dynamic brilliance of the MR2, the Miata does seem to be Old School. It doesn't throttle-steer with the adeptness of the Toyota, but it's still an impressive handler. There's character that encourages you to really fling it around like a feisty terrier playing with a rope toy."

The kid's articulate; he should be a writer.

At end of day

HOW TO CHOOSE BETWEEN TWO SUCH entertaining cars? When Doug and I totaled our subjective ratings, we each found the neo-classic Mazda just edging the new-wave Toyota. The MR2 shines in matters of dynamics and overall driving excitement. They trade points in interior and trunk, with the MR2 coming out the loser.

In matters of esthetics, the Miata is a clear winner. "Its basic lines are still superb," I identify as my writing. "Very handsome," wrote Doug, "and its 1999 changes have really grown on me."

About the MR2: "Looks like it was designed by a discordant committee," this, in my hand. "Sort of a Pokemon character on wheels," wrote Doug.

We concurred as well about the day-to-day utility of each car, the Miata getting the nod especially when pairs of people were involved. On the other hand, we must admit that "utility" per se needn't be a strong point with cars of this character. Certainly Doug's Porsche 914 isn't especially long on it. And while my Morgan *does* have a rear seat of sorts, I'd hardly call it a Malvern Link SUV.

Both the Miata and MR2 deserve to sell like hotcakes. Let's hope that this niche of the lightweight affordable sports car continues to thrive. Then, next time, more than two of us get to enjoy the fun!

Mazda
MX-5 Miata

Twelve months: Forgivably imperfect.

by Monte Doran

PHOTOGRAPHY BY GREG JAREM

Ann Arbor—

Our love affair with the original Mazda Miata has been embarrassingly well documented. It was our first Automobile of the Year in 1990, and then we gave it a record seven consecutive All-Star awards. With our hearts displayed so prominently on our sleeves, we awaited the arrival of our Four Seasons 1999 Miata with a mix of anticipation and trepidation. Would it retain all the characteristics we loved about the old Miata while improving on its few shortcomings? Or would the new Miata fail at both tasks, going down in history next to New Coke and the second round of *The Blue Lagoon*?

A year and 30,000 miles later, we found the new Miata to be worthy of our affection. As testament to its virtue, only one comment in our Miata's logbook indicated a preference for the old generation: A month after our Miata arrived, art director Larry Crane proclaimed that the new car was still an affordable sports car, "but it has lost a bit of 'Miata.' It's become a really nice little Japanese roadster full of features and upholstery…and less of the world's best Lotus. It's a great car, but I miss the Miata."

It's likely that Larry would have preferred the $20,000 base Miata without the creature comforts—air conditioning, power steering, electric windows—that most of us take for granted. We frivolously ordered every available option, save leather seats and an automatic transmission, which pushed our test car's sticker over $26,000.

The one option we regretted ordering was the $595 appearance package, which added a front chin spoiler, running boards, and rear mud guards. Every comment on the Miata's clean, attractive new sheetmetal was inevitably followed by a slanderous statement describing how the body kit detracted from that design. Production editor Ryan Simon nicely summed up the general sentiment: "The added-on body cladding looks just that—added on." Although most of us didn't like our Miata's butch look, others loved it. There were numerous accounts of strangers who complimented the car, from pedestrians who yelled, "That's a *phat* car, man," to a fellow '99 Miata owner who told Simon, "Yours is prettier than mine."

We also had few good things to say about space in the Miata's redesigned interior. Like

the *manufacturer*

Mazda North American Operations
7755 Irvine Center Drive
Irvine, California 92623–9734
President and CEO of Mazda North American
Operations: Richard Beattie
- Customer assistance: 800–248–0459
- Plant where built: Ujina, Hiroshima, Japan
- 1998 calendar year sales: 17,449
- Our car's number off the line: 11,326
- Genealogy: In the late 1980s there were no con-
temporary small roadsters to serve as a benchmark for
the Miata, so Mazda engineers purchased a late-Sixties
Lotus Elan for reference. When the Miata was introduced as a 1990 model, its smooth shape, small size,
and four-cylinder engine (a 116-bhp, 1.6-liter unit borrowed from the Mazda 323) paid homage to that Elan.
Only minor changes were enacted until the 1994
model year, when the Miata's engine was upgraded
to 1.8 liters and 128 bhp. Other improvements that
year included larger brakes, stiffer chassis tuning, and
a bigger fuel tank. The last original-body-style Miatas
were sold as 1997 models. The '98 model year was
skipped, and the new Miata was introduced late in the
'97 calendar year as a '99 model.

■ Mazda MX-5 Miata

pulling on an old pair of jeans that are snug in all the wrong places, we wondered if the Miata had shrunk in some immeasurable way—leg and headroom measurements are identical to the previous-generation car's—or if our girths were consuming more space. One explanation is the thicker door panels and door pulls, which displaced almost an inch of shoulder room. Six-foot-six copy editor Bengt Halvorson and six-foot-two design associate Darin Johnson refused to drive the Miata because their knees were wedged between the driver's door handle and the rim of the steering wheel. While this was uncomfortable, it also dangerously impeded movement of the steering wheel, a problem that easily could have been avoided with a tilt and/or telescoping mechanism.

To compensate for the diminished interior room, the trunk in the new Miata grew from 3.6 to 5.1 cubic feet. The trunk looked deceptively small but could accommodate an enormous amount of cargo with some creative packing, easily holding $100 worth of groceries or two carry-on bags. Senior editor Joe Lorio holds the record, having crammed in a full set of golf clubs and two duffel bags.

Under the new sheetmetal and larger trunk, the Miata's mechanical components are essentially carried over from the previous generation, which is fine for the most part. The double-wishbone suspension design was

modified for better steering feel and straight-line stability, and the car's cornering behavior was improved by stretching the track an additional four-tenths of an inch up front and nearly an inch in the rear. We loved the results. Said erstwhile motor gopher Reilly Brennan: "People have said the Miata drives like a go-kart. Correction: this is how go-karts are supposed to drive. The go-karts my rich friends had growing up were a bore compared with this." Jean Jennings: "The Miata is still a joy to drive, despite competition from much more expensive roadsters like the BMW Z3, the Mercedes-Benz SLK, and the Porsche Boxster."

Unfortunately, Mazda took the same laissez-faire approach with the old 1.8-liter four-cylinder engine, which has always been somewhat of a weak link in the Miata. A new head, new camshaft profiles, and a higher compression ratio squeezed an extra twelve horsepower and nine pound-feet of torque out of the old engine. But what the engine needs more than power is refinement. It still feels coarse and unsophisticated, particularly at the extreme ends of the tachometer. As one of our drivers lamented, "I'm not so crazy about the Miata's engine. Pushing deeper into the accelerator results in additional thrashing and harshness yet yields little in the way of greater acceleration."

To make the most of the currently avail-

The stubby gearshifter and gorgeous Nardi steering wheel were such a pleasure to use, they almost compensated for the claustrophobic feeling of the interior.

able power, the close-ratio manual transmission was also carried over. As before, the stubby gearshift is perfectly weighted and a joy to use. The short gearing provides acceptable acceleration, with zero to 60 mph taking 8.0 seconds. But at 85 mph—Michigan's unofficial speed limit—the engine is spinning at a frantic 4000 rpm.

Very manageable power delivery, combined with a set of Michelin Arctic-Alpin snow tires (195/55R-15 84Q, $308 from the Tire Rack, plus $71.62 for installation), a tight convertible top, and an electrically heated glass rear window made the Miata a decent winter commuter. Editorial assistant Jennifer Misaros takes the prize for foul-weather Miata motoring. On New Year's weekend, during the worst blizzard in recent memory, she ventured out to run some errands. The Miata handled the foot-deep white stuff well, but the grille did get clogged with hard-packed snow.

Our Miata held up admirably after a year of hard, continual use. It remained devoid of the cowl shake that afflicts so many convertibles. The black interior never seemed to stay clean, but it otherwise wore well.

The scheduled services totaled $319.39, which was a pittance compared with the costs of servicing our Four Seasons 1997 BMW Z3 ($900) and our Four Seasons 1998 Porsche Boxster ($800) over the same number of miles. The Miata did not require a single repair until its 30,000-mile service, when the clutch throw-out bearing was replaced under warranty to cure a moan we had been hearing when we engaged first gear. As a precaution, we spent an extra $141 for a new clutch disk in case we had radically decreased its life expectancy. During the same service visit, the dealer replaced our rear-view mirror under warranty because its arm had worked loose.

Rationally speaking, the Miata is not perfect. It falls short of a five-star rating due to its unsophisticated engine and cramped interior. But what made our Miata—and previous-generation Miatas—so captivating has little to do with reason. For the Miata is much more than the sum of its parts. This was most evident during our Automobile of the Year testing last October, when we took a similarly equipped car to Tennessee and Kentucky. The test was not very fair, as the Miata was competing with much more expensive and powerful performance cars such as the new Porsche 911, the BMW M coupe, and the Mercedes-Benz C43. Yet the Miata held its own on the twisting mountain roads, constantly nipping at the heels of these "better" cars. Pouring all of your ability into driving an M coupe only to see a four-cylinder Miata glued to your tail is truly a blow to the ego. However, driving the Miata up the tailpipes of the C43 makes you feel like a superhero. That performance caused us to give the Miata yet another trophy: The new Miata was a 1999 All-Star.

That superhero feeling made us forgive our Four Seasons Miata's flaws. The Miata is so fun to drive you forget about the rough engine, the cramped interior, your migraine headache, and the overdue mortgage payment. Somehow, the Miata makes all the world seem perfect.

Former AUTOMOBILE MAGAZINE guy Doug Weisz borrowed our Miata while he was in Ann Arbor over Valentine's Day. "Today is an unseasonably warm seventy degrees," he said, "the top's down, and there isn't a better car in the world."

our *reactions*

You can go home again.

My initial reaction to the first Mazda Miata was pretty much like everyone else's—I thought it was beautiful, and I loved the idea of an English sports car built with Japanese reliability and Japanese attention to detail. It turned out to be all that and more. When people complained that it was underpowered, I bridled. Most of these were people who had never driven a Miata and had no intention of ever buying one. Many of them were the tank-topped, gold-chained young men whose history's first sports car was a '71 Corvette. The Miata was an exquisitely balanced little sports car. If you wanted more power, I reasoned, you should buy another kind of car. I wanted a white Miata with a hard top, Cunningham-blue stripes, and old-style American Racing mag wheels.

Now we've spent a year with the more powerful new Mazda Miata. Not more powerful in the sense of Honda Civic street racers with engines that expire like artillery shells, nor like a small-block Chevy, just more of the neat little Miata we loved so much all those years ago. What I like most about it is its eager ability to run with much more powerful cars on our magazine's test trips. What it lacks in raw horsepower it makes up for with agility and poise. It won't carry three bird dogs and all your camping gear, but it most definitely is that perfect English sports car—the one that England never built.   —David E. Davis, Jr.

Gosh, how I love the Miata. Life is good on those happy occasions when I drive a Miata home from the office. Every time I sit behind the wheel of one of these wonderful little machines, my cares go out the window. The beauty is that in our Four Seasons Miata, my ten-minute drive home from the office gave me the same happy feelings as the 3000-mile trek I took last fall to Florida and back. To own a Miata must be like taking a summer vacation every day.

I would venture to guess that our yearlong Miata test will be one of the few times in my life that being five feet, five inches tall is beneficial. My six-foot, two-inch husband hated the fact that he could never really get comfortable in either the driver's or passenger's seats. But I was never cramped or uncomfortable. In fact, the Miata felt as if it were made for me. Ha ha.

The Miata is everything I want in an impractical automobile: It's beautiful, sexy, sporty, balanced, reliable, and inexpensive to purchase and operate. And the new version improves on the last one in nearly every aspect without compromising the original's charm. It's better looking, has a slightly more powerful engine, a glass rear window with defroster instead of the previous model's plastic window, and a larger trunk, and it still costs only $20,000 to $26,000. What's not to love?
    —Megan McCann

I really enjoyed driving our Miata, but I never took it on a long trip. Why? At a few hairs over six feet, six inches, I just can't get comfortable in it. Although the Miata was lauded for being more fun to drive than a go-kart, when I was at its wheel I often felt like a scrawny adolescent in a kiddie go-kart that I'd outgrown. That was a pity, because as much as I liked the Miata, it wasn't a viable option for me because of my height. If the Miata's steering wheel adjusted at all, the car would be at least tolerable for tall folks.

Call me a masochist, because I loved to suffer in the Miata's crunch-to-fit cockpit. The Miata is at its best in town and on small, tight country roads, where I had plenty of chances to flick through the gears and enjoy the direct steering response. Doran says that the Miata engine's lack of refinement is its weak link, but I never expected or wanted a more sophisticated engine. The 1.8-liter four does sound better from the tailpipe than from the driver's seat, but it's responsive and well-matched to the chassis—as long as you keep the revs up.

Any skepticism I might have had about how well the new Miata would stack up to its lofty predecessor has vanished. Mazda's roadster has been improved in nearly every aspect, but in ways that don't sacrifice its original purity of purpose. Through its endearing, uncompromised simplicity, it remains one of the few real sports cars.   —Bengt Halvorson

1999 MAZDA MX-5 MIATA ★★★★⚊

★★★★★—WRITE THE CHECK   ★★★★—SERIOUSLY CONSIDER   ★★★—PASSING GRADE   ★★—KEEP LOOKING   ★—TAKE THE BUS

running *changes*

There's not much in store for the Miata for the 2000 model year other than a limited-edition model commemorating the Miata's tenth anniversary (see page 28). Otherwise, there's the inevitable new color (a burnt orange) and some revised option packages. Halfway through the '99 model year, the base price increased from $19,770 to $20,095.

The price jump reflected additional standard equipment, which now includes fourteen-inch alloy wheels, power steering, power mirrors, power windows, a power radio antenna, and a Nardi steering wheel. With the base-price increase, a '99 Miata equipped exactly like our test car would cost $26,260, including destination charge.

in *summary*

- Superb handling and steering
- Always brings a smile to your face
- Utterly reliable
- Cramped interior
- Uninspiring engine

PROBLEM AREAS:
- Clutch throw-out bearing

PHOTOS BY GREG JAREM

the *numbers*

GENERAL:
Front-engine, rear-wheel-drive convertible
2-passenger, 2-door steel body
Base price $19,770/price as tested $26,075

MAJOR EQUIPMENT:
Standard dual air bags with passenger's-side disable switch, CD stereo; **optional** air conditioning $900, floor mats $80, anti-lock brakes $550, California emission equipment $150, appearance package (front air dam, body cladding, mud guards) $595, popular equipment package (fourteen-inch alloy wheels, Nardi steering wheel, limited-slip differential, cruise control, wind deflector, power steering, power mirrors, power windows, power antenna, power door locks, tweeter speakers) $2330, 200-watt Bose stereo with CD and cassette $550, fifteen-inch alloy wheels (dealer-installed option) $700; **not available** remote keyless entry, power top

ENGINE:
16-valve DOHC 4-in-line, iron block, aluminum head
Bore x stroke 3.27 x 3.35 in (83.1 x 85.1 mm)
Displacement 112 cu in (1839 cc)
Compression ratio 9.5:1
Power SAE net 140 bhp @ 6500 rpm
Torque SAE net 119 lb-ft @ 5500 rpm
Redline 7000 rpm

DRIVETRAIN:
5-speed manual transmission
Gear ratios (I) 3.14 (II) 1.89 (III) 1.33 (IV) 1.00 (V) 0.81
Final-drive ratio 4.3:1

MEASUREMENTS:
Wheelbase 89.2 in
Track front/rear 55.7/56.7 in
Length x width x height 155.3 x 66.0 x 48.4 in
Curb weight 2299 lb
Weight distribution front/rear 50/50%
Coefficient of drag 0.36
Fuel capacity 12.7 gal
Cargo capacity 5.1 cu ft

SUSPENSION:
Independent front, with double wishbones, coil springs, dampers, anti-roll bar
Independent rear, with double wishbones, coil springs, dampers, anti-roll bar

STEERING:
Rack-and-pinion, variable-power-assisted
Turns lock to lock 3.2
Turning circle 30.2 ft

BRAKES:
Vented front discs, rear discs
Anti-lock system

WHEELS AND TIRES:
15 x 6.0-in aluminum alloy wheels
195/50R-15 82V Michelin Pilot SX-GT tires

PERFORMANCE (manufacturer's data):
0–60 mph in 8.0 sec
Standing 1/4-mile in 16.0 sec @ 85 mph
Top speed 120 mph
Pounds per bhp 16.4
EPA city driving 25 mpg
Observed fuel economy 28.4 mpg

COMMON REPAIR ITEMS:
Headlamp unit $257.08
Front quarter-panel $216.49
Brake pads front wheels $57.16
Filters air $19.61/oil $7.19

REVIEW PERIOD:
30,254 mi
Previous articles 12/97, 2/99, 3/99, 5/99, 7/99

ACTUAL COSTS:
Warranty bumper to bumper 3 yr/50,000 mi
Scheduled maintenance 7500-mile service $27.36, 15,000-mile service $101.43, 22,500-mile service $28.10, 30,000-mile service $162.59; **warranty repairs** replace clutch throw-out bearing $194.32, replace rear-view mirror $143.62; **nonwarranty repairs** 7937 miles replace cracked windshield $272.40, 19,033 miles Michelin Arctic-Alpin snow tires $308.00, install snow tires $71.62, 26,693 miles remove snow tires $62.00, replace glove box (we broke it) $268.50, 30,042 miles replace clutch disc $140.81; **recalls** none

	EXCELLENT	GOOD	FAIR	POOR
ENGINE			•	
TRANSMISSION				•
STEERING				•
BRAKES				•
RIDE				•
HANDLING				•
ERGONOMICS		•		
SEATING COMFORT		•		
INTERIOR SPACE	•			
CARGO SPACE		•		
DOLLAR VALUE				•
FUN TO DRIVE				•

we need *your help*

If you own a 1999 Chevrolet Silverado LT 1500 4x4, Chrysler 300M, Honda Odyssey EX, Jeep Grand Cherokee Limited V-8 Quadra-Drive, Lexus LX470, Porsche 911, Saab 9-5 wagon, Suzuki Grand Vitara 4x4, or VW New Beetle 1.8T, we'd like to hear from you. We need to know your name, address, and daytime telephone; what you do for a living; your age; your car's make and model; how long you've owned it; how much you paid for it; whether there was a rebate on that amount; and whether you have had any serious mechanical problems. Also, what was your last car before this one? Most important, be specific in telling us what you like most and least about your car. If your entry is published as part of our Four Seasons report, we'll send you one of our T-shirts, too (so send us your size and color preference—black, green, or blue). Send your responses to: Four Seasons Tests, AUTOMOBILE MAGAZINE, 120 East Liberty Street, Ann Arbor, Michigan 48104.

IntelliChoice Cost Analysis

Ownership Costs

Cost Area	Five-Year Cost	Rating
Depreciation	$8686	◯
Financing ($351/month)	$4126	
Insurance (performance)	$11,263	◉
State Fees	$858	
Fuel (Hwy. 29/City 25)	$2743	◯
Maintenance	$3712	●
Repairs	$545	◯

Warranty/Maintenance Information

Major Tune-Up (60k mile int.)	$219	◯
Minor Tune-Up (30k mile int.)	$90	◯
Brake Service	$170	◯
Overall Warranty	3 yr/50k	◉
Drivetrain Warranty	3 yr/50k	◉
Rust Warranty	5 yr/unlim. mi.	◯
Maintenance Warranty	N/A	
Roadside Assistance	3 yr/50k	

Costs are based on national averages for 1998 models.

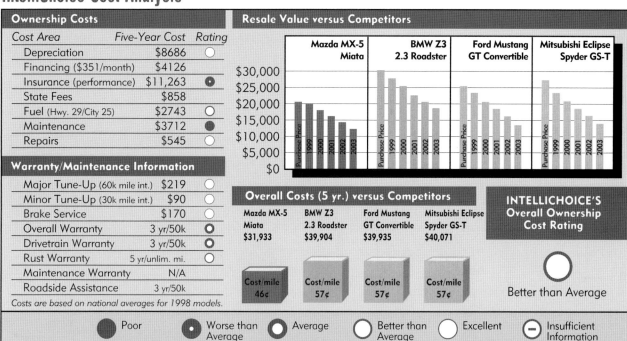

Resale Value versus Competitors

Mazda MX-5 Miata · BMW Z3 2.3 Roadster · Ford Mustang GT Convertible · Mitsubishi Eclipse Spyder GS-T

Overall Costs (5 yr.) versus Competitors

	Mazda MX-5 Miata	BMW Z3 2.3 Roadster	Ford Mustang GT Convertible	Mitsubishi Eclipse Spyder GS-T
	$31,933	$39,904	$39,935	$40,071
Cost/mile	46¢	57¢	57¢	57¢

INTELLICHOICE'S Overall Ownership Cost Rating

◯ Better than Average

Rating Legend:
● Poor | ◉ Worse than Average | ◯ Average | ◯ Better than Average | ◯ Excellent | ⊖ Insufficient Information

© 1999 INTELLICHOICE

the *competitors*

1999 BMW Z3 2.3
Base price $29,950
24-valve DOHC 6-in-line, 152 cu in (2494 cc)
Power SAE net 170 bhp @ 5500 rpm
Torque SAE net 181 lb-ft @ 3500 rpm
0–60 mph in 6.8 sec

1999 FORD MUSTANG GT CONVERTIBLE
Base price $24,870
SOHC V-8, 280 cu in (4588 cc)
Power SAE net 260 bhp @ 5250 rpm
Torque SAE net 302 lb-ft @ 4000 rpm
0–60 mph (estimated) in 5.8 sec

1999 MITSUBISHI ECLIPSE SPYDER GS-T
Base price $26,960
Turbocharged 16-valve SOHC 4-in-line,
122 cu in (1997 cc)
Power SAE net 210 bhp @ 6000 rpm
Torque SAE net 214 lb-ft @ 3000 rpm
0–60 mph in 6.5 sec

reader *reactions*

Andrew Marks, 34
Columbus, Ohio
CEO, software development company
Price as delivered: $24,077
Months owned: 4
Previous/other car: 1998 Toyota 4Runner

Likes: The new body style is more aggressive and substantial and the enhanced horsepower, torque, and exhaust note give the Miata a more complete sports car feel. The interior has a much more finished look, and the 200-watt Bose stereo is excellent even at highway speeds with the top down. The manual top is easy to operate and looks good in either the open or closed position.

Dislikes: There could be less wind noise with the top up at highway speed, and the rear window is small, which creates a dangerous blind spot (the trade-off for having a glass rear window). The interior fit and finish is good, but there are still a few squeaks that are irritating. Finally, the paint on the front fascia does not stand up to road nicks as well as it should. Even the smallest stone can leave a chip.

Bruce Hunt, 41
Tampa, Florida
Writer/photographer
Price as delivered: $19,956
Months owned: 5
Previous/other car: Isuzu Trooper

Likes: Handling is what this car is about. Turn-in is sharp and the car sticks in corners like duct tape. The Torsen limited-slip differential lets my right foot share the steering duties. The fat leather steering wheel and the short-throw shifter are great control connections between the driver and the car. I like the new look, which gives a nod to the '98 Jaguar XK8 (like the original Miata did to the 1968 Lotus Elan). No pop-up headlights means less weight over the front axle and no excess drag in night driving.

Dislikes: The engine has a nice torque curve, which works well with the gear spacing, but I wish it had a little extra grunt. Getting 140 bhp out of 1.8 liters is not much to brag about these days. Mazda should take some VTEC lessons from Honda.

James Bratek, 30
West Orange, New Jersey
Graphic designer
Price as delivered: $24,500
Months owned: 10
Previous car: 1992 VW Corrado SLC

Likes: Price is the major reason I drove home in this Miata instead of a BMW Z3 1.9. The suspension setup makes the car ride and perform like a go-kart. The car is very tossable, in a fun way, and it's easy to make handling corrections without drama. The glass rear window is a no-brainer, yet many other roadsters don't have them.

Dislikes: The engine's 140 bhp is too conservative in these high-output, cheap-gasoline times. The leather is cheap and feels like vinyl. My right knee rubs uncomfortably against the center console. The cup holders are a joke. However, even though I aspire to a Porsche Boxster, when I lower my Miata's top on a sunny day and drive along the coast or through some winding country roads, all my Miata dislikes are temporarily forgiven.

NICE ONE, SUN

S713 GKN

The MX-5 loves the sun, but can it also reign in the rain? After a 16,000-mile year in all weathers, there's only one answer

FOR the past 12 months, we've been waiting for some summer sun so we can enjoy our long-term Mazda MX-5 to the full. Finally the rain has ceased, and it's time to bid our little Mazda goodbye. Sometimes, life just isn't fair.

Mind you, the MX-5 didn't join our fleet to prove how much fun it could be on a sunny day. We already knew that in the right weather, on the right road, few cars this side of £20,000 can offer so much pure driving satisfaction. But could the sporty Mazda make the grade as everyday, all-weather transport? Would it be as pleasant to drive on the daily commute as on a country road, as relaxing on the long-haul as it is invigorating on a short blast? Time would tell.

My predecessor as *What Car?* art editor, Richard Scott, took delivery on 1 August last year, ready to bask in the combined posing appeal of a drop-top sports car and a brand new S-reg number plate. The 1.8i is already well equipped, so the only options added were metallic paint (£250) and alloy wheels (£440) to make the most of the Mazda's good looks, and a CD player (£344) to boost the standard stereo. The 1.8iS version is even better equipped, but would have set us back an extra £2000. Anti-lock brakes are the only really serious omission from the 1.8i's standard kit – they're standard on the more expensive model. But in every other respect, the more basic model is better value for money.

I took over as the MX-5's keeper in November, after Richard had already racked up 7000 miles. I'd always been a fan of the old shape MX-5, with its Lotus Elan-style

looks. The latest model is another handsome car, and with Mazda's racing bronze paintwork it certainly gets you noticed.

Truth is, image is just as important as performance for most sports car buyers, and the MX-5 has a softer, more overtly friendly visage than, say, the dynamic and aggressive-looking Elise. It's a case of personal taste, but I'd prefer a harder edge to the MX-5's image.

That's not to say there is anything soft about the performance – far from it. Show the MX-5 a stretch of open road, and 0-60mph can be dispatched in a decidedly macho 7.4 seconds.

'My commute has shown the MX-5 to be a great city car'

The 1.8-litre four-cylinder engine puts out a healthy 138bhp at 6500rpm, but the peak pulling power of 120lb ft doesn't arrive until 4500rpm. Although happy to trundle around town in a high gear, the engine saves its best for high revs.

But it's no hardship because the car is endowed with a fabulous five-speed gearbox. Everyone who drives the MX-5 comments on the swift, neat action of the 'box, which makes the rev-happy engine a pleasure to exploit to the full.

And when the sun does come out, the hood can be lowered in a flash. Undo a couple of clips on the windscreen header-rail, pull the hood back, and hey-presto – in just a few seconds, you're ready to ▷

Appearance too effete for some tastes

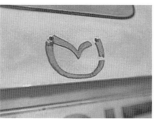

Dordogne tour placed few compromises on luggage, given car's size and remit

Badge went missing. Replacement: £7

A year in the life

40 miles

Richard Scott collects MX-5 from Tamplins of Twickenham and wastes no time in making the most of the sunshine

1500 miles

Fuel economy has yet to dip below 30mpg. Already the Mazda is showing that the motorway is not its route of choice, either hood up or down

3000 miles

Touring credentials are proven during a two-up holiday in the Dordogne. Boot provides adequate stowage and car's easy-going nature adds to holiday mood. Trip produces consistent 35mpg

5000 miles

Even though the standard-fit Yokohama tyres have bedded in, they are still unable to contain the unpredictable rear end in the wet; fine in dry, though

7500 miles

Alisdair Suttie drives hood down from London to St Andrews and back over Christmas. Decent heater and warm clothing make it quite tolerable

9000 miles

Goes in for its first service, for which Currie's in Wimbledon charges £169. At same time, rear badge is replaced, the original having been stolen. Frequent urban commuting drops fuel returns to a still very respectable 31.5mpg

12,000 miles

Yokohama tyres are swapped for a set of Bridgestones to tame the wet-road handling and give better levels of grip

◁ enjoy al fresco motoring. It's even possible to open and close the roof from the driver's seat if you're tall enough and reasonably strong. That's a real bonus at traffic lights when there's a sudden shower.

And when the rain does stop play, the fabric roof does a fine job of keeping driver and passenger snug and dry, but with the hood up rear visibility is a problem. To make matters worse, the cabin has a tendency to steam up, and the demister struggles to cope.

Wet weather driving is not the Mazda's forte. It's normally a lively yet secure handler, but show the MX-5 a wet road and even modest acceleration can provoke unwelcome sideways moments. Anyone swapping a front-wheel-

drive hatch for the rear-drive MX-5 will need to beware of the nervous back end. Ditching the standard Yokohama tyres in favour of Bridgestones after 12,000 miles was Mazda's recommendation and

'Yes, you can live happily with the MX-5 all year round'

it brought about a worthwhile improvement, but grip in the wet remains disappointing. All of which puts a frown on my face every rainy morning.

Which is a shame, because my daily 15-mile commute across south-west London has shown the Mazda to be a great city car in other respects. The willing engine, nimble handling and small size make it easy to slot into gaps in traffic, while the

In the dry, the MX-5 is a highly rewarding drive

well-weighted clutch pedal and power-assisted steering make parking simple.

Head out of the city on motorways and dual carriageways, though, and the Mazda is less at home. Wind and tyre noise quickly become irritating, more so than with such rivals as the MGF and Z3. The obvious solution is to crank up the stereo, which offers excellent sound quality, but has tiny controls that are difficult to operate when driving.

None of these flaws has stopped the Mazda racking up the miles on a couple of big trips. Deputy road test editor Andy Pringle commandeered the MX-5 for his summer holiday in the Dordogne. After well over 1000 miles of motoring on every kind of road and in every weather, he returned to Britain impressed. Andy particularly praised the MX-5's stability at speed, tracking straight and true down French autoroutes even with a fully laden boot.

By cramming in as much luggage as possible in the back of the car, and making maximum use of the shelf behind the seats, there was just enough room for Andy and his girlfriend to cram in a week's worth of holiday gear — not bad going for a small sports ▷

LOGBOOK

MODEL Mazda MX-5 1.8i
MILEAGE 16,000
TIME ON FLEET 12 months

BUYING INFORMATION
Current on-the-road price £16,655
Price when new £16,650
Best new price now £16,139*
Extras added Metallic paint (£250), alloys (£440), CD player (£351)
Trade-in value £14,000
Used forecourt price £15,000
* Supplied by Carfile (01335 360763)

PERFORMANCE
Engine 1.8-litre, 4cyl
Power 138bhp at 6500rpm
Pulling power 120lb ft at 4500rpm
Performance 0-60mph 7.4sec
Top speed 123mph

RUNNING COSTS
Leasing £365
Over 36 months/60,000 miles with maintenance. Initial payment of £1094. Supplied by British Car Contracts (0121 733 3311)

Personal Contract Purchase
£364 per month
Over 36 months/72,000 miles, deposit £1667. APR 13.0%. Final payment £5825. Total payable including acceptance and purchase fees £20,709. Supplied by Mazda Finance, Tunbridge Wells, Kent (0345 484848)

Insurance group 12
Typical quote £484

Test economy (mpg)
0-5000 miles 32.1
5000-10,000 miles 27.7
10,000-16,000 miles 30.5
Overall average 30.0
Best/worst 36.4/24.0
Official Euro-average 33.2

Servicing costs £169

Cost per mile 36.5p*
* Over 36,000 miles/three years and includes fuel, depreciation, maintenance, road tax, cost of funding. Supplied by Fleet Management Services (01743 241121)

Depreciation
£13.3k £10.8k £8.3k

PREVIOUS REPORTS
Nov '98; Mar, Jul '99

LIKES Open-top fun, easy to drive, dry weather handling
DISLIKES Wet weather handling, demisting problems

Verdict ●●●●○
Great fun until it rains

car. Destination reached, Andy was able to drop off his luggage, and set about enjoying the sinuous roads of the Dordogne. The MX-5 was in its element.

If Andy enjoyed the Mazda at its best, first prize for masochistic endeavour must go to news editor Alisdair Suttie. Last Christmas, Alisdair enthusiastically sought out the keys to the little Mazda for the holiday break. Being the season of goodwill, I was more than happy to swap the MX-5 for something with air conditioning and a proper roof.

Not content with driving a convertible in the depths of winter, Alisdair insisted on driving with the top down all the way to his family home in St Andrew's, a round trip of some 1000 freezing miles. Apparently, with a woolly hat on and the heater at full blast, it's possible to cope with the Scottish winter in reasonable comfort.

Exposed to the elements he may have been, but at least Alisdair didn't have to worry about reliability. In nearly a year's motoring, our Mazda never even skipped a beat. In fact the only unscheduled dealer

visit was not the little Mazda's fault – the 'MX-5' badge was stolen from the back of the car. We have a theory on the motive behind this unusual theft: a number of Japanese specification MX-5s, badged as Eunos Roadsters, have found their way into the UK with a market value below that of officially imported cars. We suspect that someone thought an MX-5 badge would

'Servicing bills resemble those of a far larger and dearer car'

help them to pass off their Eunos as an official UK MX-5, and so helped themselves to the badging on our car's rump. The badge was replaced for £7 at the 9000-mile service.

Currie's of Wimbledon completed all necessary work courteously and efficiently. Mind you, at £169, the bill was rather steep. If we held on to the car for another couple of months, the

Tails you lose: the rear is wayward in the wet. Bridgestones improved matters

18,000-mile service would set us back a mammoth £300. By comparison, an MGF would only need to be serviced every 12,000-miles, with the first costing in the region of £160 and the 24,000-mile service about £200. As sports cars go, the Mazda is inexpensive to buy, but the servicing costs resemble those of a far larger and dearer car.

After 16,000 miles, I'll be very sorry to see the MX-5 go. It hasn't always been the easiest of companions, but it's never let me down badly either. And when it's good, it's very good.

Is it possible to live happily with an MX-5 all year round? Yes, so long as you accept the compromises that are part and parcel of living with any convertible sports car. Sure, the Mazda is not as practical as your average hot hatch, and the wet weather handling does leave a lot to be desired. But one summery drive dispels all doubts. When it comes to running an MX-5, the sunny spells outnumber the showers. **Mark Wheeler**

Hood raised in seconds; can even be done from within car. Stereo: big noise but small buttons

THE GOOD MXER

MAZDA MX-5 1.6i FINAL REPORT Every driver who helped clock up our MX-5's 30,000 miles left smiling. The roadster just couldn't help making friends. By Peter Hodges

THE MX-5 is the car we couldn't let go of. It was originally meant to stay for just six months, but that grew to a year, which then became 18 months. Only now, after 21 months, has the Mazda gone. The reason? You can count on the fingers of one hand the cars that feel this special for this kind of money. And you'd still have fingers to spare.

To drive the MX-5 is to be reminded of why we love cars and why we love driving them. All the crucial elements are in place: the delightfully responsive steering, the short, snappy gearshift, the beautifully balanced handling. It's a car that makes even the most mundane journey feel special. My suburban commute is so much more bearable behind the wheel of the Mazda. Sometimes it's even enjoyable.

Maybe it's this user-friendliness that has resulted in the MX-5 getting a bit of a namby pamby image in some circles. There are still some who think it's funny to label it a hairdresser's car. But who cares? Those poor, benighted fools have no idea what they're missing.

We're still convinced that the basic 1.6i is the pick of the MX-5 range even 21 months down the line. The performance boost of the 1.8i isn't enough to justify another £1200, and opening the wallet for electric or leather extras is simply an exercise in gilding the lily. This car is all about having fun – fripperies add nothing to the experience.

But the ownership experience hasn't been perfect. Within a couple of months of the car's arrival, it started to suffer from an intermittent misfire at around 5000rpm. It was one of those infuriating problems that miraculously clears up when the car is taken to the garage, but then reappears the next day.

For weeks it defied diagnosis, leaving the technicians at Twickenham Mazda dealer Tamplins scratching their heads. Eventually the car was returned to Mazda UK, who managed to trace the problem

Mazda was a blast rain or shine; its popularity in the office meant 30,000 miles were racked up in 21 months

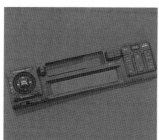

Three strikes and ropey Clarion stereo was out; aerial was a pain to remove manually, unlike quick and easy hood

MAZDA MX-5 1.6

Car run for 21 months
Introduced to the UK May 1998
Changes since then None
UK sales to date 12,320 (1.6 and 1.8)
What makes it special? This is the car that managed the feat of replacing the seemingly irreplaceable: the phenomenally successful Mk1 MX-5. The car's basic formula of front engine/rear drive and all-round double wishbone suspension was sensibly left unchanged, but stiffer bodyshell meant the handling was even better. Twin-cam 16-valve 1.6-litre engine refined to produce 108bhp/99lb ft, fractionally up from before.
Previous reports 30.9.98, 18.11.98, 17.2.99, 26.5.99, 4.8.99, 3.11.99, 16.2.00

Double wishbones all round and a stiffer bodyshell meant superb handling

to the camshaft position sensor, which helps the engine management system decide when to fire each piston. Seems it had been giving out duff information.

All was well on the car's return, the engine revving happily with its usual gruffness to the 7000rpm red line. Unfortunately, the misfire returned several weeks later; this time it was traced to a fault in the wiring loom causing the same symptoms as before.

It's testament to the Mazda's

enduring qualities that this episode failed to dampen our enthusiasm for the car. It's worth bearing in mind that neither Mazda UK, Tamplins, nor ourselves have heard of any other MX-5s suffering similar problems.

Less significant, but still niggling, have been the troubles with the stereo. The car's original Clarion radio/cassette player was never right from the start – sometimes it was impossible to adjust the volume, and other times it needed about

a dozen prods of the on/off button before it could be coaxed into life. When it finally gave up the ghost it was replaced with an identical unit. This one refused to play tapes. At the time of the last report another replacement had just been fitted, but this turned out to be no better than the original.

At this point a Sony CD unit was installed instead (now standard fit on new MX-5s). It's a thumpingly good stereo, although the bass is sometimes a little too much for the speakers.

The only other time the MX-5 has had to make an unscheduled visit to the dealer has been to have new seals fitted on the hood after the originals started coming adrift.

This problem aside, the hood design as a whole is excellent. The Mazda's heated glass rear window is a double boon: it clears condensation in a jiffy and, unlike flexible plastic, there's no risk of damaging it when folding the roof. It also promises to last a whole lot longer than a plastic window: ◗

MX-5 took on the Goodwood mud...

...and lived to tell the tale unscathed

Snappy gearchange is a joy to use

People who dismiss the MX-5 as a hairdresser's car are missing out on the most road fun to be had for £16,000

Vanity drove us to fit tasty £440 alloys, after nine months of budget driving

Lockable cubby is perfect for tapes

MX-5's 1.6i is the pick of the range

◀ it won't go opaque with age.

The hood is joyously quick and easy to operate. Who needs to be slowed down by an electric mechanism? A case in point: a few weeks ago, the Mazda was sat at traffic lights. Minutes before, it had stopped raining and the sun was re-emerging from behind the clouds. The driver thought it was time to drop the hood. So did a chap in the Peugeot 306 cabriolet in the next lane.

The Mazda's roof was down in the time it took Mr 306 to locate and press the button on his dashboard. Within moments the lights changed and the Mazda was away, but the Peugeot was still sat with its hood waving in the air, a queue of traffic backed up behind. By the time its hood was safely stowed the lights had changed

back to red. No doubt the same colour as the 306 driver's face.

The MX5's hood is so effective at keeping out the elements that there's never been any temptation to fit a hard-top, even in the bleakest of mid-winter months. Even when the seals came adrift, there was never any adverse effect on weather protection. Indeed, the Mazda has been jetwashed on a regular basis without letting a drop into the cabin, which is more than can be said for some tin-tops. There's also the fact, of course, that the hard-top costs the best part of £1500.

The Mazda's two-seat layout has never posed any serious problems. The boot's lack of depth has been criticised in a previous report, but after taking a peek inside the new Toyota MR2, the MX-5 now looks like

MX-5's rugged roof coped easily with everything from winter to jet washes

Seals were replaced after 24k miles

Boot is a decent size for a roadster

a paragon of practicality.

Running costs have been a mixed bag. Servicing hasn't been cheap, costing on average about £200, but fuel consumption around town is 32mpg, and touring remains around 40mpg.

A new set of tyres at 19,000 miles set us back £220. We decided to persevere with Yokohama rubber, despite the experiences of sister magazine *What Car?* and their MX-5. They switched to grippier Bridgestones after one wet-road scare too many. We've had similar experiences with one spin on a wet roundabout at only 25mph. When you're expecting the tail to snap out it's a real hoot – when you're not, it's a nasty shock.

It's easy to fall in love with a roadster on a sunny day; even diehard sceptics can be

bewitched by the sensations of open-top driving when the weather's perfect. But the effects of global warming aside, the reality is that the UK has a pretty ropey climate. Even fresh air freaks like myself aren't immune to the effects of hypothermia. But the Mazda is so much fun even with the roof securely fastened that being able to enjoy the wind in your hair at the drop of a roof is a bonus.

The MX-5 offers so many more of the elemental pleasures of motoring and in so much greater depth than roadsters at two or three times the price (any BMW Z3 and the Honda S2000 are examples that immediately spring to mind).

It's not just Britain's best budget roadster; in my book this car offers the most fun you can have for £16,000. ◓

LOGBOOK

TEST STARTED 18.8.98	
Mileage at start	71
Mileage now	30,021

OPTIONS	
Alloy wheels	£440

PRICES		
List price new		£15,520
Total price new		£15,960
Value now*		
Trade	Private	Retail
£10,545	£11,595	£11,845

*from What Car? Used Car Price Guide

FUEL CONSUMPTION	
Urban	26.7mpg
Extra-urban	42.8mpg

Combined	34.9mpg
Our test best	40.2mpg
Our test worst	26.1mpg
Our test average	31.8mpg

PERFORMANCE	
Top speed	122mph
0-30mph	3.0sec
0-40mph	4.5sec
0-50mph	6.4sec
0-60mph	8.9sec
0-70mph	12.0sec
0-100mph	28.2sec
30-50mph (4th)	8.2sec
50-70mph (5th)	12.8sec

SERVICING AND TYRES

MILEAGE		COST
9000	Oil change and filter	£171.00
18,000	Oil change and filter, brake fluid	£221.98
27,000	Oil change and filter, air filter	£221.98
36,000	Oil change and filter, brake fluid	£320.62
45,000	Oil change and filter	£210.00
54,000	Oil change and filter, air filter, fuel filter, brake fluid, transmission oil, differential oil, cambelt	£464.36

Sample labour rates Middlesex £67.50 per hour, Sunderland £47, Dundee £42.30

Parts costs Front bumper £254.81 (plus cost of respray), headlamp £113.99, windscreen £100.12, door mirror £91.28

Tyres 185/60 Yokohama A-460 **Typical price** £54.99 (KwikFit, fitting included)

Service costs from Tamplins, Twickenham. Parts prices include VAT but not fitting

FAULTS

5000 miles Persistent misfire caused by camshaft position sensor malfunction. Fault recurred and was traced to wiring loom

24,000 miles Hood seals replaced. Three faulty Clarion radio/cassette units replaced by Sony radio/single-CD player

COSTS OVER 29,950 MILES

Fuel	£3206	Running costs per mile	13.4p
Oil (non-service)	None	Cost/mile inc depreciation	17p
Service and parts	£812.15	Repairs Scuffed bumper resprayed	
Total running costs	£4018.15	(£99.88)	

INSURANCE

25-year-old single male, two speeding fines, five years' no-claims bonus, living in high-risk Manchester — **£1855.85**

35-year-old married male, clean licence, five years' no-claims bonus, living in low-risk Swindon — **£454.54**

Both quotes from What Car? Insurance (tel 0345 413554) and include £200 compulsory excess

WHAT WE LIKE

Superb handling, super-quick gearchange, sharp steering, excellent manual hood mechanism, heated glass rear window, styling, sheer fun factor

WHAT WE DON'T LIKE

Ugly steering wheel, poor security (needs double locks and standard alarm system), engine could be more refined, wet-weather skittishness can catch out the unwary, no anti-lock

FINAL VIEW

Still Britain's best budget roadster, though not as trouble-free as we had expected. A joy with the roof down on a sunny day, but makes even the most mundane journey a pleasure, whatever the weather.

PERFECT TIMING

STORY Michael Taylor PHOTOS Helmut Meuller

Toyota's just discovered convertibles, but Mazda's already stiffened its defences. If you thought the MX-5 was good before, be prepared for something special…

How, Mazda's problem has long been, do you improve on the best soul-cleansing apparatus to be found on the cheerful side of $100K? It's a conundrum that became suddenly pressing with the emergence of what looks, on paper, to be the MX-5's first genuine competitor.

After dodging Japan's chronic second-generation spread and surviving Generation-WRX with its reputation enhanced, history's finest budget convertible is about to face the engineering and, not insignificantly, marketing might of Toyota (page 54).

The immediate answers for the Mazda brains trust were relatively simple. They'd already trialled a six-speed gearbox here with the 10th Anniversary model early last year and anybody who used it loved it. That'll do for starters.

Then, about the only consistent call that Mazda's copped about its little drop-top has been that it could do with some more berries. And here they come.

Not that the old 1.8-litre twin-cam four-pot's been turfed completely. The existing engine block's been given what is a curiously comprehensive cylinder-head upgrade for a modest 10 percent lift in power and torque. Yet another Japanese iteration of variable valve timing (this time called Sequential Valve Timing) bumps the power up to 113 kW at 7000 rpm (from 106) and the torque lifts to 181 Nm (from 165), but 500 revs up on the old 4500 rpm peak.

In isolation, each of these two major pillars of the MX-5's upgrade would probably be enough to see it through another few years of life. Working off each other, they mount a comprehensive argument about why the drop-top status quo will take some changing.

Since its birth, the MX-5's gearbox has lead a revival in one of driving's unsung joys. Gearchanging, a task so irksome it became the domain of the software boffin, was back in town. The second-generation car's 'box aped the original with a tiny gearknob that begged to be moved – in a hurry and often.

The six-speeder is more of the same. Each shifted cog comes with a wonderfully secure feeling of metal

snicking metal, of taut engineering working in harmony and a throw so short Parkinson's sufferers would be in overdrive before they hit the roll-a-door. It also endows its operators with a teasingly short memory so that they constantly invent excuses to revisit its deliciousness. And there's no auto.

While it's encouraging to know the MX-5's lost none of its astonishing shift quality with another cog stuffed inside the casing, what's more relevant is the way it takes the torque and runs with it. Effectively, it closes up the ratios and eradicates cog-to-cog torque drop-off, meaning the second-third hole is a thing of the past. On the road, it feels like it gives the car another 30 or 40 horsepower, even though fifth is now direct drive and sixth is the only overdriven gear.

With the fourth of the odometer's tumblers still dormant, our (very early) model was way too tight to pass a concrete judgement on the engine's upgrade. Even so, using the direct-drive cog, 10 percent more power doesn't really feel like a substantial boost.

That said, it's still more willing at this early vintage to fling the tacho needle towards the redline and it's noticeably more flexible in the midrange, so disregard where the numbers say the torque peak has shifted to. It'll happily pull sixth from as little as 2000 rpm, but with this gearbox, it's almost an unconscionable act of sacrilege to find that out.

The chassis – that other MX-5 benchmark the others still chase – has been, if anything, lifted.

Both torque and power peaks are now 500 revs further around the black-on-white tacho

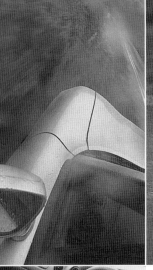

A stiffer chassis makes the Mazda classic's benchmark handling even better

FAST FACTS

body
two-door convertible

drive
rear-wheel

engine
front-mounted 1.8-litre 16-valve in-line four, variable valve timing

power
113 kW @ 7000 rpm

torque
181 Nm @ 5000 rpm

compression ratio
10.0:1

bore x stroke
83 mm x 85 mm

weight
1085 kg

weight/power
9.6 kg/kW

specific power
62.7 kW/litre

transmission
six-speed manual

final drive
3.636:1

suspension
double wishbones, coil springs, torsion bar (f); double wishbones, coil springs, torsion bar (r)

length/width/height
3975 / 1680 / 1225 mm

wheelbase
2265 mm

track
1415 mm (f); 1440 mm (r)

brakes
270 mm ventilated discs, twin-piston calipers (f); 276 mm solid discs, single-piston calipers (r), ABS

wheels
17 x 7.5-inch, alloy (f&r)

tyres
Bridgestone Potenza RE011, 215/45 R17

list price
$41,190

The wheel and tyre size has been bumped up to 16 inches, ABS is now standard, the brake rotors grow 15 mm, they've chucked Bilstein dampers at it and new truss members, while a strengthened body frame and a brace across the bonnet lift torsional rigidity by 22 percent.

And it's immediately noticeable. The ride quality is better, the balance is just as good, the steering is still amazingly telepathic and the suspension settings are so close to perfect as to render even moderate criticism picky. Call us picky, then. The back can feel too soft on bump strike. There.

Otherwise, the car is a gem. Here is a chassis that is not only happy to be punted hard, it encourages it without being imposing in daily life. It asks to take everything you can dish out to it, but isn't so impolite as to suggest you're wasting it if you don't. But when you do, the cleaner, neater and tidier you drive, the faster it gets and the more the fun accumulates. The more you let it flow, the faster it feels and the more feedback it gives and, when you get it right, the car reacts intuitively to anything the driver's thinking.

Try to turn a winding road into a ham-fisted, V8-style oversteering odyssey and it will bite back. Stand on the brakes mid-corner and the tail will come

A new brace across the strut towers helps add 22 percent to the MX-5's torsional rigidity

around. Gas it up too early and it will push into understeer. Just because its balance is perfect doesn't mean it has to reward imbeciles, and it's a better car for leaving its very best as a challenge to unearth.

Of course, the MX-5 revolutionised convertibles in more ways than one. It proved that a spare car wasn't compulsory and it can still happily chug through city life week in, week out.

There's not much room, but it's better equipped than once it was. It's picked up an in-dash CD player with a more user-friendly sound system, there's now a pair of cupholders between the console and the gear lever (though full they can interfere with the shift action) and the console swallows six CD cases.

The facia dials now run to a white background with soft amber lighting. The seats run a taller backrest and more lumbar and lateral side support, while there's now remote locking and dual airbags. Visually, the revamp's going to be hard to spot, bigger wheels aside. The tailight cluster's a bit different, the headlights are mildly narrower and so's the air-intake. But, like just like its chassis, it seems the MX-5's visual balance is not to be tampered with lightly. Neither, it seems, is Mazda's stranglehold on a market it has come to regard as its own.

It might not punch that much harder, but it's a bloody comprehensive overhaul. And one that, at $41,190, might just go down as one of the best pre-emptive strikes the Australian industry has ever seen. **LM**

Mazda MX-5 Miata
vs.
Toyota MR2 Spyder

If you can't have fun in one of these little gems, you're dead.

BY LARRY WEBSTER

No cars are closer to our editorial hearts than roadsters. Which shouldn't come as a surprise, but in case it does, listen up. Roadsters, as defined in our October 1999 issue, are open cars that can be raced in a pinch. Racing is not their main purpose; rather, roadsters should get the juices flowing and make running errands on Saturday a task worth looking forward to.

Which makes buying a roadster something other than a practical, scientific purchase. You don't buy a particular roadster because it costs $500 less than the one down the street; you buy it because it looks and feels right. But one also has to consider at least some practicality. After all, the more useful your new toy is, the more excuses you can make to drive it.

If you're a nouveau riche Internet geek and wouldn't think twice about plunking down more than 30 large for a roadster, your needs are currently well served by Honda, Porsche, BMW, and Mercedes. If,

however, the idea of spending three times the yearly income of a fast-food worker on a weekend car makes you feel guilty or you simply don't have that kind of dough, your choice was previously limited to one car—the Mazda MX-5 Miata.

But do not refer to the Miata condescendingly as "a low-priced alternative." Please. The Miata is worthy of a purchase on its goodness alone and not simply for a low price. When it was introduced, as a 1990 model, there were two similar low-buck sportsters, but neither could touch the Miata's control feel, handling, or fun quotient. By the time the Miata was redesigned for 1999, the other players had dropped out of the picture.

The Miata's virtue lies not in outright speed but rather in a oneness the driver feels almost immediately with this sports car. Few cars feel so much like an extension of the brain as the Miata does.

But now there is an alternative to Mazda's pocket gem. This year, Toyota

resurrected the MR2 name with its new MR2 Spyder. The last MR2 was a mid-engined, two-seat wedgie coupe sold here from 1985 to 1995. The MR2 Spyder seen here still has the mid-engine layout, but now it comes only as a softtop convertible.

Other than engine placement, the Miata and the MR2 Spyder are strikingly similar. Both have 1.8-liter, 16-valve DOHC four-cylinder engines, five-speed manual transmissions (only the Mazda offers an automatic), rear-wheel drive, and a manual top with a glass rear window. As a lesson in what competition can achieve, early this year Mazda, in response to this new kid on the block, lowered the Miata's price *and* increased the equipment that is standard. The as-tested price of our MR2 roadster was $23,615, and the Mazda ran up $22,735 at the checkout counter. Add the $550 optional anti-lock brakes—it's a standard feature on the Toyota—to the Miata, and they're almost identically priced.

PHOTOGRAPHY BY DAVID DEWHURST

Toyota MR2 Spyder

Highs: Stellar racetrack handling, good midrange grunt, supportive seats.

Lows: Barely room for you, a companion, and a Snickers bar; vintage-1985 Japanese interior styling.

The Verdict: Maybe the most-responsive-handling car made today, but lacks enough storage room to make it anything but a toy.

Handsome steering wheel stands out in drab interior. Shifter feels remote.

Neatly folding top is tough to operate single-handedly from the driver's seat.

We conducted our comparison test in Southern California, with mountain running, highway cruising, and track testing. We also added a lapping session on the tight 1.5-mile Streets of Willow road course. It was a tough assignment, but somebody had to do it.

Second Place
Toyota MR2 Spyder

If these two cars were strictly racing machines, the MR2 would be the easy

C/D Test Results	acceleration,* seconds							top speed, mph	braking, 70–0 mph, feet	roadholding, 300-foot skidpad, g
	0–30 mph	0–60 mph	0–100 mph	1/4-mile	street start, 5–60 mph	top gear, 30–50 mph	top gear, 50–70 mph			
MAZDA MX-5 MIATA	2.3	7.6	25.5	16.1 @ 85 mph	8.6	10.1	10.9	119	181	0.88
TOYOTA MR2 SPYDER	2.1	6.8	23.2	15.6 @ 87 mph	7.6	8.6	9.3	121	161	0.88

Vital Statistics	price, base/ as tested	engine	SAE net power/torque*	transmission/ gear ratios:1/ maximum test speed, mph/ axle ratio:1	curb weight, pounds	weight distribution, % front/rear
MAZDA MX-5 MIATA	$20,995/ $22,735	DOHC 16-valve 4-in-line, 112 cu in (1839cc), aluminum block and head, Mazda engine-control system with port fuel injection	138 bhp @ 6500 rpm/ 117 lb-ft @ 5000 rpm	5-speed manual/ 3.14, 1.89, 1.33, 1.00, 0.81/ 34, 56, 80, 106, 119/ 4.30	2380	52.9/47.1
TOYOTA MR2 SPYDER	$23,553/ $23,615	DOHC 16-valve 4-in-line, 109 cu in (1794cc), aluminum block and head, Toyota engine-control system with port fuel injection	138 bhp @ 6400 rpm/ 125 lb-ft @ 4400 rpm	5-speed manual/ 3.17, 1.90, 1.39, 1.03, 0.82/ 33, 54, 74, 101, 121/ 4.31	2260	43.4/56.6

* Our Miata was equipped with the $150 California LEV emissions package, which reduces output by 2 bhp and 2 lb-ft. The MR2 Spyder is emissions-legal in all states.

CAR and DRIVER

choice, and it finished only a single point behind the Miata. It's so balanced and neutral at the limit that the driver can choose which end to slide at will—something few of today's sports cars can do. During a short lapping session, we found ourselves braking ridiculously late for the corners and allowing the rear end to step out during turn-in, which quickly and efficiently pointed the car at the apex. The rear-end slide never felt hairy or threatening but was

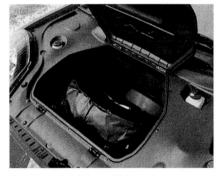

If you're a risk taker, ditching the spare tire would almost make this trunk useful.

rather a useful tool to produce quick lap times. There is nary a hint of the hair-raising, bite-you-in-the-butt potential we've encountered in some mid-engined cars, including the old MR2 and the Acura NSX.

The MR2 whipped around the road course more than a second faster than the Miata. Much of the credit for the MR2's speed goes to its excellent racetrack handling, but at 2260 pounds, it is also 120 pounds lighter than the Miata. That doesn't sound like much, but the reduced poundage pays genuine dividends in acceleration and braking distances.

The Toyota engine is a conventional DOHC 16-valve four-cylinder with variable valve timing. The little motor has quite a meaty power band. The torque peak of 125 pound-feet is eight more than has been invested in our California-reg Miata, and it occurs 600 rpm sooner. The MR2's peak horsepower equals the LEV Miata's 138 figure, and the two cars are geared nearly identically.

The MR2's more svelte profile and power-band advantage trounced the Miata

in the acceleration runs. Scooting to 60 mph takes only 6.8 seconds, 0.8 second quicker than the Miata, and the Toyota reaches 100 mph 2.3 seconds earlier, at 23.2 seconds. Standing-start runs show off an engine's peak power, but the MR2 also outshines the Miata in the top-gear tests, which illustrate the Toyota's strong midrange grunt. In both top-gear runs, the Toyota beat the Miata by at least a full second, doing the 30-to-50-mph gig in 8.6 seconds and the 50-to-70-mph test in 9.3 seconds.

The MR2 has vented disc brakes at all four corners linked to anti-lock control, and the results are impressive. In fact, hauling the little roadster down from 70 mph took only 161 feet—that's within a couple of feet of the stopping abilities of such luminaries as the Porsche 911 and the Ferrari 360 Modena. No doubt the confidence given by the excellent brakes lets the driver delay braking until the last possible moment, another factor that contributed to the MR2's fast lap times.

Still, most roadster buyers don't race their vehicles. They're more likely used for weekend getaways to view the changing colors of fall at a leisurely pace. What you need for that activity is some trunk space, and here the MR2's score is rather dismal. Most of what there is of front trunk space is used to accommodate the spare tire, leaving a paltry two cubic feet. What about behind the roadster's two seats? There's a small compartment there

road course, lap time/ average mph	emergency-lane-change maneuver, mph	interior sound level, dBA				fuel economy, mpg		
		idle	full throttle	70-mph cruising	70-mph coasting	EPA city	EPA highway	C/D 250-mile trip
1:24.50/ 63.9	61.5	47	79	76	75	25	29	18
1:23.23/ 64.9	59.2	47	85	75	74	25	30	19

dimensions, inches				fuel tank, gallons	interior volume, cubic feet		suspension		brakes, front/rear	tires
wheel-base	length	width	height		front	trunk	front	rear		
89.2	155.3	66.0	48.3	12.7	46	5	ind, unequal-length control arms, coil springs, anti-roll bar	ind, unequal-length control arms, coil springs, anti-roll bar	vented disc/ disc	Michelin Pilot SX, 195/50VR-15
96.5	153.0	66.7	48.8	12.7	46	2	ind, strut located by a control arm, coil springs, anti-roll bar	ind; strut located by 1 trailing link, 1 lateral link, and 1 toe-control link per side; coil springs; anti-roll bar	vented disc/ vented disc; anti-lock control	Yokohama Advan AO13; F: 185/55VR-15 R: 205/50VR-15,

Mazda MX-5 Miata

Highs: Communicative chassis and steering, snick-snick shifter, handsome styling, mellifluous engine note.

Lows: Cramped interior, short on midrange grunt.

The Verdict: The Japanese roadster with more soul than James Brown.

Without tonneau cover attached, folded top looks sloppy but is a breeze to raise and lower from the driver's seat.

Handsome interior's ergonomics work perfectly. Shifter is one of the best.

that might accept a briefcase, perhaps an overnight change of skivvies and socks.

Interestingly, when you're using the MR2 to absorb the fall colors at a less than breakneck pace, its neutral handling isn't apparent. Rather, the front end feels light, and the car pushes through turns. Granted, that's a safe trait, but it was a factor that contributed to our having more fun driving the Miata on the street.

Both convertible tops operate alike. Simply pop the two header latches, and manually lift and lower the top, and that can be done from the seated driver's position. The Toyota top would win a competition simply because it folds flatter. On the other hand, a seated driver will find that raising the MR2's top is more difficult because you have to reach back over the wind blocker to grasp it.

What we're about to say will no doubt start the letters-to-the-editor engine grinding. Here goes, anyway: With the top down, the MR2 is almost too comfortable. We like some wind buffeting in a convertible; we think wind in your face on a warm summer's night is part of the experience. Ironically, the MR2's designers did such a good job isolating the occupants that there's almost too little wind in evidence. You also sit low in the MR2, with the door

Size matters: Miata's larger trunk makes it more than a weekend toy.

tops level with your shoulders. Some may find this a more secure seating idea, but we're partial to the Miata's seating position, which elevates the driver and passenger into position for a gentle head mas-

sage but doesn't provide the unpleasant sensation of being hammered by Sugar Ray. Styling is a personal matter, but we have yet to find someone who thinks any part of the MR2 looks better than the Miata. And to be honest, you want to look good in your weekend toy.

Toyota must realize its car is a narrow-focus vehicle. Whereas Mazda sells about 20,000 Miatas a year, Toyota will offer just 5000 MR2s to the U.S. market in its first year. So if pure speed is your primary rationale, you'd best get in line soon.

First Place
Mazda MX-5 Miata

We can hear the harping even as we write this. "How can you numbnuts pick the Mazda—it's the same price as the MR2, but it's heavier and slower!" Let us explain.

True, the MR2 was quicker on the road course, but the Miata is not a piece of farm machinery. In the lane-change test, which demonstrates a car's agility, controllability, and willingness to change direction, our Suspension-package-equipped Miata could do the test more than 2 mph faster than could the MR2. Both cars have identical grip at 0.88 g, but the MR2 did not thread through the cones as gracefully as the Miata. The Miata digs in and hangs on; the MR2 is more sensitive to where the weight of the car is, deceleration giving grip to the front and acceleration making the front end feel light.

On the racetrack, the Miata rolls more severely than the MR2 and actually feels as though it's cornering at a higher speed. The Miata will also faithfully obey a driver's command, but it isn't as easily coaxed into a rear-end drift. Instead, it relies on crisp turn-in and balanced grip to get it through the corners. The Toyota is balanced in the way it responds to weight transfer, but it's always sliding, either pushing or oversteering. The Miata rolls into a corner, nearly bites into it, and digs its way through.

Clearly, the Miata's extra poundage affected lap times and acceleration.

Considering the 2380-pound Mazda is only 2.3 inches longer than the MR2, yet weighs 120 pounds more, we think Mazda should have done a better job of keeping the Miata light. Especially since the original 1990 Miata weighed only 2210 pounds.

At any rate, we suspect the Miata and the MR2 cornered at or near the same speed, but the MR2 easily pulled away when the course straightened out. The Miata also didn't benefit from the $550 optional anti-lock brakes, a feature that's standard on the MR2. Even so, the Miata's brakes are wonderfully communicative. We usually do about five to seven stops while measuring braking performance from 70 mph to test for fade and get a feel for how the brakes work. The Miata's were so easy to modulate that we could instantly threshold-brake without practice. Well-modulated brakes cannot beat ABS, however, and the Miata gave up 20 feet in the stopping test.

The Miata isn't just great fun to drive on a racetrack; it shines in everyday driving, too. The exhaust snarls smartly and never sounds as though you're thrashing the engine. The Mazda's shifter ties the Honda S2000's for best on the market today. You'll swear you can feel the cogs engaging. The suspension is tuned rather softly, which results in body roll while turning, but on the street, the Miata scoots around with graceful rhythm. The fun begins the moment you back out of the driveway. We love the steering feel and the feedback it offers. In our test logbook, a driver noted: "I love the way the steering wheel jitters over unseen road ripples. Perfect communication."

Comparing the practicality of roadsters is a little like debating the environmental virtues of the Ford Excursion and Chevy Suburban, but between these two roadsters, the Miata's rear trunk simply makes it more useful. Although it will accept just five cubic feet of stuff, that's more than double the MR2's space.

Voting on these two cars was extremely tough. On the one hand, the MR2 is faster and more entertaining on the track. On the other, the Miata is close to the MR2 on the track but leagues ahead in everyday driving satisfaction. So call it a virtual dead heat, except the Miata was the unanimous styling favorite and has an edge in practicality as well.

We wrote in our first Miata road test way back in September 1989 that the Miata made us cheer. It still does. ●

	engine	trans-mission	brakes	handling	ride	driver comfort	ergo-nomics	features and amenities	fit and finish	value	styling	fun to drive	OVERALL RATING*
MAZDA MX-5 MIATA	10	10	9	10	10	8	9	6	9	9	10	10	97
TOYOTA MR2 SPYDER	10	9	10	10	9	9	9	10	9	9	8	10	96

Editors' Ratings

HOW IT WORKS: Editors rate vehicles from 1 to 10 (10 being best) in each category, then scores are collected and averaged, resulting in the numbers shown above.

*The overall rating is not the total of those numbers. Rather, it is an independent judgment (on a 1-to-100 scale) that includes other factors—even personal preferences—not easily categorized.

DUSK. IT'S THAT MAGICAL TIME BETWEEN day and night when the sky becomes purple, a cool breeze kisses your face and, if you happen to be in the mountains, the air is hauntingly silent. There's no better time or place to be driving a convertible sports car, with the top down, on an empty road with only a windshield between you and the oncoming rush of air. And if your mount happens to be the new Mazda Miata, your drive can almost be a divine experience, with man, nature and machinery harmoniously coexisting. Heck, if Buddha himself were around today, he'd be singing the virtues of this nimble convertible because it now exhibits a higher level of power and control than ever before.

The Miata enters the new (true) Millennium with a significant gain in power. Its 1.8-liter 16-valve inline-4 is now equipped with variable valve timing (VVT), which continuously varies the opening/closing of the intake valves in response to load, throttle opening and engine rpm. This new technology accounts for an 11 percent boost in horsepower—from 140 to 155 bhp—and torque to 125 lb.-ft. at 5500 rpm. The revised engine comes mated to one of three gearboxes: a 5-speed manual, a 6-speed manual (available on the LS) or a 4-speed automatic.

Start the car and the twincam powerplant comes to life with a familiar growl. Rev it to about 4000 rpm, drop the clutch and the rear 205/45R-16 tires spin freely against the pave-

2001 Mazda

MX-5 MIATA

Zen and the art of top-down motoring

BY SAM MITANI
PHOTOS BY GUY SPANGENBERG

ment, sending a puff of smoke into the air. Once they grab the tarmac, the car jumps off the line with verve, momentarily pressing your back into the seat, and then accelerates in a pleasant, if not potent, nature. The car seems to reach its full stride as soon as the tachometer needle sweeps past 3000 rpm. Amid a rising storm of revs, the 7000-rpm redline comes in a blur, signaling the driver to grab the next gear. The sound and sensation are so sweet, one can't help but look forward to each upshift. The 6-speed manual gearbox of our test car was a delight to operate, with short *snickety-snick* throws and well-defined gates.

At the test track, the new Miata ran from 0 to 60 mph in 8.0 seconds and hit the quarter-mile mark in 16.2. Those of you familiar with the test data of last year's Miata may recall that it had similar acceleration times.

Mazda engineers believed that the Miata's on-road character could be significantly enhanced if improvements were made to the car's structure. Therefore, they proceeded to incorporate a formidable number of reinforcements at key locations on the car's frame and body, including the side sills and floor. There are also new crossmembers at both the front and rear, as well as a strut-tower brace.

■ Now aided by variable valve timing, Mazda's twincam 1.8-liter makes a stout 155 bhp. The 6-speed manual helps the driver keep the engine singing in its sweet spot above 3000 rpm.

The result: Torsional and bending rigidity have been improved 22 and 16 percent, respectively, over last year's model, with only this modest weight gain. And this newfound rigidity is especially noticeable when cornering. The 2001 Miata remains rock-solid stable through all types of turns with a touch of understeer through slow-speed bends. The Miata's suspension system—upper and lower A-arms at both front and rear—has firmer tube shocks that help keep the car on a level plane when cornering. Also gone is the car's overanxious tendency to kick its rear out through sharp corners, even

2001 Mazda MX-5
Miata LS

Mazda North America
7755 Irvine Center Dr., Irvine, Calif. 92623-9734
www.mazdausa.com

ROAD & TRACK
ROAD TEST

At a Glance...

0–60 mph	8.0 sec	**List Price: $23,930**
0–¼ mile	16.2 sec	**Price as Tested: $25,610**
Top speed	est 120 mph	
Skidpad	0.91g	
Slalom	62.8 mph	
Brake rating	very good	

Price as tested incl std equip. (dual airbags, leather seats, Nardi leather steering wheel, cruise ctrl, air cond, 200-watt AM/FM/CD w/4 speakers, keyless entry; power windows, mirrors and locks; strut tower brace, 16-in. alloy wheels w/locks, limited-slip differential, foglights, 6-speed manual ($650), ABS w/EBD ($550), dest charge ($480).

SCALE: 10 IN.(254mm) DIVISIONS
DRAWING BY TIM BARKER

SPECIFICATIONS

Engine

Type	**cast-iron block, alloy head, inline-4**
Valvetrain	**dohc 4-valve/cyl**
Displacement	**112 cu in./1839 cc**
Bore x stroke	**3.27 x 3.35 in./ 83.0 x 85.0 mm**
Compression ratio	**10.0:1**
Horsepower (SAE)	**155 bhp @ 7000 rpm**
Bhp/liter	**84.3**
Torque	**125 lb-ft @ 5500 rpm**
Redline	**7000 rpm**
Fuel injection	**elect. sequential port**
Fuel	**unleaded, 87 pump octane**

Warranty

Basic warranty	**3 years/50,000 miles**
Powertrain	**3 years/50,000 miles**
Rust-through	**5 years/unlimited**

Chassis & Body

Layout	**front engine/rear drive**
Body/frame	**unit steel**
Brakes: Front	**10.6-in. vented discs**
Rear	**10.9-in. discs**
Assist type	**vacuum; ABS w/ EBD**
Total swept area	**398 sq in.**
Swept area/ton	**304 sq in.**
Wheels	**alloy; 16 x 6**
Tires	**Bridgestone Turanza ER 30; 205/45R-16**
Steering	**rack & pinion, power assist**
Overall ratio	**15.0:1**
Turns, lock to lock	**2.7**
Turning circle	**30.2 ft**

Suspension
Front: **upper & lower A-arms, coil springs, tube shocks, anti-roll bar**
Rear: **upper & lower A-arms, coil springs, tube shocks, anti-roll bar**

General Data

Curb weight	**2480 lb**
Test weight	**2620 lb**
Weight dist (with driver), f/r, %	**56/44**
Wheelbase	**89.2 in.**
Track, f/r	**55.7 in./56.7 in.**
Length	**155.7 in.**
Width	**66.0 in.**
Height	**48.3 in.**
Ground clearance	**4.0 in.**
Trunk space	**6.1 cu ft**

Accommodations

Seating capacity	**2**
Head room	**36.5 in.**
Seat width	**2 x 19.0 in.**
Leg room	**42.0 in.**
Seatback adjustment	**45 deg**
Seat travel	**8.0 in.**

Drivetrain

Transmission: **6-speed manu**

Gear	Ratio	Overall ratio	(Rpm)	M
1st	3.76:1	14.70:1	(7000)	
2nd	2.27:1	8.88:1	(7000)	
3rd	1.64:1	6.41:1	(7000)	
4th	1.26:1	4.93:1	(7000)	
5th	1.00:1	3.91:1	(7000)	1
6th	0.84:1	3.28:1	est (5800)	1

Final drive ratio **3.91**
Engine rpm @ 60 mph in 6th **29**

Instrumentation

150-mph speedometer, 8000-rpm tachometer, coolant temp, oil level, fuel lev

Safety

dual front airbags
seatbelt tensioners
anti-lock braking with
electronic brake-force distribution

PERFORMANCE

Acceleration

Time to speed	Seconds
0–30 mph	**2.6**
0–40 mph	**4.1**
0–50 mph	**5.8**
0–60 mph	**8.0**
0–70 mph	**10.8**
0–80 mph	**14.1**
0–90 mph	**18.1**

Time to distance	
0–100 ft	**3.3**
0–500 ft	**8.7**
0–1320 ft (¼ mile)	**16.2 @ 85.6 mph**

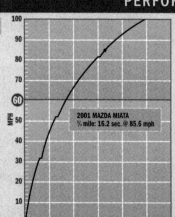

2001 MAZDA MIATA
¼ mile: 16.2 sec. @ 85.6 mph

Braking

Minimum stopping distance
From 60 mph	**124 ft**
From 80 mph	**215 ft**
Control	**excellent**
Brake feel	**very good**
Overall brake rating	**very good**

Fuel Economy

Our driving	**est 24 mpg**
EPA city/highway	**23/28 mpg**
Cruise range	**est 280 miles**
Fuel capacity	**12.7 gal.**

Handling

Lateral acceleration
(200-ft skidpad) **0.91g**
Balance **mild understeer**
Speed through
700-ft slalom **62.8 mph**
Balance **moderate understeer**
Lateral seat support **very good**

Interior Noise

Idle in neutral	**52 dBA**
Maximum in 1st gear	**82 dBA**
Constant 50 mph	**75 dBA**
70 mph	**79 dBA**

Subjective ratings consist of excellent, very good, good, average, poor; na means information is not available.

Test Notes: Launching the Miata off the line is effortless. Hold the engine at 4000 rpm then drop the clutch. The car scoots briskly through the quarter mile guided by a precise 6-speed gearshift. Through the slalom, the Miata feels nimble, with the tail controllable by throttle modulation. Around the skidpad, the Mazda mildly understeers and exhibits only a small amount of bodyroll.

Test Conditions:

Temperature	Humidity	Elevation	Wind
74° F	52%	1010 ft	calm

when depressing the brake pedal in mid-turn. And although the rack-and-pinion steering system remains unchanged, the car's improved chassis makes it feel more precise than ever. It's easy to recall the Miata's motto of "oneness between man and horse" while driving the agile roadster because everything seems to work in harmony. The brakes, whose pedal feel has been dramatically improved, have larger discs (on models with 16-in. wheels) and EBD (Electronic Brake-force Distribution) that automatically optimizes braking of the front and rear wheels evenly, so the new roadster stops better than ever. Ride quality is excellent for such a small convertible, with the suspension soaking up road irregularities in sports-sedan manner. Simply put, the new Miata is a car that exhibits the solidity of a much larger car on the open highway while retaining its nimble nature on twisty roads.

The Miata's 0.91g on the skidpad is roughly the same as the previous model, but its 62.8-mph dance through the slalom is a few steps quicker than before—a testament to its left/right transitional stability.

The 2001 Miata receives a slight facelift, but unless you park it next to the current model, you'd be hard-pressed to see what's changed. For one, the headlights appear slightly more triangular than before, and the front

■ The world's best-selling roadster—better than ever without losing that crucially important balance. Below: a road made for the Miata...

bumper and air-dam have been moderately spiced up. At the rear, the taillights feature a new lens design. Also, sporty 5-spoke 16-in. alloy wheels, standard on the LS and optional on the base, give the new roadster a more athletic profile.

Inside, the changes are equally subtle. The gauges within the instrument cluster now have white faces with dark lettering, and chrome rings border the speedometer and tachometer. The seats are also new, redesigned to provide better support without sacrificing comfort. Taking center stage here continues to be the compact 3-spoke Nardi steering wheel that looks as good as it feels.

To date, Mazda has sold more than 565,000 Miatas since 1989, a feat recognized by *The Guinness Book of World Records* as the world's best-selling 2-seat sports car. And with a base price of $21,180, this number will no

doubt become much larger in time.

As Mazda has proved time and again with its Miata, what's most important about a sports car is not how quickly it can accelerate. Rather, it's how it makes its driver feel behind the wheel. And on a secluded mountain road, the 2001 Miata makes you feel as if you're part of the environment. In the words of Robert M. Pirsig, author of the cult classic, *Zen and the Art of Motorcycle Maintenance,* the new Miata makes you feel "completely in contact with it all. You're in the scene, not just watching it anymore, and the sense of presence is overwhelming. That concrete whizzing by five inches below your foot is the real thing, the same stuff you walk on, it's right there…and the whole thing, the whole experience, is never removed from immediate consciousness."

Fresh élan

MAZDA MX-5

A ROADSTER revolution is taking place in this country. Yesteryear's readily affordable "two-seater on a small family car chassis", initiated by the post-war MG T-series, has metamorphised into a new kind of topless four-wheeled fun without frills. By modern we mean a dedicated chassis, the inclusion of some luxury, and a degree of sophistication. Sadly, though, such progress brings with it a price tag (in SA's case, in excess of R200 000) that categorises such motoring pleasure as accessible rather than affordable. But the country's manufacturers and importers obviously believe there are enough potential buyers to justify offering these dream (for most of us) machines on the local market. One such, the Mazda MX-5, has made a couple of appearances on our shores before. Now a new facelifted version is here carrying a bit more conviction.

Leaving Porsches out of the equation – they are in a different league, really – the rear-wheel drive MX-5 1,8-litre joins the mid-engined Toyota MR2 1,8 and front-wheel drive Alfa Romeo Spyder 2,0 at SA's entry level of roadster revelry, with the mid-engined MGF 1,8 due early in 2002. (The ostensibly similar Honda S2000 is priced way above these runabouts.) No more than a handful of models to choose from, then, yet the choice is teasingly varied. Of them all, the Mazda is the most classic in conception.

The MX-5 first appeared in February 1989, unwittingly (or *was* it intentional?) reviving interest in nimble simple roadsters that had all but disappeared following the demise of Austin Healey Sprites, MG Midgets and suchlike. Where Mazda scored a bullseye was with the styling, an unabashed crib of the '60s Lotus Elan that was, and still is, considered one of the best sports cars ever. What Mazda offered,

"Immediately feels like a fun package"

though, were the looks and roadholding matched with Japanese engineering and reliability, aspects that Colin Chapman's mass-produced creations almost invariably lacked. The MX-5 – known as Miata and Eunos in other markets – quickly saw off the copycat slurs and became a big hit, particularly in the USA. Just

Bonnet bulges seductive when viewed from inside. Tombstone seats upholstered in leather. Well-stacked facia set off by Nardi steering wheel. Instrumentation includes an oil pressure gauge.

250 of the first 1,6-litre models were alloted to SA.

A facelift and the introduction of a 1,8-litre engine occurred in 1993, and 115 examples were exported here. For the 1998 model year, a new MX-5 was introduced to the world, with more rounded and less Elan-like styling, including "proper" headlights in place of the previous pop-ups. Last year, the model received a mild freshening, and it is this latest second-generation MX-5 that now forms part of Mazda SA's ongoing product line-up. Priced at R225 000, which includes a factory hardtop, it is around R5 500 cheaper than an MR2 with its optional solid roof, and we can expect the MGF to be in this ballpark, too. So, amongst these three topless babes at least, we can expect a bit of a catfight for supremacy, with each having its own devoted fan club.

In this regard, the MX-5 is already ahead of the game. Whenever did you hear of a model's enthusiasts' club being invited to the launch of a new derivative? Mazda did just that with this latest MX-5, and the owners' opinions were eagerly sought – and given – exemplifying the strong bond that exists between the cars and their patrons. Is such loyalty justified, or not, we wondered?

The MX-5 continues to be a good-looking car, with – like most small roadsters – a slightly feminine persona brought about mainly by its size and soft contours. But that is not to suggest it is effete. The classic front engine/rear-wheel drive chassis is powered by a spirited 1 840 cm³

Makes a change to find a modern four-cylinder mounted longitudinally up front, driving the rear wheels. Twin-cam 16-valve engine delivers its max power of 107 kW at the 7 000 r/min red line. Performance is brisk, economy reasonable.

twin-cam, 16-valve, four-cylinder motor featuring sequential valve timing. It pumps out 107 kW at a red-lined 7 000 r/min, and 168 N.m of torque at 5 000. A six-speed gearbox takes drive

"The brakes are supercar good"

through a Torsen limited-slip diff to the rear wheels, which, like the fronts, are independently suspended by double wishbones and coil spring/gas damper units. There are anti-roll bars at both ends. Brakes are discs all round, ventilated up front, and they boast the car's only "modern" driver aid, namely ABS with EBD. All the ingredients, then, for a spirited drive.

Climb in and be sure to extend your right leg down into the footwell before closing the door, otherwise you are likely to trap your knee between the door panel and the steering wheel rim. Use your arms to lever yourself into a comfortable position and your left

elbow will likely drop into the tunnel console drink-holder's flip-back cover. Put a drink in the holder and it will get in the way of gearchanging. Belt up, start up, then engage first and you

will find your hand brushing the handbrake. By now you will be aware that the MX-5's cockpit is, er, snug…

But activate the drilled accelerator pedal and thoughts on the interior's shortcomings begin to dim as the little Mazda warms to its task: quicker, it has to be said, than the heater manages to circulate warm air on chilly mornings. So that is why heated seats are standard… Hood down (why else buy a roadster?) and with the minimal – but effective enough – draught deflector

erected, the MX-5 immediately feels like a fun package. The view over the bonnet is quite sexy, the gentle bulges over the wheelarches and engine having a classic Jaguar-esque seductiveness about them. Using the power exterior mirrors to look behind is spoilt by their being sited aft of the fixed quarterlights, demanding head rather than mere eye movement to view.

A classy Nardi three-spoke wheel controls the power-assisted steering, but the reaction around the straightahead position is sensitive, which means you can almost think the car through gentle sweepers but need to be wary of winding on lock too sharply through the twisties. Once you are used to the steering response – there is 2,65 turns from lock to lock – the MX-5 can be hustled and enjoyed for its dynamic vigour. There is enough life in the handling to feel sporty without an abundance of torque to call upon to get the tail wagging at will. The ride is stiff – less intimidating at speed than when pottering around – even though the meaty 205/45 tyres on 16-inch alloys are pressurised to a gentle 180 kPa all round. Scuttle shake is not an issue. Shifting the six-speeder is not ultra-slick (4th to 5th changes need delibera-

Cockpit is narrow, and the floor console is uncomfortable to rest arm upon. Use the drink holder and the container will hinder gearchanging. Remote boot and fuel flap levers in lockable compartment.

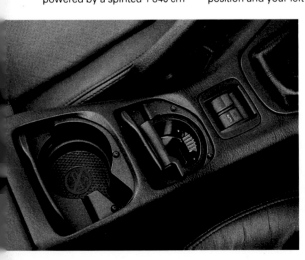

Smart alloy wheels with low-profile rubber provide excellent grip but a hard low-speed ride. Superb all-disc braking system. Headlights are excellent on dip and main beam.

tion), but once warm it is easy enough to keep the motor up where it belongs, challenging the red line. Peak power is at maximum usable revs, remember, and the engine spins willingly. To reach 100 km/h from rest involves two upshifts, the second at just over 90 km/h, but the elapsed time of 8,86 seconds is respectable enough. The kilometre marker is passed in just a fraction over the benchmark 30 seconds at 171,4 km/h, at which point the bonnet lifts and stays that way right up to the 197 km/h averaged top speed. Naturally, it gets noisy inside at high speeds with either hardtop (test

condition) or soft-top erected. But in the kind of motoring the MX-5 will be generally used for, there is no major cause for complaint. Roadsters are for having fun in, not necessarily for going fast.

Braking performance is excellent, practically in Porsche territory. Yes, the Mazda feels like it is standing on its nose if full braking effort is applied, but our test 10-stops from 100 km/h average of 2,8 seconds is supercar good. Other safety features include dual front airbags and

seatbelts with pretensioners and load limiters.

Creature comforts include leather upholstery with perforated inserts for the tombstone-backed seats, air-con (the facia vents are awkward to adjust), electric windows, remote central locking, a two-speaker/two-tweeter radio/front-loader CD sound system, and remote releases for the fuel flap and bootlid. White dial instrumentation (including an oil pressure gauge), with black/red graphics adds to the sporty environment.

The soft-top is fairly simple to lower, but takes some muscle power to pull taut enough to secure the latches when erecting. There is ample headroom with the hood up. When it is folded, there is a fiddly tonneau cover to contend with. Both tops have glass backlights with heating elements.

Hey, and the MX-5 has a usable boot, too. A capacity of 112 dm^3 may not sound a lot, but it is enough to make any Toyota MR2 owner green with envy. Use soft bags rather than our

Use of space-saver spare realises useful (for a roadster) boot space.

Likes and dislikes

DESIGN
- ✔ No fussy detail, no appendages, styling links with Lotus Elan not so obvious now, but it is still a classic roadster shape
- ✔ Rigid body
- ✘ Bonnet lift at high speed

POWERTRAIN
- ✔ Not quite the silky engine/slick-shifting experience we were expecting, but will probably loosen up over time

COMFORT AND FEATURES
- ✔ Hardtop part of the spec
- ✔ Superb headlights
- ✔ View over the bonnet
- ✘ Some aspects of cockpit layout annoying
- ✘ Cramped for most over average build

PERFORMANCE AND BRAKING
- ✔ Quick enough to satisfy most, and on par with rivals
- ✔ Outstanding brakes

FUEL ECONOMY
- ✔ What one would expect

RIDE AND HANDLING
- ✔ Entertaining without a host of back-up driver aids. Adheres to a classic roadster profile
- ✔ Ride sporting but almost too hard
- ✘ Over-sensitive steering

VALUE FOR MONEY
- ✔ Given the level of equipment, currently it is the most affordable practical roadster available locally

ISO-standard blocks and the boot will hold a bit more. Loading height is 750 mm, and for a roadster that, by definition, is not meant to be a heavy goods carrier, it is surprising that headlight beam height adjustment is provided. The headlights, incidentally, are superb on dip and main. A space-saver spare wheel and the battery are located under the boot mat.

Test summary

As a roadster practical enough to be used as everyday transport, the MX-5 fits the bill convincingly. Aspects of the cockpit layout annoy, though, which takes a little shine off the overall driving pleasure the Mazda provides. Toyota's MR2 is more spirited but less practical, and the Alfa Spyder is perhaps more tourer than sportster. Our experience with the upcoming MGF suggests it will be the cat amongst the pigeons. In the meantime, we reckon the reasons for the original MX-5's cult following may not immediately apparant with this new model. Still, its classic configuration and all-round ability still rate it as a desirable for those who can afford it. ●

Mazda MX-5 ★★★★☆

SPECIFICATIONS

ENGINE:

Cylinders	four in-line
Fuel supply	electronic multipoint injection
Bore/stroke	83,0/85,0 mm
Cubic capacity	1 840 cm³
Compression ratio	10,0 to 1
Valve gear	d-o-h-c, four valves per cylinder, variable valve timing
Ignition	electronic
Main bearings	five
Fuel requirement	unleaded

ENGINE OUTPUT:

Max power ISO (kW)	107
Power peak (r/min)	7 000
Max usable r/min	7 000
Max torque (N.m)	168
Torque peak (r/min)	5 000

TRANSMISSION:

Forward speeds	six
Low gear	3,76 to 1
2nd gear	2,27 to 1
3rd gear	1,65 to 1
4th gear	1,26 to 1
5th gear	1,00 to 1
Top gear	0,84 to 1
Reverse gear	3,56 to 1
Final drive	3,64 to 1
Drive wheels	rear, with LSD

WHEELS AND TYRES:

Road wheels	16x7J alloy
Tyre make	Bridgestone Turanza ER30
Tyre size	205/45 R16
Tyre pressures (front)	180 kPa
Tyre pressures (rear)	180 kPa

BRAKES:

Front	270 mm ventilated disc
Rear	276 mm disc
Hydraulics	ABS, with EBD

STEERING:

Type	rack and pinion, power-assisted
Lock to lock	2,65 turns
Turning circle	9,2 metres

SUSPENSION:

Front	double wishbones, coil spring/damper unit, gas shocks, anti-roll bar
Rear	double wishbones, coil spring/damper unit, gas shocks, anti-roll bar

CAPACITIES:

Seating	2
Fuel tank	50 litres
Boot space	112 dm³

WARRANTY AND SERVICE INTERVALS:
3 years/100 000 km
Service every 15 000 km

TEST CAR FROM:
Ford Motor Company, Mazda division

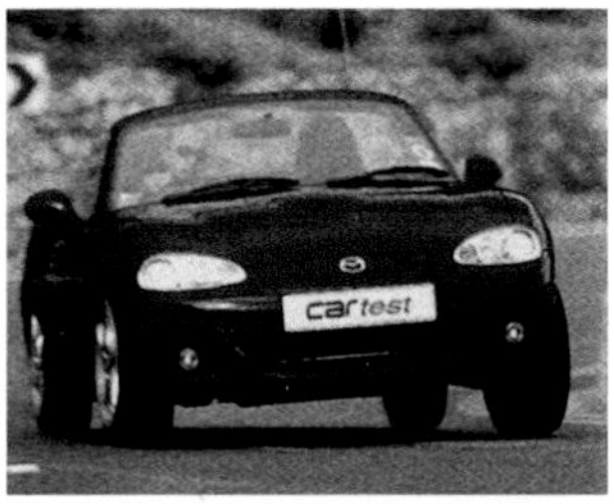

POWER AND TORQUE

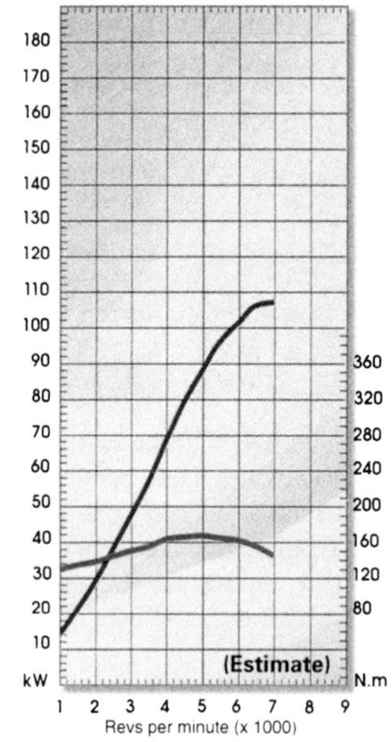

kW
10
20
30
40
50
60
70
80
90
100
110
120
130
140
150
160
170
180
N.m
80
120
160
200
240
280
320
360
(Estimate)
1 2 3 4 5 6 7 8 9
Revs per minute (x 1000)

ENGINE SPEED

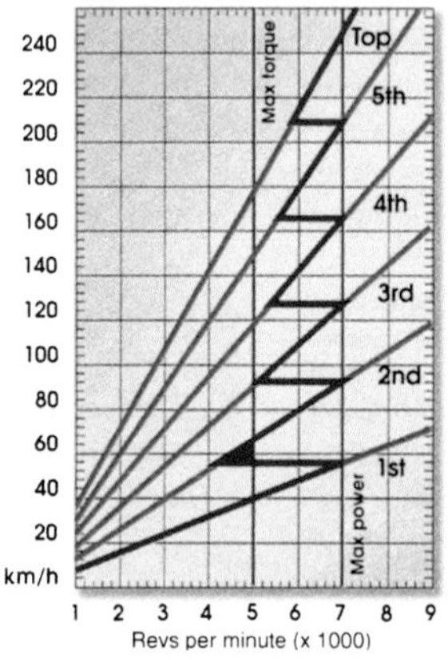

km/h
20
40
60
80
100
120
140
160
180
200
220
240
Max torque
Max power
Top
5th
4th
3rd
2nd
1st
1 2 3 4 5 6 7 8 9
Revs per minute (x 1000)

ACCELERATION

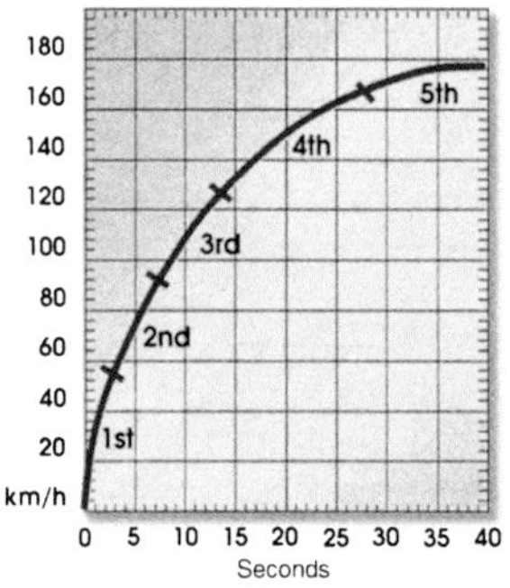

km/h
20
40
60
80
100
120
140
160
180
1st
2nd
3rd
4th
5th
0 5 10 15 20 25 30 35 40
Seconds

TEST RESULTS

MAXIMUM SPEED (km/h):

True speed	197 at 5 556 r/min in top gear
Speedometer reading	206

(Average of runs both ways on a level road)

Calibration:	60	80	100	120
True speed:	57	76	96	114

Odometer error: 0,4 per cent under

ACCELERATION (seconds):

0-60	3,89
0-80	6,07
0-100	8,86
0-120	12,34
1 km sprint	30,20
Terminal speed	171,4 km/h

OVERTAKING ACCELERATION (seconds):

	3rd	4th	5th	Top
40-60	3,23	4,53	6,05	8,07
60-80	3,21	4,51	5,95	8,13
80-100	3,27	4,59	6,22	8,76
100-120	3,76	4,95	6,89	9,85
120-140	–	5,62	7,86	12,45

FUEL CONSUMPTION (litres/100 km):

60	5,45
80	6,25
100	7,55
120	8,53
*Fuel index	10,57 litres/100 km 9,46 km/litre
Estimated tank range	473 km

(*Calculated overall consumption)

BRAKING TEST:
From 100 km/h

Best stop	2,61
Worst stop	2,92
Average of 10 stops	2,80

(Measured in seconds with stops from true speeds at 30-second intervals on a good bitumenised surface.)

GEARED SPEEDS (km/h):

Low gear	55*
2nd gear	92*
3rd gear	126*
4th gear	165*
5th gear	208*
Top gear	248*

(Calculated at engine power peak* – 7 000 r/min and at max. usable r/min – 7 000 r/min.)

INTERIOR NOISE LEVELS (db, A-weighted):

	Mech	Road
Idling	40	–
60	61	–
80	63	70
100	67	74
120	70	76

PERFORMANCE FACTORS:

Power/mass net (W/kg)	93
Frontal area (m²)	2,04
km/h per 1 000 r/min (top)	35,46
Mass as tested (kg)	1 155 (incl h/top)

(Calculated on "mass as tested", gross frontal area, gearing and ISO power output)

TEST CONDITIONS:

Altitude	at sea level
Weather	mild, calm, hazy
Fuel used	95 octane unleaded
Test car's odometer	3 832

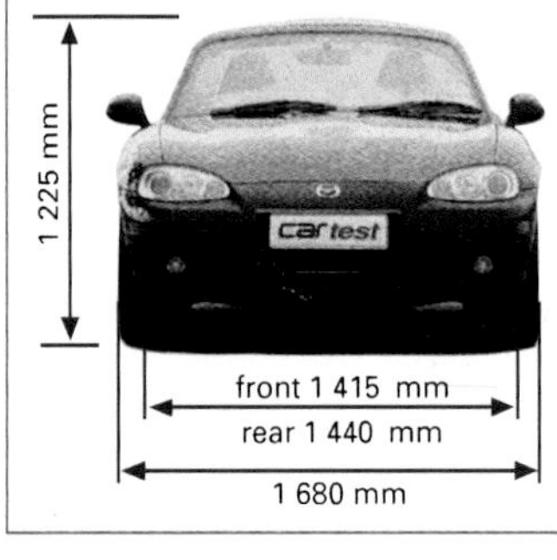

1 225 mm
front 1 415 mm
rear 1 440 mm
1 680 mm

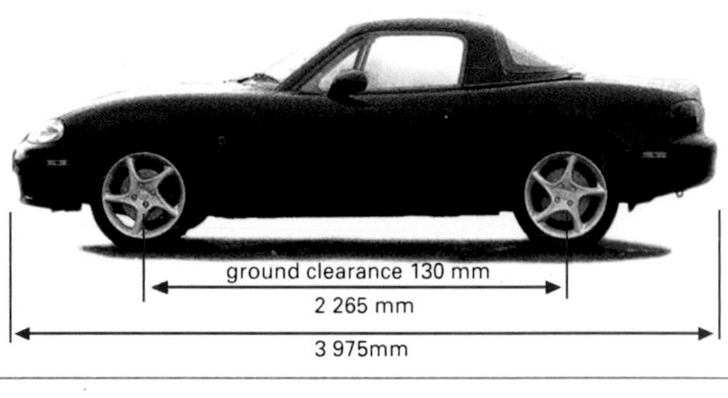

ground clearance 130 mm
2 265 mm
3 975mm

MAZDA MX-5

LOG BOOK **MILEAGE:** 2200 **PRICE:** £17,495
AVERAGE FUEL CONSUMPTION: 27.7MPG
DATE ACQUIRED: OCTOBER 2001 **COSTS TO DATE:** NIL

AMID GENERAL HILARITY WITHIN THE *CAR* office, my new long-termer appears to be the smallest roadster we could find, given to me just before we bid adieu to the last of the summer sun and welcome the vagaries of the British microclimate. But, in keeping with my determinedly wayward attitude to such things, our new MX-5 Sport will be used to the fullest extent during its stay with us.

So far, this has included driving it in the rain with the roof down, falling out of it (foot entanglement issues) on the high street — to the great amusement of several bystanders — and entering it into Performance Car of the Year on the basis that it is quite probably more fun than cars with twice the power and price tag. Nobody could accuse us of not putting our cars through their paces, but this was quite an extreme introduction into the long-term car park.

After a substantial period of extra care and attention during the first few miles (the car was delivered with only 100 miles under its wheels), the MX-5 was subject to more raucous throttle operation in preparation for its PCOTY debut later in the month. Everyone is left wanting more. The easy familiarity of the chassis dynamics, the effortless rear-drive feel and sharp steering puts this original into the top flight. The six-speed gearbox feels snappier than the left-hooker I tested in Germany, the clutch and brakes similarly light and well matched. More power and torque would be nice, but we've heard talk of the forthcoming MPS version having just that, so we'll wait and see.

From the restyle we get a slightly more angular look, but to be honest, you'd have to be a bit of a spod to tell at a glance new from old. Rest assured, new MX-5 won't be confused with a Boxster, but nor will it be confused for anything but a two-seat sports car — important in this market.

On the minus side, the cabin seems inexplicably smaller than I remember when I tested the left-hand-drive version in Germany earlier this year, with the non-adjustable steering wheel sitting so close to the top of my legs that it feels as if I'm reaching down to it, drawing the driving position into a yogic contortion. The interior redesign still impresses, though, with classier dials lending the baby Mazda a more refined air, although the elbow-operated cupholder lid is still a massive annoyance. We will see if these irritations remain minor in the next few months.

Saying that, cruising seems to be achieved with painless nonchalance, that extra gear giving a bit more range and a bit less noise.

After our first month together, I'm left wondering where people got their image of this car. During research into attitudes to the MX-5 phenomenon, the overpowering response from men was that of quiet condescension, but for the knowledgeable few. My advice is to get out and drive one, see what all the fuss was about in the first place, because despite its minimalist dimensions, this is a car with a big heart.
TOM FORD

MAZDA MX-5

A new six-speed gearbox and subtle facelift will help keep the crown of Mazda's 12-year-old king of roadsters well polished

AUTOCAR
ROAD TEST
Number 4518

MAZDA MX-5
Model tested 1.8i SPORT
List price £17,495
Top speed 125mph
30-70mph 8.2sec
0-60mph 8.2sec
60-0mph 2.7sec
MPG 24.1

For Looks, handling, grip, kit, value, hood, practicality, quality
Against Low-speed ride, noise, performance, economy drop

Imagine you run a big car company and you've produced the perfect car. Your designers and engineers have got it absolutely right first time; the car has been launched to critical acclaim and is selling by the shipload. What you'd most like to do is just leave it alone to seduce the public and swell your bottom line.

But you can't. A car this good is guaranteed a long life. Younger rivals will try to steal its laurels, and you'll need to make subtle changes that keep your car fresh without disrupting its essential, unfathomable alchemy. Improving it is almost impossible; ruining it is horribly easy.

Mazda has been struggling with this problem since it launched the MX-5 in 1989. In 1998 it put revised mechanicals into an all-new bodyshell and sighed with relief as sales continued to set records. Now we have the latest round of changes – they're less obvious to the eye but almost as far-reaching, and hope to ensure the MX-5 retains its king of the roadsters status until the all-new car arrives in 2003.

Almost all the changes are included in the 1.8i Sport tested here. At its heart is the same 1839cc four-cylinder, twin-cam unit offered in the MX-5 since soon after its launch; an updated version of the original 1.6 also remains. The 1.8 now gets Mazda's S-VT sequential valve timing, a continuously variable system aimed at improving power, torque and economy across the rev range.

On paper it barely betrays its presence; power is up by 6bhp to 146bhp at

HISTORY Launched in '89, Mazda's MX-5 singlehandedly revived the roadster. Openly inspired by the '60s Lotus Elan, it had a four-pot engine at the front, rear-wheel drive, double wishbone suspension and a pretty body – the standard roadster recipe. Mazda could not have predicted its popularity; it has sold over 600,000 units and has inspired a raft of rivals, the MGF and BMW Z3 among them. The first major change came in '98: revised engines and an all-new bodyshell which lost the pop-up headlamps but kept the charm and proportions of the original.

7000rpm and torque by 5lb ft to 124lb ft at 5000rpm, both peaks arriving 500rpm later than in the old engine. At the test track the new car actually fares fractionally worse, hitting 60mph in 8.2sec and 100mph in 24.2sec, respectively 0.4 and 1.7sec behind the times we recorded for the post-facelift 1.8 in 1998. Getting from 30 to 70mph through the gears takes 8.2sec and we clocked a maximum speed of 125mph, 1mph behind the '98 test car.

Two factors mainly account for this. At 1100kg the new car is seven percent heavier and despite its extra grunt the power-to-weight ratio drops three notches to 133bhp per tonne. The new six-speed manual gearbox – the second major change – gives slightly shorter gearing in the lower ratios, necessitating two changes to hit 60mph.

But the shortfall in performance is slight, and straight-line speed was never what the MX-5 was about. It is still competitive, though; the BMW Z3 1.9 is 0.2sec slower to 60mph, the Toyota MR2 0.7sec quicker. It's more important that the

> "Pure speed is not what this car is about – being fun to drive is more important"

powertrain be fun to use, and this one is; throttle response is alert, the engine gathers revs eagerly and the new 'box retains the MX-5's hallmark short, accurate action. The gearing is well chosen; the extra cog helps keep the engine on the boil under hard acceleration and it also delivers a relatively relaxed cruise for a roadster at 22.6mph per 1000rpm in sixth.

Despite this, and Mazda's claims for the economy of its S-VT system, the revised MX-5 is actually thirstier than the old car; we recorded an average of 24.1mpg on test, 4.6mpg less than before. Mazda's claim has dropped slightly, too, from a combined 33.2mpg for the old car to 32.5mpg for this one.

The chassis changes are as wide-ranging but rather more successful. The sills and scuttle have been strengthened and several bolt-on stiffeners have been added, most noticeably the beefy strut brace linking the tops of the front suspension towers. Mazda claims the bodyshell is now 22 percent more rigid. It supports the same double-wishbone suspension, now fitted with Eibach dampers tuned to improve rebound performance. Bigger 16in wheels are standard on the Sport and the rack-and-pinion steering is revalved to give greater weight and feedback. ▸

Performance and specifications

Engine

Layout 4 cyls in line, 1839cc
Max power 146bhp at 7000rpm
Max torque 124lb ft at 5000rpm
Specific output 79bhp per litre
Power to weight 133bhp per tonne
Torque to weight 113lb ft per tonne
Installation Front, longitudinal, rear-wheel drive
Construction Alloy head, iron block
Bore/stroke 83.0/85.0mm
Valve gear 4 per cyl, dohc with SV-T
Compression ratio 10.0:1
Ignition and fuel Electronic multipoint fuel injection, petrol

Gearbox

Type 6-speed manual
Ratios/mph per 1000rpm
1st 3.76/5.1 **2nd** 2.27/8.4
3rd 1.65/11.6 **4th** 1.26/15.1
5th 1.00/19.0 **6th** 0.84/22.6
Final drive 3.64

Maximum speeds
6th 118mph/5220rpm **5th** 125/6570
4th 107/7100 **3rd** 82/7100
2nd 59/7100 **1st** 36/7100

Acceleration from rest
(Surface dry)

True mph	sec	speedo mph
30	2.9	32
40	4.2	43
50	6.0	54
60	8.2	64
70	11.1	75
80	15.5	86
90	19.6	97
100	24.2	108

Standing qtr mile 16.6sec/81mph
Standing km 30.5sec/106mph
30-70mph through gears 8.2sec

Acceleration in gears

mph	6th	5th	4th	3rd	2nd
20-40	15.7	11.4	8.3	6.0	4.3
30-50	14.4	10.3	7.4	5.4	3.5
40-60	15.8	10.4	7.3	5.8	-
50-70	17.4	12.3	7.3	6.8	-
60-80	18.4	13.1	7.0	-	-
70-90	21.4	13.1	7.6	-	-
80-100	25.5	14.2	10.5	-	-

Layout

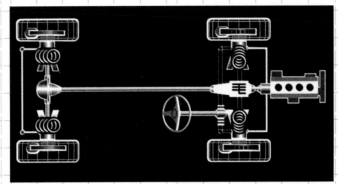

Steering

Type Rack and pinion, power assisted
Turns lock to lock 2.7
Suspension
Front Double wishbones, coil springs, anti-roll bar
Rear Double wishbones, coil springs, anti-roll bar
Wheels & tyres
Wheels 7Jx16in **Made of** Alloy
Tyres 205/45 WR16 Bridgestone Turanza
Spare Space saver, steel
Brakes
Front 269mm ventilated discs
Rear 276mm solid discs
Anti-lock Standard, with electronic brake force distribution

Gearing

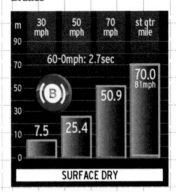

Brakes

60-0mph: 2.7sec

	30 mph	50 mph	70 mph	st qtr mile
	7.5	25.4	50.9	70.0 (81mph)

SURFACE DRY

Fuel consumption test results

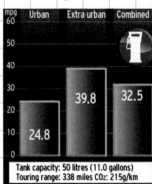

Average	Touring	Best	Worst
24.1	30.7	30.7	15.2

Fuel consumption claims

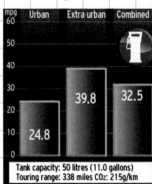

Urban	Extra urban	Combined
24.8	39.8	32.5

Tank capacity: 50 litres (11.0 gallons)
Touring range: 338 miles CO2: 215g/km

Noise

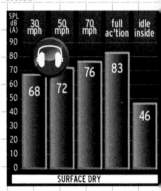

30 mph	50 mph	70 mph	full ac'tion	idle inside
68	72	76	83	46

SURFACE DRY

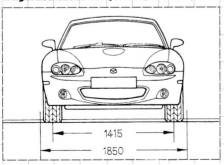 bp All Autocar road tests are conducted using BP Cleaner Unleaded Fuel or BP Cleaner Diesel with additives to help keep engines cleaner

AUTOCAR ROAD TESTS...

...are the most exhaustive published in the UK. Each car is measured in detail, then performance, speed and brake tested. We also try to cover at least 500 miles on all types of road, and measure economy in all conditions. In the interests of safety all performance testing is conducted at a neutral proving ground by our trained road testers.

Body 2dr roadster **Cd** 0.37 **Front/rear tracks** 1415/1440mm **Turning circle** 9.2m **Min/max front legroom** 900/1080mm **Front headroom** 900mm **Interior width** 1270mm **Min/max boot width** 960/1400mm **Boot length** 600mm **Max boot height** 275mm **VDA boot volume** 144 litres **Kerb weight** 1100kg **Weight distribution front/rear** 50/50 **Width** (inc mirrors) 1850mm

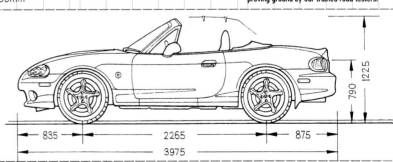

1415
1850

835 — 2265 — 875
3975

790
1225

IAN HOWATSON

The performance figures were taken with the odometer reading 2009 miles. **AUTOCAR** test results are protected by world copyright and may not be reproduced without the editor's written permission

Better handling and better grip

Roof rarely used, except in rain...

...when it's simple to operate...

Bigger 205/45 tyres boost grip; body control continues to impress. 1.8i four's power boosted to 146bhp   **...and fits snugly and securely**

The car may have been re-engineered, but the MX-5 genes have been preserved intact. Body control is excellent, fiercely resisting roll and pitch under braking. Sweet, neutral handling is also retained. The car will turn in cleanly and without understeer; it encourages you to use the throttle to adjust your line, but the back end never feels wayward. The bigger, wider wheels and low-profile tyres increase grip and traction considerably and let the car perform this way at higher speeds. Push beyond their limits and it will understeer safely; lots of extra grip and little extra power mean oversteer is only readily available in the wet.

Thankfully the MX-5 remains free from electronic traction control, despite now having ABS and brakeforce distribution as standard across the range. The Sport gets a Torsen limited-slip differential and although it aids traction, the MX-5 only rarely has a surfeit of power over grip and it is only likely to be of real benefit when you're driving hard in poor conditions.

Problems? Road noise and the low-speed ride over choppy surfaces are both adversely affected by the switch to bigger tyres, and although the steering isn't as light as the previous incarnation, we'd like it to be weightier still, offering more response and feedback through the 45 degrees around dead-ahead.

Changes to the car's styling are limited to subtle surgery around the nose and tail. Both sets of lamps have been gently redrawn and the creases around the front lamps are sharper to match the new front fogs and bigger air intake. The five-spoke alloys look graceful and fill the arches more convincingly. The hood remains virtually unchanged since '89, and with good reason; it's a tough, snug, simple device. The addition of a heated glass rear screen only makes the process simpler; the old perspex item had to be unzipped first.

Inside, all models get new seats with integrated headrests; they are heated on the Sport and the leather upholstery, Nardi steering wheel and gearknob all come as standard. At £17,495, this level of kit represents excellent value; the basic BMW Z3 lacks even alloys but is nearly £1500 costlier. The Toyota MR2 is £500 more but lacks leather and storage space.

The driving position remains excellent despite a fixed steering wheel and no seat height adjustment, although drivers over six feet tall will find their heads rubbing the roof. The quality of interior plastics has been improved, and the MX-5's finish betters that of its rivals, including the Z3's.

Air-con remains a £1299 option; it's largely redundant on roadsters with strong heaters. They can be driven with the roof down until it starts to rain heavily. But in traffic, our MX-5 radiated a great deal of heat from the central drive tunnel into the cabin, and it became uncomfortable when rain forced us to keep the roof up.

The redesigned central console is another irritation; the covered cupholders and ashtray lie directly under your left elbow and open as soon as you lean on them. And the bonnet began to bow alarmingly at speeds in excess of 110mph.

In truth, with the exception of the extra kit and grip, the long inventory of changes has done little to alter the appeal of the MX-5. That's probably just what Mazda intended: sharpen the looks, outflank the opponents with a few trick bits, but otherwise leave the car alone and drivers will continue to love it. It's a tactic that's worked.

What it costs

On-the-road price	£17,495
Total as tested	£17,495
CO₂	215g/km
Cost per mile	50.9p
Contract hire per month	£345.26
Equipment	
Air-conditioning	£1299
Cruise control	–
Auto 'box	–
Sat-nav	–
Electric seats	–
Hard-top	£1475
Metallic paint	●
Airbag driver/passenger/side	●/●/–
Alarm/immobiliser	●/●
RDS stereo/CD player	●/●
● standard – not available	
Insurance group	13A
Typical quote	£600
Warranty	
36 months/60,000 miles, 6 years rust	
Servicing	
9,000 miles minor, 18,000 miles major	

Fiddly Sony stereo replaced by unique-fit, big-button item

Leather-rimmed Nardi wheel standard on Sport

Powerful heater and heated seats let you keep roof down in cold weather

New high-backed seats are excellent. Sport gets leather trim as standard

Six-speed 'box has MX-5's usual short, sharp action

Quality of plastics, fit and finish all improved over previous MX-5

PETE GIBSON

Still the benchmark roadster

STORY Todd Hallenbeck PHOTOS Ellen Dewar

PACEMAKER

The only thing soft about Mazda's potent new turbocharged MX-5 SP is its top

The time would be better spent standing in a field waiting to be struck by lightning, and for the past 13 years that's exactly how you may have felt waiting for Mazda to turn up the wick on its darling little MX-5. Well, you can stop keeping the cows company because as of January, Mazda will release a first-run batch of 100 turbocharged MX-5 SPs.

Alan Horsley, the hoarse voiced ex-race team manager, performed a minor miracle in 1992 when he modified a handful of RX-7s and set them loose on race tracks against the might of Porsche's 993 911. His success was duly noted with permanent marker on the walls at Mazda HQ in Hiroshima by Takao Kijima, RX-7 and MX-5 project manager. Since then Horsley's small workshop in the Sydney suburb of Kingsgrove has become a semi-factory skunkworks.

Although impressed with Horsley's RX-7 SP project, Kijima enforced a hands-off policy with MX-5. His direct approach explains why the MX-5 is, after 13 years in production and 600,000-odd sales, so simple, so agile and so light. Without the kilos the MX-5 does not need an extra kilowatt, Kijima would say in 1998 at the launch of the second generation MX-5. "More power means a bigger engine, stiffer chassis and more weight," he'd rattle several times in our conversation. "That would not be an MX-5."

It is hard to argue with a man so obsessed with simplification and reduction that on his business card he's trimmed an 'I' from his name (Kijma).

He knows every intimate detail about the Aussie-developed MX-5 SP, a car that hammers flat all of Kijima's credos with 150 kilowatts and 280 Newton-metres using a Garrett turbocharger, air-to-air intercooler and 7.5 pounds of boost. It is within his dictator's power to veto the MX-5 SP, but instead Kijima approved the project. He's fanged the prototype and climbed out smiling.

"The MX-5 SP is more complex than the RX-7 SP," said Horsley, counting 215 unique parts. Not that the spanner work is difficult as Horsley claims it takes 10 hours and you never need to lift the cam

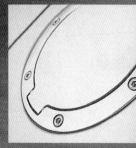

Turbo, intercooler, trick carbon fibre airbox and metres of tubing are part of the mods to MX-5 SP's 150 kW mill

The SP will pound a WRX, a 200SX and *a Porsche Boxster over 400 metres*

cover, although two holes are drilled to remount the windscreen washer bottle. Both in and out manifolds are changed, the aluminium intercooler mounted forward of the radiator and several metres of bent steel piping duct it all together like a hollow pretzel. Horsley's racing experience shows in the tidy installation and attention to every detail, while his focus on performance shouts from the rear wheels.

Bigger brakes seem likely to accompany the mule kick up the backside. Horsley says otherwise, seeing no reason to improve stopping power since the MX-5 SP weighs within a couple of kilos of the standard MX-5, and then again it adds to the complexity of the car and conversion.

Prodrive, the UK-based performance tuner which just purchased Tickford and with it Falcon XR and T-Series production, will assemble 100 turbocharged MX-5s at its Melbourne shop. With facilities in the UK, US and Japan, Prodrive is a handy consort if the MX-5 SP goes international. Mazda US is presently evaluating the MX-5 SP in Los Angeles, and there are sniffs of interest from Europe.

Have I mentioned the MX-5 is light? I'll mention it again – 1119 kg. It is the key to the awesome performance of the MX-5 SP. If Kijima believes increasing power will overplay the balance of the MX-5's chassis, he is utterly wrong. Believe it, the MX-5 SP is totally involving to punt.

The speedo and tacho are constant witnesses to the modification. Both move at about the same rate, somewhere between blur and unbelievable. You rarely meet the 7200 rpm rev limiter in the nat-atmo MX-5,

but in the SP you greet it in almost every gear, and there are six nicely gated and weighted gears coming at you in Uzi-like rapid fire.

Kijima's brilliant chassis controls the effect of 33 per cent more power and 55 per cent more torque like it was built for it. The qualities which make it great in standard form, such as its gearing, steering and body rigidity, are the same that make it greater in turbocharged SP trim.

So how great is it? The MX-5 SP will pound a Subaru Impreza WRX, a Nissan 200SX *and* a Porsche Boxster by as much as half a second over 400 metres, and the MX-5 SP matched the best ever time we've clocked in a 5.7-litre Commodore SS. At 14.36 seconds from zero to 400 metres it basically hauls arse. Zero to 100 km/h in 6.24 seconds proves the

Omigosh! This MX-5's swallowed an intercooler

So rapid is the SP, that photographers struggle to capture the FULL car in frame. Ellen!

only soft spot on the MX-5 SP is the top.

Wait for it because here comes the rub. All except the Boxster are less expensive. At $55,540 (without air-con) the MX-5 SP is exactly $12,055 more than the base car. You be the judge, but it's a price jump that would intimidate Evel Knievel.

The turbo bangs on the boost from very damn low in the revs, like around 2000 rpm and keeps the pressure up until the fun limiter stops the excitement.

The engine block is, of course, the same at that used by Mazda in the turbocharged 323 Familia and Ford KF Laser TX3. Max boost flutters from 7.5 psi to 8.0 psi. So it doesn't boost as much as a WRX, but so what? The MX-5 SP is bang-on quicker and far less furious in its power delivery. Off boost, the MX-5 SP drives like a standard MX-5, and on boost

it can turn both rear wheels in the first three gears. You know immediately that the MX-5 SP is quick, but you overlook how relaxing it is to drive. Torque does that to a car, and 280 Nm does it effortlessly.

The Garrett turbo has an ally in the engine's Sequential Valve Timing system, which according to engine speed alters the intake valve timing by retarding or advancing the camshaft through 40 degrees. By freak luck, S-VT works on cue with the turbo's boost curve to march out more power than Horsley had originally planned when he started tinkering with the pre-S-VT MX-5 two years ago.

There comes a problem when you lift the right foot, and the blowoff valve vacates boost pressure from the metres of tubing that comprises the intake system. Akin to turbo lag, but not exactly the same, it takes a moment or two for the turbo to re-pressurise the intake system before the engine returns to full power. It's noticeable when attacking a series of flowing corners balancing oversteer at the limit with the slightest of throttle inputs – as you do.

The purist may say Aussie Alan Horsley buggered the world's best sports car. That's probably exactly what Kijima first thought, until he dropped his backside into the MX-5 SP. The MX-5 now has the power to match its brilliant chassis.

FAST FACTS

body	two-door convertible
drive	rear-wheel
engine	front-mounted turbocharged, intercooled 1.8-litre 16-valve DOHC four
power	150 kW @ 6800 rpm
torque	280 Nm @ 4600 rpm
compression ratio	10.0:1
bore x stroke	83 mm x 85 mm
weight	1119 kg
weight/power	7.46 kg/kW
specific power	83.3 kW/litre
transmission	six-speed manual
final drive	3.636:1
suspension	double wishbone with coil springs, anti-roll bar (f); double wishbone, coil springs, anti-roll bar (r)
length/width/height	3975/1680/1225 mm
wheelbase	2265 mm
track	1415 mm (f); 1440 mm (r)
brakes	270 mm ventilated discs, two-piston calipers (f); 276 mm solid discs, single-piston calipers (r), ABS
wheels	16 x 6.5-inch (f&r), alloy
tyres	Bridgestone Turanza, 205/45 R16 (f&r)
fuel	48 litres, PULP
list price	$55,540

FAST FIGURES

0-10	0.43
0-20	0.91
0-30	1.38
0-40	1.82
0-50	2.32
0-60	3.08
0-70	3.61
0-80	4.32
0-90	5.28
0-100	6.24
0-110	7.16
0-120	8.28
0-130	9.72
0-400m	14.36 @ 160.6 km/h

MX-5 SP cocks a hind leg when you sink the right slipper – bewdie!

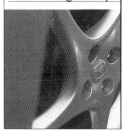

Contenders

Mazda MX-5 1.8i Sport — £17,495

More power and a six-speed 'box aim to keep the first of the new-age roadsters at the top of the class

MG TF 135 — £17,245

Britain's best-selling roadster gets a complete make-over – but is it as good to drive as its rivals?

Peugeot 206 CC 2.0 SE — £16,195

A retractable hard-top and two extra seats give the chic Peugeot more practicality than a roadster

IT'S THAT TIME OF YEAR WHEN ONE RAY OF sunshine sends us delving for a pair of shorts, and we start daydreaming of summer evenings driving sporty soft-tops with the sun setting in the background. Of course, the reality is we still spend most of May to September with the convertible roof up, but the optimistic among us will be pleased to hear that the MGF and Mazda MX-5 roadster have both been given a make-over.

Over the past six years, the MGF's dinky looks and comfortable, easy-to-drive manner have made it the best-selling roadster in the UK. Now it has morphed into the MG TF and, supposedly, the relaxed character of old has given way to a car that looks meatier and, thanks to a new suspension set-up and more powerful engines, drives with more panache.

There are four new TFs, all mid-engined as before, with the engine sitting behind the driver but ahead of the rear wheels. The core model will be the 135, using a more powerful version of the previous 1.8-litre engine and it costs £17,245.

To coincide with the MG's relaunch, Mazda has given its MX-5 a face-lift. Power has increased slightly, equipment levels have improved and the interior has undergone a mild tweak. The revised 1.8-litre engine is available in two different sets of tune, and with either a five- or six-speed manual or an automatic gearbox. To match the MG TF on price, we have chosen the range-topping 146bhp 1.8i Sport, with its six-speed 'box, alloy wheels and hide-covered seats for £17,495.

The third car here, the Peugeot 206 CC, offers an interesting and more practical alternative to the roadsters. Of all the cars here it's most suited to the 'roof-up, roof-down' nature of British summers thanks to a hard-top that retracts neatly into the boot at the push of a button; plus it has two small rear seats.

The 2.0-litre SE matches the power of the other two, and its chassis is based on that of the 206 GTi, so it promises an entertaining drive. Its already long equipment list has also recently been boosted to offer such useful gadgets as rain-sensitive wipers and, even though it's the most comprehensively specced CC in the range, it costs just £16,195. ▷

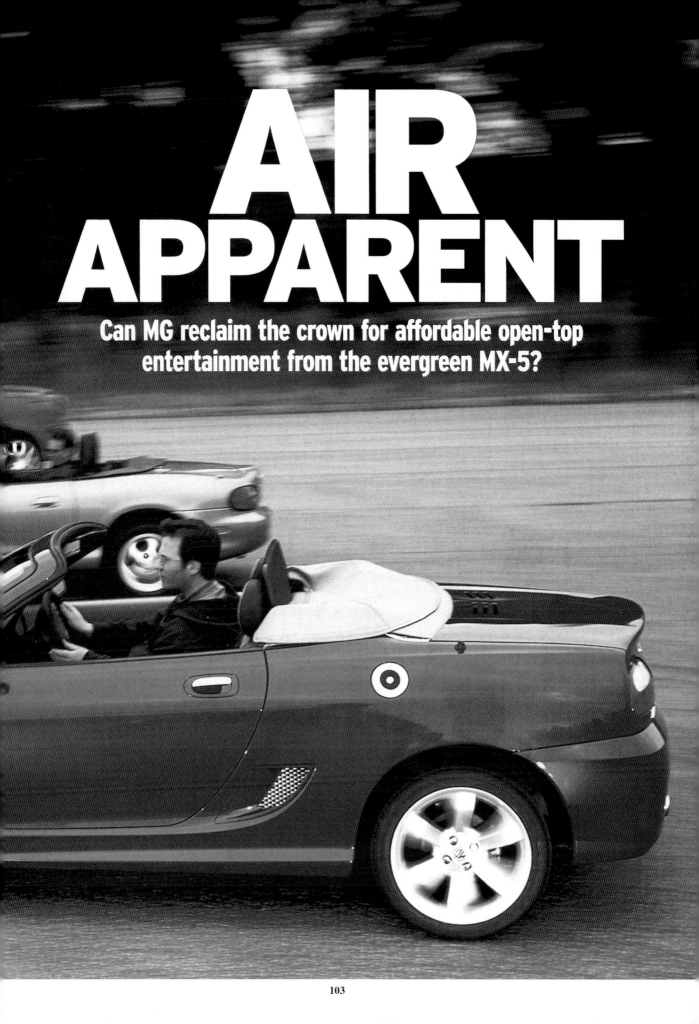

AIR APPARENT

Can MG reclaim the crown for affordable open-top entertainment from the evergreen MX-5?

Mazda MX-5 1.8i Sport £17.495

Leather, heated seats are comfortable and supportive, although they don't adjust for height

Cabin is well built but plain, and switchgear looks dated; stubby gearlever is a joy to use

Lively Mazda is most at home in corners

Boot is the smallest, but is a practical shape

MX-5 may not be quickest in a straight line, but its precise handling is a delight, and its ride is most supple

FOR

Precise handling; tactile controls; driving position

AGAINST

Price; high running costs; too much gear changing

VERDICT

A pure and simple roadster that's a joy to drive all day, every day

ON THE ROAD

Mazda	●●●●○
MG	●●●○○
Peugeot	●●○○○

WE'VE ALWAYS PRAISED the MGF's supple ride, but one of the major changes MG made when transforming the mild-mannered F into the TF was to stiffen up its rear suspension.

The company has abandoned its Hydragas system for a more conventional spring-and-damper arrangement. The resulting firmer settings and lowered ride height have improved the MG's control and balance, but have ruined its ride comfort. The TF crashes over the smallest pock-marks and feels jittery at all speeds. The steering wheel now feeds back every lump and bump to the driver.

The TF has been given quicker steering with part-electric rather than engine-driven power assistance, but apart from a lot of kickback, it doesn't provide much feedback. The car turns into corners well, but any feel through the wheel is artificial. Because of its limited range of

adjustment, no one in the road test team found it comfortable to hold, either. A vague gearchange makes it even harder to drive smoothly.

While MG's engineering team was starting over with the TF, their peers at Mazda were working on the age-old 'if it ain't broke, don't fix it' principle.

The MX-5's major controls are all beautifully weighted, a feature that's glaringly obvious after driving the other two here. The steering is sharp and responsive, the throttle responds eagerly to every blip, and the stubby gearlever snicks crisply into place.

Best of all is the way the MX-5's rear-wheel-drive chassis remains so firmly planted on the road, no matter how fast you go. And if the back end does become a little wayward, it's easily corrected. You always know exactly where you are

> **'Mazda's chassis remains firmly planted, no matter how fast you go'**

and what the car's doing. Its ride is a little firm, but it's the most comfortable here and does the best job of smoothing out rutted tarmac.

It's a set-up that quite simply embarrasses the 206. Granted, it is not a bespoke roadster, but Peugeot has made some alterations to compensate for the loss of stiffness when you fold away the roof. The suspension is a softened version of the 206 GTi's, but its ride is too fidgety, especially at speed. It does make a better job of soaking up urban bumps than the MG TF, however.

The Peugeot corners quite flat, but runs out of front-end grip too easily, and the rear hops about on roughly surfaced tight corners. The gearchange has the same loose feeling found in the rest of the 206 range, and the steering wheel constantly tugs at the driver under

hard acceleration. The main problem, however, is that at speed the body shakes and shudders, while the front tyres are often left furiously grappling for traction as they try to cope with the power from the 2.0-litre engine.

Despite being the heaviest car here, and only fractionally more powerful than the MG, the Peugeot is no slouch. It's the slowest when accelerating in any of its gears, but it has well spaced lower ratios and a healthy dose of pull as the revs start to rise, so it reaches 60mph quicker than the others. Its engine is impressively smooth and pulls cleanly to the red line.

The MG's engine features variable-valve timing, which continuously adjusts the length of time the valves stay open to maximise efficiency and increase performance. Thanks to some tweaks which improve its breathing, the TF certainly feels more responsive and willing to rev than its predecessor. And despite having the lowest power output here and the least pull, its 1.8-litre unit ▷

MG TF 135 £17,245

Driving position is quite upright, and seat does not adjust for height; footwell feels cramped

New mix of materials brightens cabin, but effect is tacky; wheel adjusts for height only

MG corners with gusto; it has plenty of grip

Deep rectangular boot betters the MX-5

MG TF's engine makes a satisfying growl and it's quick, but its ride is dreadful; alloy wheels are optional

FOR

Able handling; good brakes; attractive styling

AGAINST

Poor ride; plastic rear window; poor equipment list

VERDICT

Make-over has taken the TF a few steps back rather than forward

◁ keeps up well with the other two. It's actually quicker off the mark than the Mazda, and beats it in the sprint to 60mph.

The MX-5 also has variable-valve timing for the first time, and its engine is the most powerful of this trio. However, its six-speed gearbox hinders rather than helps its progress. You have to change up too often to keep it spinning in the best rev band and make the most of the 146bhp, particularly in the lower gears. This makes pulling cleanly away from junctions quite an art. That said, its taller top gear helps economy and refinement at speed.

Because these cars are all convertibles, none cruises along in silence at high speeds. The Mazda's engine is the quietest of the trio but once at constant open-road pace, tyre roar and wind noise would drown it out, anyway. It's still not as bad as the MG, though. A great deal of wind noise gets through the TF's cloth-top, which makes it the noisiest car here.

We knew Peugeot would be the quietest, because of its hard-top,

however, because the side windows are frameless, there's a fair amount of wind noise at motorway speeds, supplemented by road roar.

IN THE CABIN

Mazda	●●●○○
MG	●●○○○
Peugeot	●●●○○

NOWHERE ARE THE 206's hatchback origins more evident than from the driver's seat. Roadster fans won't appreciate perching so high up, although the CC's driving position is lower than in other 206s, and there's no seat-height adjustment to compensate.

The height is not the only problem. The steering wheel has no reach adjustment, which means taller people, in particular, have to compromise in the way they sit, adopting a straight-arm, bent-knees posture to get their hands on the wheel. And the seat itself seems to have been designed for people with cast-iron lumbar regions. No matter what shape or

size you are, it's difficult to find a natural driving position in the 206, let alone a sporty one.

Neither the MG nor the Mazda's steering wheel adjusts back and forth, nor do their seats move up and down, but both provide a more comfortable position than the Peugeot. You still sit quite high up in the MG TF, though, so it does not provide as involving a driving position as the low-down posture you adopt in the MX-5. The TF's narrow footwell is a bit claustrophobic, too, because the pedals are so low to the floor. The Mazda's driving position is the best for long journeys because it's the most laid-back, so you emerge free from aches and pains.

Once ensconced behind the wheel, all three have clear, well sited instruments. Head- and legroom are good in all three with the roofs

'TF certainly feels more responsive and willing than its predecessor'

in place. The extra rear seats in the 206's cabin make it feel the most spacious, but the extra pews are only suited to giving quick lifts around the corner. Even then, both people up-front have to pull their seats well forward to create some legroom. With the roof up, there's precious little headroom in the back, either. The rear seats do come in useful as extra storage space, however. When the roof is in the boot, they are even commodious enough to take a pram. The Peugeot also has some useful stowage spaces up-front and it's the only car here to have decent-sized door pockets.

The main advantage the Peugeot has over its rivals is its electric hard-top. Unclip two hooks, press a button and the tin roof folds away neatly into the boot. The cloth roofs of the MG and Mazda have to be ▷

Peugeot 206 CC 2.0 SE £16,195

Driver sits high, in a tiring arms-straight, knees-bent position; leather trim costs £700

Interior is stylish and offers plenty of toys, but it squeaks and rattles when crossing bumps

Back end tends to hop about on fast corners

Biggest boot is smallest with the roof down

Peugeot is least engaging on the road; ride is awful; gearchange feels vague and wheels scrabble for grip

FOR
Electric hard-top; practicality; residual values

AGAINST
Driving position; gearchange; poor ride and handling

VERDICT
Good value for money; stylish and desirable, but not a true sports car

●●●○○

◁ raised or lowered manually, and then covered by a tonneau.

Access to the 206's load bay is poor once the roof is stowed, and there's scarcely enough depth for a briefcase, never mind a few bags of shopping. That said, with the roof in place, the boot becomes by far the largest of the three, and is more than capable of carrying several sports bags. It also has the widest entrance and lowest load lip, which helps when loading heavy items.

To save space, the 206 comes with two cans of tyre weld to make an emergency repair rather than a spare wheel. A space-saver spare wheel is available for £54, but has to sit in the boot. The MX-5 has its space-saver stashed in a wheel well beneath the boot floor, while the MG TF keeps one in the load area underneath its bonnet.

The rear load bays of the two roadsters are very different shapes but can both carry a decent amount of food shopping. However, when the sun goes in and the roofs go up, their tonneau covers take up space. Storage up-front in both is almost

non-existent, apart from a couple of small bins in which to put mobile phones or sunglasses.

Mazda's recent make-over included the addition of white, chrome-ringed instruments, but they don't do much to brighten up its dark and rather dated cabin. The quality is good, however, and nothing squeaks. The glass heated rear window is a bonus.

The MG's plastic rear window lets it down, but the company insists using plastic rather than glass allows a larger window area.

Despite its make-over, the TF's cabin looks cheaper than the others. The plastics are hard and the silver painted gearknob looks tacky. Buyers would have to pay an extra £175 for the Bright Pack featured on our car, including shiny door handles, ashtray and handbrake release button; plus another £200 for the carbon-fibre door inserts.

The windblockers in both the MG and Mazda work well, so you get the wind-in-your-hair treat without the need for a thick scarf and warm, woolly hat.

BUYING & OWNING

Mazda	●●●○○
MG	●●●○○
Peugeot	●●●●○

A ROUND OF PHONE calls to dealerships to ask about discounts proved fruitless in every case. Mazda and MG dealers were unwilling to deal because their cars are so new, and there are still waiting lists for the new CC, two years after its launch.

This is great news for its residuals, though, as used 206s are still selling for close to their original list price and even after three years you should recoup more than half what you paid.

We had more luck on the web. Snoop4Cars.com could sell us an imported CC 2.0 SE for £12,929, a £3000 saving on a UK-sourced car, with a three-month wait. Drivethedeal.com was quoting £16,630 for a UK-sourced MX-5, but none of the websites we tried offered discounts on the TF.

The MG is the most sparsely equipped car here, lacking the passenger airbag and alloys of its

rivals. These will set you back a total of £800. Mazda has enhanced the MX-5's equipment list, so the Sport now has a full list including alloy wheels, leather seats and electric windows. The 206 CC is the cheapest, but it is also very well equipped, offering side airbags, an electric roof and climate control.

The Mazda is not only the most expensive to buy, it's also the dearest to run. Its combined fuel return of 29.8mpg compares poorly with the 35.3 and 35.6mpg of the Peugeot and the MG respectively. As a result, it will cost well over £1000 a year, or 10,000 miles to fuel, despite the sixth gear which helps touring economy.

Because it has to be serviced every 9000 miles, it will probably be the most costly to maintain, too. Over three years, Mazda owners will spend somewhere in the region of £813, compared to £663 for the Peugeot. Servicing prices have yet to be confirmed for the MG.

The MG is the cheapest to insure as it falls into group 12; the 206 is the most expensive, in group 14.

Key

Our Choice

		MAZDA	MG	PEUGEOT
MAKE		MAZDA	MG	PEUGEOT
Model		MX-5 1.8i Sport	TF 135	206 CC 2.0 16v SE
	Performance	●●●●○	●●●●○	●●●●○
	Ride and handling	●●●●●	●●●○○	●●●○○
	Refinement	●●●○○	●●●○○	●●●○○
	Behind the wheel	●●●●○	●●●○○	●●●○○
	Space and practicality	●●○○○	●●○○○	●●●○○
	Equipment	●●●○○	●●●○○	●●●●○
	Safety equipment⁹	●●●○○	●●○○○	●●●●○
	Reliability	●●●●○	●●●○○	●●●○○
	Security equipment¹	●●●○○	●●●○○	●●●○○
	Buying and owning	●●●○○	●●●○○	●●●●○
VERDICT		●●●●●	●●●○○	●●●●○

What they cost

	MAZDA	MG	PEUGEOT
On-the-road price²	£17,495	£17,245	£16,195
What Car? Target Price	£16,739	£16,392	£15,111
Sample leasing cost³	£351	£309	£340
Cost per mile⁴	49.9p	tbc	45.8p

Equipment

		MAZDA	MG	PEUGEOT
T	Automatic gearbox	na	na	na
M	Metallic paint	£250	£345	£250
●	Alloy wheels	●	£525	●
✿/✳	Air-conditioning/climate control	£1300	£1125	✳
	Manual/electric roof	◠	◠	◠
	Power steering	●	●	●
	Steering adjust	●	●	●
	Central/remote locking	●	●	●
D	Deadlocks	D	D	D
	Alarm/immobiliser	●/●	●/●	●/●
	Airbags – driver/passenger/side	●/●/na	●/£275/na	●/●/●
	Manual/electric driver's seat adjust	●	●	●
	Anti-lock brakes	●	●	●
	Leather seats	●	£875	£700
	Rear centre 3-pt belt	na	na	na
	Front elec windows	●	●	●

Your price⁵

	MAZDA	MG	PEUGEOT
Before discount including your choice of options	£	£	£

Running costs

	MAZDA	MG	PEUGEOT
Official mpg (urban/extra-urban/combined)	21.7/37.7/29.8	25.3/46.9/35.6	25.2/45.6/35.3
Fuel cost (10,000 miles)⁶	£1187	£994	£1003
Tank capacity (litres)	50	50	47
CO₂ rating (g/km)	215	189	191
Service (3yr/36,000 miles)⁷	£813	tbc	£663
Service interval (miles)	9000	15,000	20,000
Insurance group/typical quote³	13/£600	12/£566	14/£628
Warranty (months/miles)	36/60,000	36/60,000	36/60,000
Anti-rust/paint warranty (yrs)	6/-	6/3	12/-
Replacement due	New car	New car	Not imminent

Performance

	MAZDA	MG	PEUGEOT
Engine (cc/type)	1839/4cyl	1796/4cyl	1997/4cyl
Peak power (bhp/rpm)	146/7000	134/6750	138/6000
Peak torque (pulling power) (lb ft/rpm)	124/5000	122/5000	143/4000
Kerb weight (kg)	1100	1150	1152
0-60mph (sec)	8.8	8.6	8.3
Max speed (mph)	124	127	127
30-70mph (sec)⁸	8.7	8.8	8.2
30-50mph in 3rd/4th/5th/6th (sec)	5.0/6.8/9.4/12.5	5.1/6.9/11.0/na	5.5/8.0/10.3/na
50-70mph in 3rd/4th/5th/6th (sec)	5.0/6.9/9.4/13.6	5.6/7.0/10.5/na	5.2/7.7/10.4/na
Braking 30-0mph/70-0mph (m)	9.1/54.6	6.6/51.9	na/51.1

Dimensions

	MAZDA	MG	PEUGEOT
Length/width/height (mm)	3975/1850/1225	3943/1807/1261	3835/1880/1373
Front headroom/legroom	acceptable/good	good/exc	exc/good
Rear headroom/legroom	na/na	na/na	poor/poor
Boot size min/max (litres)	144	210	175/410
Turning circle (m)/Turns lock-to-lock	9.7/2.7	10.5/2.8	10.9/3.3

WINNER MAZDA MX-5 1.8i SPORT ●●●●○

WHAT CAR? KNOW WHAT'S WHAT TEST WINNER ✓

DESPITE THE MG'S MAJOR overhaul and the Peugeot's value, the MX-5 is still the best car here. It's still a thrill to drive and has the most comfortable driving position. It might be more expensive to buy and run, but we would pay the premium and reap the rewards every time we took it out of the garage, come rain or shine.

The 206 takes runner-up spot because of its style and added practicality, plus its excellent residual values.

The new MG is better to drive than the Peugeot, but if your priority is driving fun, then you should buy the Mazda. The supple ride and easy nature of the old MGF have been spoiled, and the result is one of the most disappointing cars we have driven in recent months.

Peugeot 206 CC 2.0 SE ●●●○○

MG TF 135 ●●○○○

*ROAD*STARS

STORY **ANDREW FRANKEL** PHOTOGRAPHS **PETE GIBSON**

The affordable roadster market has been shaken up with newcomers from Ford
and Smart, while Peugeot is in there slugging. But they must all get past the MX-5

IT'S STRANGE how things come around. Thirteen years ago, Mazda launched the MX-5 as an unabashed homage to the original Lotus Elan, re-invented the affordable roadster and has cashed in ever since. I wrote the *Autocar* road test and was aware that I was in the presence of greatness from the moment I stepped aboard. But not even I would have dared predict that, three prime ministers later, it would still be with us.

Now we have a new generation of affordable roadsters, the poacher has turned gamekeeper and it is the Mazda to which these others now look and its sales,

longevity and image to which they aspire.

There are two distinct ways of going down the roadster route. The one chosen by the established Peugeot 206 CC and Ford StreetKa newcomer: take the tin-snips to the roof of an existing hatch-back. Or you can do what Mazda did and create a new car from scratch. This is the path chosen, for the most part at least, by the new Smart Roadster; it's not quite an entirely new design, though, but because it shares less than 30 per cent of its components with the Smart City-Coupé, per-haps it deserves to be seen as such.

Nor is it a coincidence that the con-

vertible Smart and Mazda are better looking by far than their cabriolet rivals. Pretty though the Peugeot and Ford are, both look high-sided and dumpy next to the true roadsters. Deciding between the Mazda and Smart is not difficult either: with its recent facelift, the MX-5 lost much of the original's elegance, while the Smart is one of the five best-looking cars on the road. It works from almost any angle.

It is also the only true radical here. Whereas the others put normally aspir-ated four-cylinder engines of between 1.6 and 1.8 litres driving five-speed manual gearboxes under their bonnets,

the £13,495 Smart uses a 0.7-litre, turbo-charged three-cylinder engine running through a six-speed sequential semi-automatic 'box sited directly behind the driver. And while its 79bhp may sound impossibly puny next to the 144bhp Mazda, 110bhp Peugeot and 94bhp Ford, this needs to be seen in the context of its weight: at 790kg, it has a weight advantage of over 200kg over the next heaviest car. What does that mean in real terms? Only the Mazda has a better power-to-weight ratio.

But that's not how it feels either on the road or on paper. Drive the Smart hard ▶

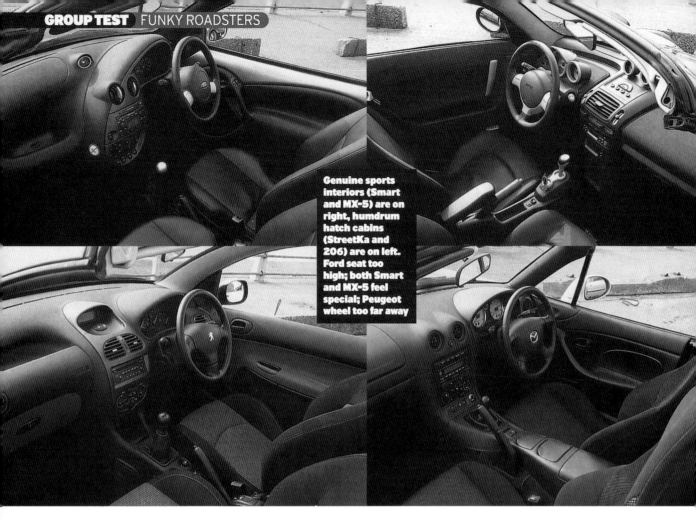

Genuine sports interiors (Smart and MX-5) are on right, humdrum hatch cabins (StreetKa and 206) are on left. Ford seat too high; both Smart and MX-5 feel special; Peugeot wheel too far away

and the engaging rasp of its engine, the flutter of its wastegate and the paddle-operated gearbox all contrive to con you into thinking it's much faster than it actually is. All I can tell you is that after a frenzy of flutters, several ratios and a lot of noise you look down at the speedometer and cannot believe just how slowly you're travelling. For those wishing to enjoy themselves while remaining within the limiting confines of the national speed limit, this is a neat trick. The rest might find it mildly frustrating.

StreetKa's lump unrefined at speed; Smart's uses turbo power

206 CC produces 95bhp per tonne but MX-5 tops out with 135

Ultimately it will hit 60mph in 10.9sec and carry on to a roof-up max of 109mph

In fact, the £14,480 Peugeot is quite substantially faster. The temptation is to let the 1.6 206 CC disappear into the shadow of its 2.0-litre sister but the perceived wisdom around here is that it's actually the better car. It never feels gutless or underpowered, its twin-cam engine is sweet enough not to grate and sufficiently gutsy to hit 62mph in 10.2sec and carry on to 120mph, which is more than enough to allow it to hold its head

high in this company.

Which is more than can be said of the StreetKa: £13,745 in Luxury trim. There are sound financial reasons why Ford uses its South Africa-sourced eight-valve 1.6-litre motor for the StreetKa rather than the unrelated 16-valver found in the Focus, but in this company it is very much the poor relation. It's noisy and coarse and provides neither the quantity nor quality of performance to give the StreetKa a convincing turn of speed. It takes over 12.0sec to reach 60mph – while the others better 11 – and it's all over by 108mph, the lowest top speed of the lot. Compared with the £15,495 Mazda's 8.5sec sprint to 60mph and 127mph top speed, that's some deficit. Even if we'd used a 1.6-litre MX-5 (9.7sec to 60mph and 119mph), it would still seem slow, but as another £500 buys 144bhp instead of 110bhp, why would you?

But bald performance never was much of a guide to available fun and, staggering though it might sound on the evidence provided so far, the Streetka is actually more fun to drive than all bar one.

That one is the Mazda. Don't let anyone tell you that just because this car was designed in the 1980s it has somehow had its day. Mazda could so easily have made this car with front-wheel drive and simple, cheap, strut suspension. But it didn't and there was a reason that Mazda put its engine in the front, its driveshafts at the back and suspended the whole by double wishbones: it made the car handle like a dream. And to this day it possesses a balance and feel you'll not

find in any rival. It feels like what it is: a proper sports car you can drive on the throttle with a precision that makes you feel like a hero.

You won't get the same feeling from either of the two converted hatches but both are still fun on a winding road. The StreetKa is the more convincing of the two acts: it has considerably better steering than the Peugeot, a little more grip and a few more answers when it finally runs out. The 206 is game enough and makes few mistakes but, ultimately, it turns in a little less readily and communicates less clearly than its new rival.

Which leaves the Smart. Weighing little more than a Lotus Elise and enjoying a brilliantly stiff chassis, the Roadster should be able to run rings around all the others, Mazda included, and the fact that it is, in many ways, the least fun to punt down a favourite road shows by how far Smart has missed its target. The obvious problems are its needlessly slow steering – 3.5 turns across an unremarkable lock whether you choose the optional power assistance or not – and the wincingly long pause between each gearchange. It might have six paddle-operated sequential gears, but I'd take the simple H-pattern five speeders of its rivals any day.

But there's more to it than that. The Smart probably generates more pure grip than any of the others but it's accompanied by little feel and even less balance. Even the 206 feels lively by comparison. Given its weight, newness and purpose-built design, this car should outhandle its opponents with ease; in fact it is

All have their individual charms but Smart (right) wins on looks. Facelift did Mazda no favours but it's still a favourite; Peugeot's tin-top gives it unique appeal; Ford roof simple to work

Factfile

	FORD STREETKA	SMART ROADSTER	PEUGEOT 206 CC	MAZDA MX-5
How much?	£13,745	£13,495	£14,480	£15,495
How fast?				
0-62mph	12.1sec	10.9sec	10.2sec	8.5sec
Top speed	108mph	109mph	120mph	127mph
How thirsty?				
Combined	35.8 mpg	55.4mpg	40.9mpg	32.5mpg
CO_2 emissions	191g/km	122g/km	166g/km	210g/km
How big?				
Weight/fuel tank	1061kg/42 litres	790kg/35 litres	1152kg/50 litres	1065kg/50 litres
Engine				
Layout	4 cyls in line, 1597cc	3 cyls in line, 698cc	4 cyls in line,1587cc	4 cyls in line, 1839cc
Max power	94bhp at 5500rpm	79bhp at 5250rpm	110bhp at 5800rpm	144bhp at 7000rpm
Max torque	99lb ft from 4250rpm	81lb ft at 2250rpm	110lb ft at 4000rpm	124bhp at 5000rpm
Power to weight	89bhp per tonne	100bhp per tonne	95bhp per tonne	135bhp per tonne
Installation	Transverse, front-wheel drive	Transverse, mid, rear-wheel drive	Transverse, front-wheel drive	Longitudinal, front, rear-wheel drive
Gearbox	5-speed manual	6-speed manual	5-speed manual	5-speed manual
Steering				
Type	Power assisted rack and pinion	Power assisted rack and pinion	Power assisted rack and pinion	Power assisted rack and pinion
Lock to lock	2.8 turns	3.5 turns	3.2 turns	2.7 turns
Brakes				
Front	258mm vented discs	203mm vented discs	266mm vented discs	255mm vented discs
Rear	203mm drums	140mm drums	2247mm solid discs	251mm solid discs
Wheels and tyres				
Size	6.0J x 16in	6.0J x 15in (f), 7.0 x 15 (r)	6.0J x 15in	6.0J x 15in
Tyres	195/45 R 16	185/55 R 15	185/55 VR 15	195/50 R 16

OUR CHOICE (Mazda MX-5)

THE AUTOCAR VERDICT

Great dynamics but engine is coarse and underpowered	Best looking car here let down by gearchange and steering	Strong engine and hard-top marred by awful driving position	13 years old and still going strong – great all-round performer

◆ the least enjoyable of all.

Smart may well argue that a car like this makes you feel better about yourself than the others do, just by sitting in it. As we shall see, with one as cute, well-proportioned and thoughtfully detailed as this, that's a surprisingly powerful argument. In the meantime both the StreetKa and 206 have deeply compromised driving positions – the Ford's seat is too high and will not recline sufficiently to let six footers get comfortable, while the 206 still suffers from the age-old problem

of siting its steering wheel too far away from the driver. Both also have disappointingly humdrum cabins, too closely related by far to the humble hatches on which they are so obviously based.

The Mazda is better; it at least has a true sports car driving position where you sit *in* rather than on the car, but there's no doubting that while the rest of the car was discovering the secret of eternal youth, its switchgear was dozing somewhere else. It's the Smart alone that feels special, with a surprisingly spacious

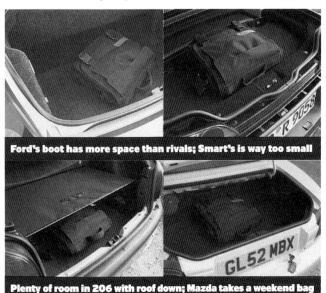

Ford's boot has more space than rivals; Smart's is way too small

Plenty of room in 206 with roof down; Mazda takes a weekend bag

cabin, low-slung driving position and neat, funky instrumentation including an amusingly hyperactive turbo boost gauge.

Few people will buy the Smart as an only car, so it is perhaps not important that it is by far the least practical of the four. Shorn of the Roadster-Coupe's hard-top, it will take less luggage than a Caterham, offering just a flat shelf at the rear and a miserably small pocket in the front. It is a day-tripper or, at most, a weekender. All thoughts of longer breaks away should be dismissed. It also has the most fiddly roof, requiring you to fit longitudinal rails to either side of the car before the canvas top slides into place at the touch of a button.

The Mazda is hardly generous with its space, but its boot is just big enough to countenance a driving holiday, while its roof remains simplicity itself: haul it over your head and slam shut the two latches that attach it to the windscreen. It takes comfortably less than 10 seconds.

And, of course, it is here that the Peugeot shines. The StreetKa's roof is almost as easy as the Mazda's and stows neatly away, but the 206's folding steel top has a unique appeal. Roof up, its boot is generous and even with it down, there are always the rear seats to fill with luggage – heaven knows, you wouldn't choose to use them for human habitation. The Ford has no such space in its cabin, but its boot is surprisingly large. With the roof hidden where its back seats once were, Ford quotes a larger boot capacity for the StreetKa than for the Ka hatch on which it is based.

If you're looking for an only car, the argument in favour of the Peugeot is overwhelming. Not only is it the most refined by far with the roof up, so it is with the roof down. You could truly live with it as you would a coupé and just enjoy dropping the roof on those rare occasions in this country when the sun shines for more than 10 minutes at a time.

But it's less stylish than the StreetKa and less fun to drive, and for many of the young, single and overwhelmingly female customers, the Ford may prove more tempting still. I'd place it ahead of the 206, but only just.

Yet neither occupies either the top or bottom spot in this comparison and I'll deal with the difficult one first. If looking good is your only concern, buy the Smart, but if you want to drive, as readers of this magazine surely will, it will likely disappoint. Truly this car had the potential to demolish the opposition in this test, but its slow steering, slow gearbox and lacklustre handling place it at the far end of the group.

Which leaves the Mazda to take the honours once again. It's less pretty than the Smart, less practical than the Ford or Peugeot but it has the one vital commodity these young guns lack: it is genuinely thrilling to drive. This should not surprise us because we have known for 13 years that the MX-5 is an honestly conceived and properly engineered sports car. And until someone else has the foresight to build another and sell it at the same price, it looks likely to rule this particular roost for a while yet. ●

Mazda MX-5 Miata

AUTO JOURNALISTS TEND TO BE A somewhat dour lot. That's in no small part due to the fact that when we're allowed out of our cages long enough to interact with humans, we're inevitably asked that question—"What is the best car?"—with no thought to how difficult it is to answer. It's enough to make one rend one's garments.

SPECIFICATIONS:

Layout	rwd
Wheelbase	89.2 in.
Track, f/r	55.3/56.3 in.
Length	155.3 in.
Width	66.0 in.
Height	48.4 in.
Curb weight	2387 lb
Base engine	1.8-liter dohc 16V I-4
Bore x stroke	83.0 x 85.0 mm
Displacement	1839 cc
Horsepower	142 bhp @ 7000 rpm
Torque	125 lb-ft @ 5500 rpm
EPA city/highway	25/29 mpg
Optional engine(s)	none
Transmission	5M, 6M, 4A
Suspension, f/r	ind/ind
Brakes, f/r	disc/disc
Tires	P205/40R-16
Luggage capacity	5.1 cu ft
Fuel capacity	12.7 gal.

WARRANTY:

Bumper-to-bumper	3 years/50,000 miles
Powertrain	3 years/50,000 miles
Rust-through	5 years/unlimited miles

www.mazdausa.com

But here's an answer: Mazda's Miata. Waitwaitwait. Hang with us for this page and we'll make our case.

But first, a brief look at the changes for 2003. The base car now has the strut-tower brace, 16-in. alloy wheels and wider tires that previously belonged to the LS model or in the optional suspension package. Both the MX-5 and the LS get sprinklings of aluminum-like trim in the interior, and there are a few more color choices. And that's it. Not that Mazda's entertaining little roadster needed much to gild perfection.

Now, as to what makes the Miata the best car, let's start with the engine. A 1.8-liter dohc inline-4 with Sequential Valve Timing (S-VT) that alters intake-valve timing according to throttle-opening, rpm and load, it punches out 142 bhp at 7000 rpm, and matches to manual 5-speed, or 6-speed (available on the LS) gearboxes, or a 4-speed auto. Regardless, the Miata, at only 2387 lb. (base model), sprints to 60 mph in 8 seconds or so. That is excellent performance, sufficient to satisfy all but the most testosterone-poisoned enthusiasts, more than enough for hauling passengers, and will

AT A GLANCE:

MODEL	MSRP	ENG	TRAN	ABS	SEATS	A/C
MX-5	$21,605	I-4	5M	NA	2	OPT.
LS	$24,385	I-4	5M	OPT.	2	OPT.

yank the headlights right out of any stock minivan.

Okay, you want more proof? How about the Miata's handling? Independent front and rear suspension, relatively lightweight, responsive rack-and-pinion steering and near-ideal balance of grip to horsepower all conspire to make the Miata one of the most tossable platforms around. It's wonderfully forgiving, too, and will help keep novices from rotating into the scenery. They will, naturally, have excellent environs from which to practice vehicle control. Plus, if you have to get grandmom to church, Jacob to cello lessons, or Ciara to her lacrosse finals, once again the Miata comes to the fore. Just ignore their shouting.

All of this automotive greatness comes with most of the available options expected on today's cars, and with a shockingly reasonable price.

What? You say the Miata only carries one passenger? And has little to no room for shopping or grocery items? Look, do we have to do all the thinking around here? Try to keep up: If you have more people or cargo to haul, then make more trips. Then you can begin to truly appreciate the Mazda MX-5 Miata's many virtues. Or just buy one for every member of the family.

No one ever said perfection was easily attainable.

Ego-Booster

Words Tim Nevinson Photos Sean Craig

GT NEWCOMER | MAZDA MX-5 TURBO

Since its launch in 1989 the MX-5 has become recognised as the world's top-selling two-seater roadster ever, gaining a swag of awards and almost unanimous admiration. There was really very little to complain about, and much to be admired. Those who did complain fixated on a perceived lack of grunt and minor comfort issues.

Following the lead of independent performance houses – who have resorted to increasing muscle via turbo or supercharging – Mazda has now had a go at improving its small sportster's perceived power deficiencies.

Blown away

The factory Mazda MX-5 Turbo model (debuted at the Tokyo Motor Show last year) is now available in New Zealand, and cheap too at $43,995.

Fitted with a single-scroll turbocharger with 7.25psi maximum boost and an air-to-air intercooler, the 1.8-litre dohc engine now delivers 121kW at 6000rpm – 14 per cent more than the standard car, with the peak 1000rpm below the non-turbo engine – and 206Nm at 4500rpm, almost 23 per cent more than standard, and peaking 500rpm earlier.

The six-speed manual transmission feeds power to the 205/40 R17 tyres through a new torque-sensing limited slip differential with a revised final drive ratio. Mazda's results from these changes show acceleration times from 0-100kph being reduced by 0.6 of a second, to about 7.8 seconds for the new turbo version.

From the outside, changes include stylish 17-inch alloy wheels, a new front spoiler incorporating an extra-large air duct flanked

by recessed fog lamps, a boot spoiler and rear under-spoiler. Despite, no doubt, adding extra weight, these changes really do enhance the appearance. It is a shame, however, that Mazda chose to leave the weedy-looking silver intercooler in the middle of the car's mouth, contrasting with the dark background to give a sort of toothless grin that draws attention to the intercooler's diminutive size.

Inside, the interior also boasts a number of luxury features including an in-dash six-disc CD player with six speakers, aluminium foot pedals and black cloth trim with red inserts on the seats – a colour scheme carried through to the leather steering wheel, gear knob and hand brake lever.

Palpable excitement

Probably the most unnecessary feature of a new MX-5 is Mazda's comprehensive three year unlimited kilometre warranty, and Mazda 'on Call 24-Hour roadside assistance' for the same period. In addition Mazda pays for scheduled servicing for the first three years or 100,000km (whichever comes first). Perhaps the heat and complication of the turbocharger will bring with it some new issues, but in our experience one of the MX-5's most endearing features is that it just doesn't break down.

If style is important to you, the new turbo scores. The new colours are superb, and the wheels and body kit make the car very eye-catching, and more 'macho' than any MX before it, if a little tall – the car sits high on its new wheels. The new wheel and tyre combo also likes to follow the camber of the road, and with the power steering set quite heavy about centre, the effort required to maintain straight ahead becomes tiresome. The level of grip available is quite impressive, but the steering does not possess the balletic qualities of the old MX-5, and nor is the handling anything like as progressive.

Cog-Swapping

Balancing the poise of an MX-5 on the throttle through bends is one of

MAZDA MX-5 TURBO

○ **Engine**	1800cc dohc in-line four cylinder, turbocharged.
○ **Transmision**	Six-speed manual transmission
○ **Brakes**	Four wheel disc brakes
○ **Suspension**	Double wishbone; front and rear
○ **Price**	$43,995

life's simple pleasures, but unfortunately the Turbo's torque curve does not present those opportunities.

The power required to unlock the rear is in a small range at the top of the power band, where you are really thrashing the engine and close to an up-change. Its not pleasant to listen to, nor practical to use. There is no-one at home unless the turbo is spooled up, and that only happens at the top of the rev range. This means plenty of cog swapping to keep up good progress and enjoy the benefits of reducing understeer with the throttle. Quick and precise gearchanges are not as easy with the six-speed as they were with the older five-speed, creating another frustration to those used to the agile original. The net result is a car that may well be faster on paper, but is substantially less rewarding to drive smoothly and quickly. The axiom about gilding lilies comes to mind, as well as the proverb 'all that glisters is not gold.'

Coming to the new MX-5 Turbo from some other make, or if you never appreciated the dynamic qualities of the original MX-5, I'm sure you would be more than happy with the new Turbo – but some of us have been spoiled for life. ∎

A Miata with muscles, for a pittance more.

BY BARRY WINFIELD

PHOTOGRAPHY BY DAVID DEWHURST

Perhaps the biggest surprise we got from the new Mazdaspeed MX-5 Miata—other than its remarkable bargain price—is how much of the elemental Miata flavor has been retained. We suspected that a higher-output Miata would require heavier transmission components, a harder ride, and a heavier feel. But the car doesn't manifest any of those characteristics in enough quantity to dilute the essential charm of Mazda's iconic roadster.

From the moment it appeared in 1989, we've been big fans of the little Miata. It made our 10Best list in its original form, and then again when the fixed-headlight version debuted in '98. The Miata was never a powerful car, but it has always been light and nimble—and very entertaining. Evidently, we were not alone in our admiration. From the car's debut until last New Year's Day, Mazda has sold 311,666 Miatas in the U.S.

But here's the best reason ever to buy one: an IHI ball-bearing turbo blowing

seven-and-a-quarter pounds of boost into combustion chambers with fractionally reduced compression ratios (9.5 versus 10.0:1). That gives the Mazdaspeed Miata 178 horsepower—36 more than its tamer sibling—to spur it through the quarter-mile in 15.2 seconds. The turbo car has a redline 500 rpm short of the standard model's 7000, but it rips to the red in quick blasts.

We recorded a 6.7-second sprint to 60

mph and expect slightly faster results from production cars. We had to promise to be gentle with the prototype vehicle you see in these pictures, but even so, the car was 1.4 seconds quicker to 60 mph and over a second faster through the quarter than the last Miata we tested.

Mazdaspeed's Miata is based on the normal model's LS trim level and is equipped with the optional six-speed transmission. Beefing up this gearbox for its bigger job involved shot-peening of internal gearwheels along with a fourth-gear ratio change so slight you have to go to three decimal places to appreciate it. The action is thus as light and direct as it has ever been and preserves one of the car's most important entertainment assets.

Gear shifting is critical in a car that gobbles ratios during hard acceleration like a bear in a Burger King Dumpster, and the Miata can be shifted as fast as is humanly possible. But since midrange engine response is stronger in the turbo Miata, too, there is less call for downshifting on the open road. A top-gear 50-to-70-mph time of 7.6 seconds is pretty respectable and four seconds better than the 142-hp model's.

On a purely subjective level, the Mazdaspeed car feels wholly transformed, capable of top-gear traffic slaloms at just a jab of the pedal. The turbo itself

is virtually transparent—you can't even hear it with the top up—and it suffers so little lag that the car mostly feels naturally aspirated.

Unlike the Mazdaspeed Protegé, which has a turbo kit supplied by Callaway, Mazda's hot-rod Miata wears a factory-developed and -installed turbocharger kit, as well as a heavier-duty clutch and revised suspension. Both cars are big fun, but we've observed the Protegé's performance to fluctuate from one vehicle to another, hinting at production variations. We doubt this will be a problem with the Miata.

The installation is what you'd expect from a big-name factory: tidy and professional, with neat touches such as induction resonators to cut obnoxious noise. Certainly, the car is endowed with a wonderful sense of integration, offering crisp throttle response and clean transitions even when being shifted violently at the redline.

Mazdaspeed's chassis modifications have been equally careful, and the car suffers little, if any, extra ride harshness from its shortened and stiffened (and red-painted) springs or its bigger anti-roll bars. The car wears Bilstein shocks, too, which are extraordinarily good at snubbing unnecessary body motions while soaking up bump shock.

The ride quality isn't a problem on any half-decent surface, but tire noise from the

17-inch Toyo Proxes R28s can be, especially since the fabric top does not provide an enormous amount of acoustical attenuation. But this is a sports car, right? And a hot version of one at that. If you want a quiet ride, you might want to buy something else.

On any interesting road, the only tire noise you need to hear is the song of the Toyos as they approach their limit, and the rasp of the turbocharged four takes precedence over the 225-watt Bose stereo, even with the additional speakers now built into the wind blocker's base. We expected the MX-5 to be a little quivery atop its new stiff springs and bars, but the front shock-tower brace seems to have kept the usual Miata compromise between structural

rigidity and lightness about where it was.

Certainly, the extra roll stiffness and the stringent body-motion disciplines are welcome in the canyons along with the quick steering, everything contributing to decisive turn-in and a great sense of stability.

Although the Mazdaspeed car was pretty loose on the skidpad, where it could be throttled into a rear-wheel slide at any time (aided perhaps by the Bosch torque-sensing limited-slip diff), it felt simply responsive on the road. There, it was quick to heed the wheel and able to change direction nimbly. Throughout these little games, the Mazdaspeed Miata revealed a surprising degree of civility.

And now for the best part: the price. With a generous load of standard features—power windows, a CD changer, a wind blocker—the Mazdaspeed Miata costs $26,020. A standard Miata LS—with leather, but without a six-speed, turbo, or suspension upgrades—costs just $827 less, or $25,193. It's a screaming deal because any decent aftermarket turbo kit would cost at least three grand and wouldn't come with Mazda's warranty *or* the suspension bits.

Mazda also boasts that the car's performance is almost equal to that of a BMW Z4 2.5 at a price that is thousands of dollars lower. At first it seems an inappropriate comparison. But the latest Miatas

have poise and refinement brought by numerous structural upgrades, painstaking chassis tuning, and patient tweaking of all the integrated systems.

Even the interior has been upgraded to first-class. Mazdaspeed's so-called Grand Touring package—leather seats and red-stitched wheel and gear-lever covers—teams with a silver-colored center stack and white-faced gauges to push the Miata's interior upmarket. The other Mazdaspeed signatures—an exhaust tip, a unique front air dam, Racing Hart wheels—put the finishing touches on a desirable product. At the price, this car's almost an unbeatable deal, but be aware that production is limited to just 4000 a year.

Hey, nothing's perfect. ∎

C/D TEST RESULTS

ACCELERATION
	Seconds
Zero to 30 mph	2.3
40 mph	3.5
50 mph	5.1
60 mph	6.7
70 mph	9.0
80 mph	11.3
90 mph	14.7
100 mph	18.3
110 mph	24.1
120 mph	32.0
Street start, 5–60 mph	8.1
Top-gear acceleration, 30–50 mph	9.1
50–70 mph	7.6
Standing ¼-mile	15.2 sec @ 91 mph
Top speed (redline limited)	127 mph

BRAKING
70–0 mph @ impending lockup	168 ft

HANDLING
Roadholding, 300-ft-dia skidpad	0.90 g
Understeer	**minimal** moderate excessive

FUEL ECONOMY
EPA city driving	20 mpg
EPA highway driving	26 mpg
C/D-observed	21 mpg

INTERIOR SOUND LEVEL
Idle	47 dBA
Full-throttle acceleration	79 dBA
70-mph cruising	75 dBA

CURRENT BASE PRICE* dollars x 1000
- VW New Beetle GLS 1.8T convertible
- Mazdaspeed MX-5 Miata
- Honda S2000
- Nissan 350Z Touring convertible

0 8 16 24 32 40
*Base price includes freight, any performance options, and applicable gas-guzzler taxes.

ACCELERATION seconds ■ 0–60 mph ■ ¼-mile
- Honda S2000
- Nissan 350Z Touring convertible
- Mazdaspeed MX-5 Miata
- VW New Beetle GLS 1.8T convertible

0 4 8 12 16 20

BRAKING 70–0 mph, feet
- Honda S2000
- Mazdaspeed MX-5 Miata
- Nissan 350Z Touring convertible
- VW New Beetle GLS 1.8T convertible

155 160 165 170 175 180

ROADHOLDING 300-foot skidpad, g
- Honda S2000
- Mazdaspeed MX-5 Miata
- Nissan 350Z Touring convertible
- VW New Beetle GLS 1.8T convertible

0.50 0.60 0.70 0.80 0.90 1.00

EPA CITY FUEL ECONOMY mpg
- VW New Beetle GLS 1.8T convertible
- Honda S2000
- Mazdaspeed MX-5 Miata
- Nissan 350Z Touring convertible

0 5 10 15 20 25

MAZDASPEED MX-5 MIATA

Vehicle type: front-engine, rear-wheel-drive, 2-passenger, 2-door roadster

Price as tested: $26,720

Price and option breakdown: base Mazdaspeed MX-5 Miata (includes $520 freight), $26,020; Grand Touring package (consists of red-stitched leather interior and black cloth softtop), $700

Major standard accessories: power windows and locks, remote locking, A/C, cruise control, rear defroster

Sound system: Bose AM-FM radio/CD changer, 6 speakers

ENGINE
Type	turbocharged and intercooled inline-4, iron block and aluminum head
Bore x stroke	3.27 x 3.35 in, 83.0 x 85.0mm
Displacement	112 cu in, 1840cc
Compression ratio	9.5:1
Fuel-delivery system	port injection
Turbocharger	IHI RHF5
Maximum boost pressure	7.3 psi
Valve gear	belt-driven double overhead cams, 4 valves per cylinder, variable intake-valve timing
Power (SAE net)	178 bhp @ 6000 rpm
Torque (SAE net)	166 lb-ft @ 4500 rpm
Redline	6500 rpm

DRIVETRAIN
Transmission	6-speed manual
Final-drive ratio	4.10:1, limited slip

Gear	Ratio	Mph/1000 rpm	Max test speed
I	3.76	4.4	28 mph (6500 rpm)
II	2.27	7.3	47 mph (6500 rpm)
III	1.65	10.0	65 mph (6500 rpm)
IV	1.26	13.1	85 mph (6500 rpm)
V	1.00	16.5	107 mph (6500 rpm)
VI	0.84	19.6	127 mph (6500 rpm)

DIMENSIONS
Wheelbase	89.2 in
Track, front/rear	55.7/56.7 in
Length/width/height	155.7/66.1/48.0 in
Ground clearance	4.0 in
Curb weight	2540 lb
Weight distribution, F/R	52.8/47.2%
Curb weight per horsepower	14.3 lb
Fuel capacity	12.7 gal

CHASSIS/BODY
Type	unit construction
Body material	welded steel stampings

INTERIOR
SAE volume, front seat	46 cu ft
luggage	5 cu ft
Front-seat adjustments	fore-and-aft, seatback angle
Restraint systems	manual 3-point belts, driver and passenger front airbags

SUSPENSION
Front	ind, unequal-length control arms, coil springs, anti-roll bar
Rear	ind, unequal-length control arms, coil springs, anti-roll bar

STEERING
Type	rack-and-pinion with variable hydraulic power assist
Steering ratio	15.0:1
Turns lock-to-lock	2.3
Turning circle curb-to-curb	30.2 ft

BRAKES
Type	hydraulic with vacuum power assist, anti-lock control, and electronic panic assist
Front	10.6 x 0.9-in vented disc
Rear	10.9 x 0.4-in disc

WHEELS AND TIRES
Wheel size/type	7.0 x 17 in/cast aluminum
Tires	Toyo Proxes R28, 205/40R-17 80W
Test inflation pressures, F/R	29/32 psi
Spare	high-pressure compact

Spool**sport**

For 15 years, Mazda spurned requests to add a
turbo to its brilliant MX-5. Resistance proved futile...

WORDS **JONATHAN HAWLEY**
PHOTOS **CRISTIAN BRUNELLI**

N A time when the word turbo is
used to sell everything from vacuum
cleaners to razors, Mazda seems
remarkably coy about confessing to
precisely what powers its new MX-5
SE. Pop the bonnet, and you need a
torch, mirror, and a bit of imagination
even see there's a turbocharger nestled
eep on the left-hand side of the engine.
alk around the car, and there's not a turbo
dge to be seen. Only the intercooler
eking out from under the front bumper
ves the game away, but it could also be
istaken for a radiator.

Even cranking the ignition key and
ing for an exploratory drive isn't totally
nclusive. There's no spooling up of power
a wild peak, no manic thrust in the
nall of the back. Unless you were totally
customed to the standard car's somewhat
aemic delivery, this feels like a quicker
rsion of the original, not one that's copped

a wholesale boost in performance.

The thing is, there was a whole lot more
to developing the SE than just bolting on a
snail, winding up the wick, and letting it rip.
Bluntly, that was more the preserve of the
Australian-developed MX-5 SP. But don't get
me wrong – that car's 150kW rendition of
petite sports car power was exhilarating, and
hardly rough around the edges. It's just that
the SE adopts a more softly-softly approach to
MX-5 performance enhancement. With 0.5 bar
(7.25psi) maximum boost, it produces 14kW
more than the atmo engine's 107kW output,
although torque is more significantly improved
from 168 to 206Nm.

Despite the relatively modest power and
torque increases, a remarkable amount of
other hardware has been upgraded. The
drivetrain, for instance, gets a beefier
clutch, stronger tailshaft, and torque-sensing
differential, while the cooling system has
also been upgraded.

Suspension is controlled by Bilstein
dampers, spring rates are increased by 20
percent, anti-roll bars are thicker, and ride
height is lowered seven millimetres. Spidery
five-spoke 17-inch alloys are shod with wider
and lower-profile rubber.

The SE even looks different, thanks to a
body kit comprising a bulkier front airdam,
re-profiled back bumper, and a smallish wing
on the boot lid. Inside, there are a few visual
changes such as bright red inserts on the
cloth seats (optional leather is a dull black,
by contrast) and a silver-hued centre console.

Remarkably, all this has led to a price
increase of just $5000 over the naturally
aspirated MX-5. In fact, now that the Nissan
200SX has disappeared, if you are looking
for another turbocharged, rear-drive two-
door, it's hello to the Mercedes S600L – and
goodbye to 350 grand. At $45,490, the SE is
also some $10,000 less than the much more
powerful SP, so anyone who bought the latter

Point-to-point, the SE leaves the standard MX-5 for dead

will probably be wondering whether they paid too much.

We can't put their minds at ease. The MX-5 SE has better than adequate performance, accelerating strongly through all six of its manually selected gears (no auto is offered), with just a hint of turbo lag low in the rev range to indicate this is a force-fed motor. On full throttle the exhaust can give a pop as boost is off-loaded close to the rev limit, but, for the most part, acceleration is distinctly non-turbo-like, and as linear as the standard car. There's just more of it.

The output certainly isn't enough to overwhelm traction, which is probably as much to do with the tricky diff and wider rubber as anything. Despite the increase in torque, even full-blooded standing starts are unlikely to produce wheelspin, but neither does the engine bog down if traction is maintained. It simply hooks up and gets busy, accompanied by a nice raspy exhaust note that's more than familiar from previous MX-5s.

If you're starting to get the idea that the SE was carefully tuned to maintain the MX-5's renowned balance of power, grip, and handling, then you're pretty much there. It's as easy to drive as ever, with the very quick, short-throw gearshift and crisp clutch making it fine for commuting, even if a revised steering rack has led to less turns lock to lock and a bigger turning circle than before.

Driving the SE is fun in its purest sense, whether it's wheeling around the 'burbs – using twice as many gearshifts as necessary, given the increase in grunt – or, as more likely, out on the open road.

The stiffer suspension barely seems to have affected the ride quality, rather it has given the whole chassis a more meaty feel without added harshness. There are a few shudders through the open body over successions of ripples, but it's not too bad for a convertible. Braces joining the front strut towers and one joining the ends of the chassis rails probably account for the added rigidity.

There's noticeably more grip than in the atmo MX-5, meaning anyone who likes to hang the tail out will have to try harder. But the upshot is that as well as being appreciably faster in a straight line, point-to-point the SE leaves the standard car for dead. The steering is quicker off-centre and there's less roll oversteer. What's been maintained is the delicious feedback from suspension, brakes, and steering that made the MX-5 one of the best and most tactile sports cars available – it's just that now the rate of arrival has edged upwards another notch.

The cockpit is a one-size-fits-all affair with no adjustment for steering column or seat height, so the steering wheel may snag on meaty thighs. That said, the seats have plenty of lateral grip without resorting to overt bolstering and, as always, flipping the roof back is as easy as two latches and a bit of muscle. Roof on, taller drivers almost have to peer under the windscreen header rail.

What's apparent is that the SE isn't so much a hyper version of the existing MX-5 compromised by the quest for speed, but more a natural and incremental progression of its strengths. Perversely, it has taken plenty of engineering to hold things in check, but the main thing is that, for a scant $45,000, the SE is even more entertaining than the original. And that's saying plenty. ⦿

Turbo or not turbo?
That *was* the question

The MX-5 SE is the first factory turbo version of one of the world's best-selling sports cars, but it might not have been that way. Before the roadster's debut in 1989, a team at Mazda investigated adding a turbo option to the then-unnamed MX-5. Ironically, the original NA-series car's 1.6-litre four was a direct, naturally aspirated development of the turbocharged Mazda B6T engine used in the 323 SS16V and KE-series Laser TX-3.

The idea sounded good to everyone except one crucial guy: MX-5 program manager Toshihiko 'Pops' Hirai, father of the MX-5. A resolute and intensely focused engineer, Hirai-san was determined to adhere to the basic product concept, wishing to avoid additional variants that would distract the development team.

Hirai remained inflexible to persistent proposals to expand the MX-5 range with a turbo, but after Hirai retired in the mid '90s the MX-5's chief chassis engineer, Takao Kijima, was promoted to program manager. And the more pragmatic Kijima-san has never met an extra kilowatt he didn't like. For the next-generation NC-series MX-5 due in 2005, however, Kijimi is adopting a development focus that has more in common with the original. 'Pops' Hirai would definitely approve. **BOB HALL**

MAZDA MX-5 SE

$45,490 / As tested $48,443**

Drivetrain

Engine	in-line 4, dohc, 16v, turbo
Layout	front engine (north-south), rear drive
Capacity	1.839 litres
Bore/stroke	83.0/85.0mm
Compression	9.5:1
Power	121kW @ 6000rpm
Torque	206Nm @ 4500rpm
Redline/Cutout	6600/6750rpm
Transmission	6-speed manual
km/h 1000rpm	7.8 /13.0/17.8/23.4/29.4/35.0
Gear ratios	3.76/2.27/1.65/1.26/1.00/0.84
Diff ratio	3.64

Chassis

Body	steel, 2 doors, 2 seats
L/W/H	3983/1680/1225mm
Wheelbase	2265mm
Front/rear trck	1415/1440mm
Weight	1122kg
Boot capacity	144 litres
Fuel/capacity	95 octane/48 litres
Fuel consumption	10.6L/100km (test average)
Suspension	**Front:** double wishbones, coil springs, anti-roll bar **Rear:** double wishbones, coil springs, anti-roll bar
Steering	power rack and pinion
Turning circle	10.4m/ 2.3 turns lock to lock
Front brakes	ventilated discs (270mm)
Rear brakes	solid discs (276mm)
Tyres	Toyo Trampio Vimode
Tyre size	205/40R17 80W

Safety hardware

Active	ABS
Passive	dual front airbags, pre-tensioner/force-limiter seatbelts
NCAP rating	4 (2001, LHD)

Performance

Power to weight: 108kW/tonne
Speed at indicated 100km/h: 97

Speed in gears

➊	54km/h @ 6750rpm
➋	87km/h @ 6750rpm
➌	120km/h @ 6750rpm
➍	157km/h @ 6750rpm*
➎	198km/h @ 6750rpm*
➏	220km/h @ 6100rpm*

Standing-start acceleration

0-60km/h:	3.4sec
0-80km/h:	5.3sec
0-100km/h:	7.8sec
0-120km/h:	10.7sec
0-400m:	15.5sec @ 147km/h

Rolling acceleration: 3rd/4th/5th/6th
80-120km/h: 5.2/6.0/8.2/10.6sec

Verdict: ★★★★☆

☑ All the charms of the atmo MX-5, but faster. Well priced

☒ **Air-con optional, interior looking dated**

Track: Oran Park, dry. Temp: 22°C Driver: Nathan Ponchard. Warranty: 3yr/unlimited km. Servicing to 50,000km: $235 + 6.2hrs. Redbook 3-year resale: 60%. AAMI insurance: $966. *Manufacturer's claim or estimated. **Including leather and air-con

Turbo 1.8 huffs and puffs, but does not blow doors down. Does open up enjoyable new dimensions, though

Add a turbo, get a silver console. SE cabin sports detail changes; snug-fitting functionality remains

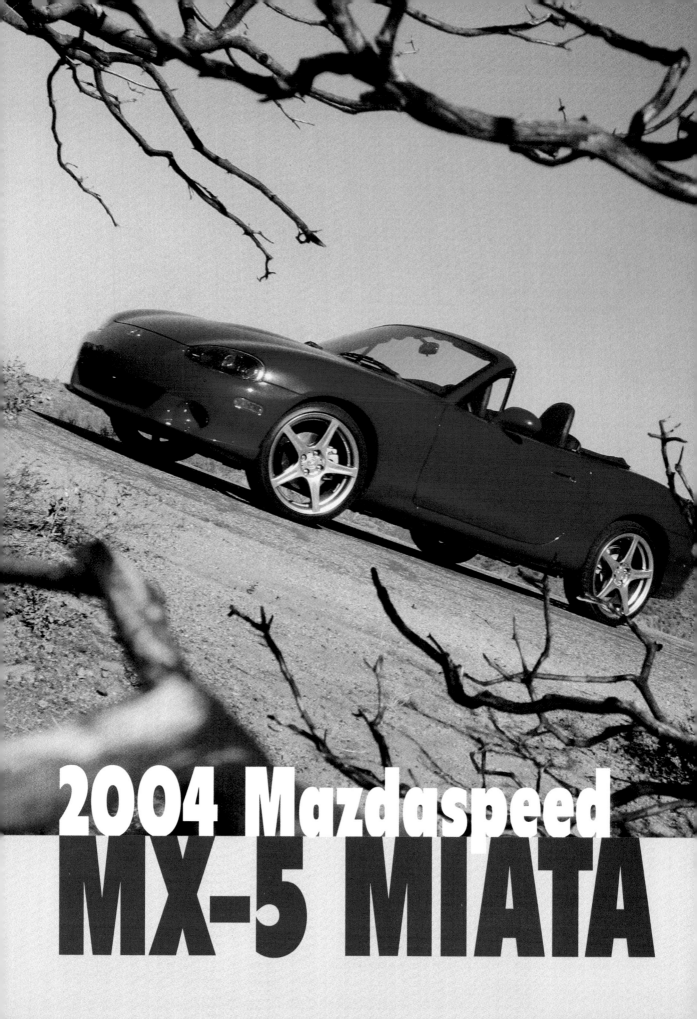

2004 Mazdaspeed
MX-5 MIATA

R O A D
R&T
T E S T THE AFTERMARKET HAS BEEN turbocharging Miatas almost since the car's inception, so you have to wonder why it took Mazda 14 years to add a turbo themselves. The answer is they've been worried from the beginning that too much power would upset the car's world-renowned balance.

But since the Miata made its debut in 1989, about the only thing lacking for it to be a serious sports car (as opposed to just a seriously fun car) was power. It's been a chassis waiting for a real driving force. Finally, it's here. And while the extra power doesn't transform the Miata into a take-no-prisoners sports car, it does take it to a level of straight-line performance that has simply never been part of the Miata's résumé.

The key to the Mazdaspeed MX-5 (Mazdaspeed is Mazda's tuning division) is, of course, the turbo, which is a single-scroll unit that provides 7.25 psi at maximum boost. A Denso front-mounted air-to-air intercooler is fitted in the lower air intake. The intercooler was painted silver on the prototype we first drove, but the production car's units are painted black, most likely to make the intercooler—which is quite small and a little wimpy looking—less obvious. Engineers also ditched the VVT cylinder head, claiming it isn't necessary when running forced induction. Other engine modifications include lowering the compression ratio from 10.0:1 to 9.5:1 along with a modified engine block to accommodate the oil line for the turbocharger, while the oil cooler plate and engine radiator have more cooling capacity. The 6-speed manual transmission, clutch, pressure plate, driveshaft and differential have all been reworked to withstand the turbo's wrath.

The extra power added to the 1.8-liter inline-4 comes out to 178 bhp at 6000 rpm and 166 lb.-ft. of torque at 4500, increases of 25 and 33 percent, respectively, over the normally aspirated Miata. Because the turbo doesn't start getting serious until about 4000 rpm, the driveability is not as good as many modern turbo powerplants; the MX-5 goes from not-much-power to

Better late than never

BY MIKE MONTICELLO • PHOTOS BY RON PERRY

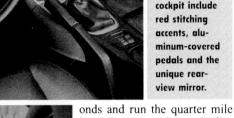

■ Mazdaspeed's touches in the cockpit include red stitching accents, aluminum-covered pedals and the unique rearview mirror.

suddenly a whole bunch. Get caught in the wrong gear or at low revs and you'll get smoked. However, if you make sure the tachometer stays above 4000 rpm you'll give BMW Z4 owners fits leaving stoplights.

Despite the fact the engine's power delivery is less than seamless, the bottom line is that it is by far the fastest production Miata we've ever tested. It can sprint to 60 mph in just 6.8 sec-

onds and run the quarter mile in 15.2 sec. at 91.2 mph. But those numbers also show that every Dodge SRT-4, Subaru WRX, Mitsubishi Lancer Evolution and Nissan 350Z sidling alongside will blow the Mazdaspeed off the road, despite the MX-5's commendably light curb weight of 2550 lb. You still need power to go fast, and it is a little surprising that after making the Miata Maniacs wait all these years for more performance, all Mazdaspeed can come up with is an additional 36 bhp (over the stock 142 bhp).

Despite Mazda's belief about the power/balance issue, we're confident the Miata's chassis/suspension package can handle more than 200 bhp—probably even 250—without disturbing its

inherent forgiving nature. Mazdaspeed must have felt the same way, because the changes they made to the suspension to handle the extra speed the car generates are fairly minimal, though they do have a positive effect.

Larger front and rear anti-roll bars (23.0 mm front/14.0 mm rear), shorter, stiffer springs (ride height was dropped by 0.3 in.) and Bilstein shock absorbers with Mazdaspeed-specified damping rates improve the handling while a front strut tower brace increases chassis rigidity. Hot-looking Racing Hart alloy wheels with 205/40R-17 Toyo Proxes R28 tires give the car more stick and more show. Mazdaspeed also gave the car a slightly quicker steering ratio. The brakes remain identical to the standard Miata's, with 10.6-in. vented front and 10.9-in. solid rear discs with ABS.

All these minor suspension changes mean that...not much has changed. The car responds to inputs better and has more grip due to the sticky tires, but the ride is also a touch harsher. Its slalom speed of 67.9 mph shows how easily the MX-5 changes direction. All the traits you've always loved about the Miata's handling are still there—quick, accurate steering, minimal body roll and

2004 Mazdaspeed MX-5 Miata

Mazda North American Operations, P.O. Box 19734, Irvine, CA 92623; www.mazdausa.com

List Price: $25,500
Price as Tested: $30,720

Price as tested incl std equip. (ABS, front airbags, air conditioning, 225-watt Bose AM/FM radio/6-disc CD audio system, keyless entry, foglights, Mazdaspeed exhaust, stainless-steel scuff plates, aluminum pedals, floormats; pwr windows, mirrors & door locks), Grand Touring package (black cloth top, leather seats with red stitching) $4700, dest charge ($520).

At a Glance	
0–60 mph	6.8 sec
0–¼ mile	15.2 sec
Top speed	est 127 mph
Skidpad	0.87g
Slalom	67.95 mph
Brake rating	very good

SCALE: 10 IN.(254mm) DIVISIONS
DRAWING BY TIM BARKER

© HACHETTE FILIPACCHI MEDIA U.S., INC./ROAD & TRACK

SPECIFICATIONS

Engine

Type ....cast-iron block & alum. head, turbocharged inline-4
Valvetrain .....dohc 4-valve/cyl
Displacement ....112 cu in./1840 cc
Bore x stroke ....3.27 x 3.35 in./ 83.0 x 85.0 mm
Compression ratio 9.5:1
Horsepower (SAE) ....178 bhp @ 6000 rpm
Bhp/liter 96.8
Torque ....166 lb-ft @ 4500 rpm
Redline ....6600 rpm
Fuel injection ....elect. sequential port
Fuel .....premium unleaded, 91 pump octane

Warranty

Basic warranty .....4 years/50,000 miles
Powertrain .....4 years/50,000 miles
Rust-through .....5 years/unlimited miles

Chassis & Body

Layout......front engine/rear drive
Body/frame......unit steel
Brakes: Front....10.6-in. vented discs
Rear....10.9-in. discs
Assist type....vacuum, ABS
Total swept area......413 sq in.
Swept area/ton....240 sq in.
Wheels....cast alloy; 17 x 7
Tires   Toyo Proxes R28, P205/40R-17 80W
Steering....rack & pinion, elect. pwr asst
Overall ratio....14.7:1
Turns, lock to lock....2.3
Turning circle....34.2 ft
Suspension
Front: upper & lower A-arms, coil springs, tube shocks, anti-roll bar
Rear: upper & lower A-arms, coil springs,tube shocks, anti-roll bar

General Data

Curb weight......2550 lb
Test weight......2730 lb
Weight dist (with driver), f/r, %....52/48
Wheelbase......89.2 in.
Track, f/r....55.7 in./56.7 in.
Length....155.7 in.
Width....66.1 in.
Height....48.0 in.
Ground clearance......4.0 in.
Trunk space......5.1 cu ft

Accommodations

Seating capacity......2
Head room....35.3 in.
Seat width....2 x 16.0 in.
Leg room....42.5 in.
Seatback adjustment......25 deg
Seat travel....8.0 in.

Drivetrain

Transmission: 6-speed manual

Gear	Ratio	Overall ratio	(Rpm)	Mph
1st	3.76:1	15.42:1	(6600)	28
2nd	2.27:1	9.31:1	(6600)	47
3rd	1.65:1	6.77:1	(6600)	65
4th	1.26:1	5.17:1	(6600)	85
5th	1.00:1	4.10:1	(6600)	107
6th	0.84:1	3.44:1	est (6600)	127

Final drive ratio....4.10:1
Engine rpm @ 60 mph in top gear 3000

Instrumentation

150-mph speedometer, 8000-rpm tachometer, coolant temp, fuel level, oil pressure

Safety

front airbags
anti-lock braking
seatbelt pretensioners
(all standard equip.)

PERFORMANCE

Acceleration

Time to speed	Seconds
0-30 mph	2.4
0-40 mph	3.5
0-50 mph	5.2
0-60 mph	6.8
0-70 mph	9.0
0-80 mph	11.2
0-90 mph	14.8
0-100 mph	18.5

Time to distance	
0-100 ft	3.1
0-500 ft	8.3
0-900 ft	11.9
0–1320 ft (¼ mile)	15.2 @ 91.2 mph

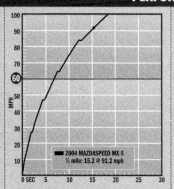

2004 MAZDASPEED MX-5
¼ mile: 15.2 @ 91.2 mph

Braking

Minimum stopping distance
From 60 mph......125 ft
From 80 mph......219 ft
Control......excellent
Brake feel......very good
Overall brake rating......very good
Subjective ratings consist of excellent, very good,good,average, poor; na means information is not available.

Fuel Economy

Normal driving......19.4 mpg
EPA city/highway......20/26 mpg
Cruise range......227 miles
Fuel capacity......12.7 gal.

Handling

Lateral acceleration
(200-ft skidpad)......0.87g
Balance......mild understeer
Speed through
700-ft slalom......67.9 mph
Balance......mild understeer
Lateral seat support......good

Interior Noise

Idle in neutral......53 dBA
Maximum in 1st gear......83 dBA
Constant 50 mph......76 dBA
70 mph......78 dBA

Test Notes:

For launch, let the tachometer hover around 4000 rpm before engaging the clutch. A quick 1–2 and 2–3 shift is necessary to get up to 60 mph, and care is needed for the vague 4–5 shift. • The skidpad is done in 2nd gear with the engine kept on boost at around 4500 rpm. The car's balance is close to neutral and it can be throttle steered easily. • The slalom test is best accomplished with progressively increased speed. Tight steering and stiff suspension cause the rear end to step out during fast transitions.

Test Conditions:

Temperature	Humidity	Elevation	Wind
76°F	54%	350 ft	calm

■ The turbocharger adds much-needed power to the Miata. Rear wing, chrome exhaust tips and more aggressive front spoiler are Mazdaspeed upgrades.

excellent absorption of bumps—yet this is the first Miata that wants to powerslide the tail out exiting 2nd-gear corners! You feel as though you can do no wrong with the Miata. The car is so predictable in everything it does that you'd have to do something really boneheaded to put one off the road. Better response to drop-throttle would be welcome; however, because it doesn't respond on a knife's edge means it won't bite the unsuspecting driver with a crazy attitude change heading into a corner under hard braking.

Subtle exterior changes on the Mazdaspeed MX-5 include a more aggressive front spoiler, smoked headlamps, a rear undertray, rear wing, a larger exhaust tip and a body-color inside rearview mirror with the

Mazdaspeed logo clearly visible.

And underneath the hood, Mazdaspeed didn't just bolt on a turbocharger and call it a day. They also painted a red crackle finish on the cam cover. The oil fill cap is made of anodized aluminum and you can't help but notice the silver finish of the turbo's piping and strut tower brace.

The interior follows the minimal-change philosophy of the rest of the car. Red stitching accents the seats, the grippy, perfectly sized leather-wrapped steering wheel, the short little shifter and the handbrake. The aluminum-covered pedals are perfectly placed for proper rev-matching heel-and-toe downshifting while you keep a close eye on the tachometer and the rest of the silver-backed gauges. The stainless-steel side sills add a bit of flair to what is otherwise a Spartan (but all business), yet slightly outdated interior.

The Mazdaspeed MX-5 is not perfect. "Better late than never" is one way of describing it, as we're glad to finally have the turbo power. But a more appropriate phrase may be "too little, too late," especially with an all-new 2006 Miata on its way soon. There is more than a little cowl shake, and vibrations over bumps are felt through the steering wheel and seats. Also, there is a lot of wind noise with the cloth top up—plus noises coming from the top itself—and the optional leather seats are surprisingly lacking in lateral support; why not give us some real sport seats, Mazdaspeed? If you're more than 6-feet tall, good luck fitting comfortably into the Miata's cozy cockpit; and have fun squeezing luggage into the tiny, 5.1 cu.-ft. trunk.

On the positive side, the Miata is the car that defines the phrase "snicks from gear to gear," with its incredibly precise, short-throw 6-speed gearbox. And let's not forget it is the reliable reincarnation of the classic British roadster, only now with some real power. So even if it sounds like we think Mazdaspeed didn't go far enough with the MX-5, we still can't help loving the car. Despite the fact many cars in its price range—our test car was closing in on $27,000—are far faster (and many with four doors), the bottom line is that the Miata is serious fun; and now it's even more so with the Mazdaspeed version. Whether it makes sense versus other performance cars is up to you. But if you love Miatas—or absolutely need a convertible—we can guarantee this car will put a smile on your face every time you get behind the wheel. And on a winding mountain road, you'll experience pure Miata magic. ⊙

Every control is easy to find in simple cockpit

Driving position is not perfect for taller drivers

Shallow boot can cope with two large bags

Mazda MX-5

PRICE £15,000-£18,000 **TARGET PRICE** £13,853-£17,100 **NCAP** Crash test ⊕⊕⊕⊕ **NVSR** Security rating 4/2	
SEATS 2 **DOORS** 2 **ENGINES** 1.6, 1.8 **TRIM LEVELS** Nevada, Angels, Euphonic, Icon, Arctic, Sport	

PERFORMANCE ★★★☆
The 1.6 and 1.8 engines both offer sprightly performance, but it's worth spending the extra on the 1.8 to make the most of the MX-5's chassis. Thanks to variable valve timing, power is up to 146bhp without affecting driveability at lower revs, and the top-spec Sport comes with a close-ratio six-speed 'box.

RIDE & HANDLING ★★★★☆
The MX-5 is still the standard-setter for low-cost roadsters. The chassis is impressively stiff, so the cabin remains largely free from shakes. The car's delicacy sets it apart from rivals. The steering is precise and full of feel, and the rear-drive chassis helps it cling to bends. It's wonderfully easy to control. An over-firm ride is its only vice.

REFINEMENT ★★★☆☆
Put the roof down in a cabrio and you

expect to get assaulted by the outside world. The MX-5 is no different in this respect. Roof up, plenty of tyre noise comes into the cabin, which means the Mazda can get tiring on long motorway jaunts. You hear plenty of wind roar coming through the soft-top, too.

BEHIND THE WHEEL ★★★☆☆
The simplicity of the MX-5 extends to its cockpit. The few controls are where you want to find them and are easy to use. The driving position is snug, but the seats, despite their thin padding, are not uncomfortable. Taller drivers will struggle to find a decent driving position, though. Aside from a small central bin there are few cubbyholes.

SPACE & PRACTICALITY ★★☆☆☆
Unlike its Toyota MR2 or MG TF rivals the Mazda does get a decent-sized boot. It's shallow but more than capable of

swallowing two overnight bags. With the hood up, most drivers will have decent head- and legroom. However, getting in and out may be a concern if you're really rangy.

EQUIPMENT ★★★☆☆
Mazda has addressed the MX-5's previously poor equipment level. The cockpit has been made more attractive by the inclusion of new high-backed leather seats on the top model, a new centre console and white-faced dials. All models come with power steering and electric windows. The range-topper gets electric mirrors and alloy wheels.

BUYING & OWNING ★★★★☆
The MX-5 retains its value well, holding on to more than half its new price over three years. Fuel economy is sensible and so are insurance groups for a sports car, so it's not expensive to run. Carbon

dioxide emissions with the 1.8 are quite high, though, which will affect company car tax. Although this shape car is still popular, an all-new MX-5 is scheduled to arrive later in 2005.

QUALITY & RELIABILITY ★★★★☆
The high number of 10-year-old MX-5s you see in pristine condition should answer any doubts over durability. They're simple and super-reliable if regularly serviced. The cabin and hood are durable, but the soft-top may need some attention to keep it watertight.

SAFETY & SECURITY ★★☆☆☆
All models get twin front airbags, but no side 'bag protection is available. Anti-lock brakes are standard. The MX-5 has an electronic immobiliser and an alarm but there are no deadlocks. It took us only 20 seconds to break in, but the immobiliser resists drive-away.

PICK OF THE RANGE
Length/width/height(mm) 3975/1680/1225 Boot min/max (litres) 144 Warranty 3yr/60k • 6yr anti-rust • 3yr paint • 3yr breakdown

MODEL	1.6i	1.8i
On the road price (from)	£15,000	£15,500
What Car? Target Price (from)	£13,853	£14,314
Estimated retained value (3yr/36,000miles)	53%	53%
Sample leasing cost (from)/Cost per mile (pence)	£257/34.9	£262/36.6
Insurance group/typical quote	11/£416	12/£440
Service cost (3yr/36,000 miles)	£828	£781
Power (bhp)/Torque (lb/ft)	108/99	146/124
0-60mph (sec)/Max speed (mph)	9.7/119	8.8/120
CO2 rating (g/km)/tax liability	188/24%	215/30%
Official mpg (urban/extra-urban/combined)	27.7/44.1/36.2	24.8/39.8/32.5

MX-5: precise and extremely easy to control

VERDICT ★★★★☆

FOR Rear-drive, and the steering and driving position to let you exploit it

AGAINST Cabin looks dated, but that was deliberate. The 1.6 is sluggish

VERDICT Just what a sports car should be to drive. The MX-5 is still one of the best roadsters around

BEST BUY 1.8i
BEST AVOIDED 1.8i Sport

Mazda MX-5 Miata

AT A GLANCE:

MODEL	MSRP	ENG	TRAN	ABS	SEATS	A/C
MX-5	$22,098	I-4	5M	NA	2	STD
LS	$24,093	I-4	5M	OPT.	2	STD
Mazdaspeed MX-5	$25,780	I-4t	6M	STD	2	STD

t turbocharged

THE MIATA DOES MANY THINGS WELL, but one of them isn't laying down two lurid black stripes of rubber when the skinny pedal is pinned to the floormat. Enthusiasts have been lusting for more power since the sweet-handling reincarnation of the 1960s' British roadster appeared in 1989, but the official response has been something along the lines of, "We must not upset the delicate balance between horse and rider." Yeah, right.

Well, this Shetland pony now has Seabiscuit aspirations in the form of the Mazdaspeed version (introduced in mid-2004), with 178 bhp and 166 lb.-ft. of torque from its 1.8-liter dohc inline-4 courtesy of a ball-bearing turbocharger that packs 8.5 psi of intercooled boost into the combustion chambers. This engine, coupled to a standard 6-speed manual transmission, easily lops a full second off the 0–60 time (now in the high 6-second range) while trading away minimal low-end performance.

Firmed-up suspension with Bilstein shock absorbers, a lower ride height and suitably aggressive Racing Hart 17-in. wheels shod with 205/40R-17 tires improve both handling and looks, while two new Mazdaspeed-exclusive colors (Lava Orange Mica and Black Mica, added to the original mid-2004 shades of Velocity Red Mica and Titanium Gray Metallic) identify this Miata as the heavy lifter of the lineup. There are a host of other changes exclusive to the Mazdaspeed

version that include a front shock-tower brace, a red wrinkle-finish cam cover, stainless-steel scuff plates on the door-sills, a body-color inside rearview mirror and unique front and rear spoilers.

The less powerful Miatas, available in both base and LS trim levels, are still entirely satisfying sports cars, powered by the same 1.8-liter 16-valve engine sans turbo that puts out 142 bhp at 7000 rpm and 125 lb.-ft. of torque at 5000, using regular-grade fuel. The standard gearbox on both is a 5-speed manual whose short, direct lever throws have become an industry standard. Optional is a 4-speed automatic, which does sap some of the joy from the driving experience. And optional on the LS is a 6-speed manual, which is paired with a shorter 4.10:1 final drive ratio.

The base car is no slouch where standard equipment is concerned, with an AM/FM/CD sound system, air conditioning (via the engine-driven compressor or by simply lowering the manual, two-latch cloth top), and power windows and mirrors. Step up to the LS and you can revel in such additional amenities as leather seats, cruise control, remote keyless entry, power door locks, a 6-speaker Bose AM/FM/CD audio system and a limited-slip differential. Two new colors—Nordic Green and Razor Blue—are the only changes for 2005.

Whatever the version, all Miatas have near 50/50 weight distribution, responsive rack-and-pinion steering, and a disc brake and double A-arm suspension at each corner. Couple

those attributes with the agility that comes from a relatively low curb weight of 2387 lb. and you have a driving experience that could make even the Grinch crack a smile.

Others to consider: BMW Z4, Lotus Elise, Toyota MR2 Spyder. ◎

SPECIFICATIONS:

Layout	rwd
Wheelbase	89.2 in.
Track, f/r	55.7/56.7 in.
Length	155.7 in.
Width	66.0 in.
Height	48.4 in.
Curb weight	2387 lb
Base engine	1.8-liter dohc 16V I-4
Bore x stroke	83.0 x 85.0 mm
Displacement	1839 cc
Horsepower	142 bhp @ 7000 rpm
Torque	125 lb-ft @ 5000 rpm
EPA city/highway	25/29 mpg
Optional engine(s)	1.8-liter turbocharged dohc 16V I-4, 178 bhp
Transmission	5M, 6M, 4A
Suspension, f/r	ind/ind
Brakes, f/r	disc/disc
Tires	P205/45WR-16
Luggage capacity	5.1 cu ft
Fuel capacity	12.7 gal.

WARRANTY:

Bumper-to-bumper	4 years/50,000 miles
Powertrain	4 years/50,000 miles
Rust-through	5 years/unlimited miles

www.mazdausa.com